The publishers would like to express their gratitude to
FNB
for their generous sponsorship which has greatly assisted
in financing the production of this book.

Larger Carnivores
OF THE
African Savannas

J. du P. Bothma

Centre for Wildlife Management,
University of Pretoria, Pretoria, South Africa

AND

Clive Walker

Lapalala Wilderness, Vaalwater, South Africa

J. L. van Schaik

Published by J.L. van Schaik Publishers
1064 Arcadia Street, Hatfield, Pretoria
All rights reserved
Copyright © 1999 Authors

First edition 1999
ISBN 0 627 02411 4

Cover design by Brightmark, Pretoria
Cover photograph Alf Schroelkamp
Typesetting in 11/14 pt Bembo by Pace-Setting & Graphics, Pretoria
Printed and bound by NBD, Drukkery Street,
Goodwood, Western Cape

This book is dedicated to all those who have shared numerous campfires with us. Although the ashes of those fires have been dispersed long ago by the ever-restless winds of Africa, the memories will remain with us forever.

ACKNOWLEDGEMENTS

We wish to thank the following people and institutions who contributed greatly to this work. First and foremost, J.L. van Schaik Publishers of South Africa and Springer-Verlag of Germany for their interest and faith in the book. Theresa Papenfus of J.L. van Schaik Publishers was a particular and immense source of inspiration and help, and she deserves special mention, as do Magdaleen du Toit, Ernst Schlatter and Andrew Ford for the preparation of the book. Mrs B. Bothma diligently prepared numerous drafts of the manuscript. But for her, all this work would have been of little avail. The University of Pretoria provided logistic and moral support, and allowed J. du P. Bothma to take substantial study leave to prepare the manuscript. Dr I. Plug of the Transvaal Museum gave valuable advice on the prehistory of life on earth. Prof F.C. Eloff is thanked for allowing us the use of his leopard photograph on page 62. Dr A. Hall-Martin and Dr P. Richardson are acknowledged for reference material on the brown hyeana and the aardwolf consulted by Clive Walker. Margaret Hitge, Joan Lötter and Alexa Webb are acknowledged for their valuable editorial services. Finally, the staff of the Centre for Wildlife Management at the University of Pretoria bore the brunt of additional work during the study leave mentioned above. We extend our sincere thanks to them all.

FOREWORD

I am honoured to contribute the Foreword to this remarkable book – the product of many years of dedication and commitment by Prof. Koos Bothma and my friend and mentor Clive Walker. These two men have worked together since 1973 on this and many other projects. Their combined talent will, I have no doubt, produce more such wonderful records of the wildlife of our beautiful, but fragile country.

Koos Bothma, who holds the Eugène Marais Chair of Wildlife Management at the University of Pretoria, has had a longstanding research connection with the Kalahari and the Kunene Province, formerly known as the Kaokoveld, Namibia. His scientific work was focused mainly on predators, particularly leopards, but it ranges widely in the field of wildlife ecology. His highly acclaimed book *Game ranch management* has become the standard reference work in this field.

Clive Walker was the founder and former Executive Director of the Endangered Wildlife Trust in the Waterberg Mountains as well as chairman of the Wilderness Trust of Southern Africa. He is also a major wildlife artist.

It is true that few people who visit the 'wild' country are entirely satisfied until they have seen carnivores in action. Carnivores possess a certain magical attraction that cannot be denied, or easily described. This book will lead to an even greater appreciation and deeper understanding of these animals. Most interesting and at times touching, is the description of the family life of each carnivore species of the great savannas.

The author and artist of *Larger Carnivores of the African Savannas* have succeeded in making their research accessible and enjoyable to a diverse readership. Scientific information, presented in a natural, accessible style, makes this book equally valuable to the researcher, student and lay person. Botha's description of the African savannas and the larger carnivores, enhanced by Walker's sensitive drawings 'invites' the reader to picture these fascinating animals in their natural surroundings. I admire the expertise and dedication that went into the making of this work.

The vision of the publisher JL van Schaik, and the personal commitment of Theresa Papenfus and Ernst Schlatter in ensuring the successful publication of *Larger Carnivores of the African Savannas* is to be admired. I am delighted to have been a part of this book, in however small a way and look forward with anticipation to forthcoming 'archives' by Koos Bothma and Clive Walker.

To quote Ian MacDonald, Chief Executive WWF SA: 'It has become one of nature conservation's truisms that people will only conserve what they love, that they will love only what they understand and that they will understand only what they have been taught.'

Let us therefore be taught, understand and love, thus making the world a better place for all who share its fragile state!

STEVE BALES
Group Art Custodian
FNB – a Division of FirstRand Bank Limited

Johannesburg
July 1999

CONTENTS

1

Introduction

Africa has been thought of as a stable continent for so long, one is tempted to believe that its vast and immensely varied flora and fauna have existed since early times. Yet this is not so, because man's history on earth is relatively recent, and even after Africa became a separate continent it took millennia for the savannas to develop. In fact, many of the savannas and their related large herbivores and carnivores have appeared only recently in geological time. Any date ascribed to events far back in the earth's history can naturally never be accurate, and the following sequence of events in the earth's development is therefore only approximate.

The earth, with its great land and water masses, is in a state of constant physical change. Although much of this happens gradually, our world has already experienced 4 billion years of change, some of it slow, but other periods much more abrupt and even cataclysmic. These changes are driven by the immense heat which originates from the earth's centre, and which has provided the energy for vast changes in the nature and distribution of the oceanic basins and land masses over time. At present there are known to be 16 huge tectonic plates on earth. These rigid plates are demarcated by chains of active volcanoes and form part of the earth's cold crust which varies in thickness from about 3 to 75 km. The plates move about on an upper mantle some 640 km thick. New magma is produced along the boundaries of these plates causing adjacent plates to move apart. Elsewhere the plates may meet, causing some of them to sink into deep oceanic trenches where they melt again in the hot mantle below the crust. Mixing with sea-water, the newly melted crusts fuel violent volcanoes and earthquakes such as those commonly found along the Ring of Fire in the Pacific Ocean. As the plates converge or pull apart, they take vast land masses with them, continually altering the face of the earth by forming and subdividing the great continental land masses.

The earliest known land mass on earth was a supercontinent known as Rodinia. Its southern half included what was later to become Amazonia, Greenland and the South Pole. It lay mostly along the South Pole, but its northern half straddled the equator and included parts of what is today South Africa, the Congo, Australia, South China and the North Pole. Although the latitudes of this and other subsequent ancient supercontinents are known, little is known about their longitudes of occurrence. However, it is believed that much of Rodinia was submerged under the sea. At that time, the earth was already 4 billion years old. About 750 million years ago, Rodinia began to split apart under the relentless movement of the continental plates. Over the next several hundred million years, its pieces reassembled, only to break apart again, some pieces migrating thousands of kilometres to eventually form the continents of the earth as we know them today. Some 600 million years ago, all the fragments of Rodinia had reunited to form a new supercontinent, Pannotia. Then a fragment of Pannotia tore away to drift north, leaving most of what became Gondwana at the South Pole. As this fragment reached the equator, it split into three parts: Laurentia (North America and Greenland), Baltica (Northern Europe) and Siberia. These three land masses were mostly submerged. Between them lay a warm, shallow sea where animals with exoskeletons first appeared some 570 million years ago.

As these ancient continents began to push against each other, the oceanic basins widened and sea levels fell, resulting in the emergence of more land above the sea. In this process, the North American part of Laurentia collided some 390 million years ago with Baltica (Northern Europe) and later with Avalonia (Great Britain and New England). These collisions thrust a fragment of Gondwana upward to form the Caledonian and northern Appalachian Mountains. About 300 million years ago, Gondwana and some of the northern continents collided to form Pangaea. This huge land mass stretched from Pole to Pole. It was surrounded by the Panthalassic Ocean, the ancestor of the current Pacific Ocean. This led to the extinction of most of the reptile-like life forms of that time, 250 million years ago. The surviving reptiles then spread over Pangaea again, and later evolved into the dinosaurs. No sooner had Pangaea formed, than it began to break up again, rifting into three main parts. One part contained Eurasia and North America, the second contained Africa and South America, and the third Antarctica, Australia and India. Each of these pieces also started to separate about 120 to 200 million years ago, isolating new evolutionary lines such as the marsupials. India eventually collided with Asia 50 million years ago after a journey of 150 million years. At the same time, Africa collided with Europe, creating new migration routes for the life forms emerging then, including most of Africa's carnivores or their ancestors. India's collision left most of Central Asia dry and cool.

In terms of life on earth, multicellular animals with exoskeletons first appear in the fossil record 570 million years ago, after 3 billion years of primitive life. This period is called the Cambrian Explosion. Life continued to ebb and flow. As the continents continued to squeeze together 390 million years ago, the oceanic basins continued to widen, and sea levels fell. This process uncovered more land and withdrew saltwater barriers between river systems and the large lakes. Freshwater fishes started to migrate, and plants began to colonise the land masses. About 65 million years ago, an asteroid or comet weighing a trillion tonnes and moving at a speed of 160 000 km per hour, slammed into the Yucatan Peninsula and the Gulf of Mexico. This collision formed the 182 km wide Chicxulub Crater which now lies submerged in the Gulf of Mexico. This massive impact caused violent storms, tidal waves or tsunamis, and global forest fires. The consequent immense dust and soot clouds left the earth cold and dark for many years, and led to the extinction of half of the world's animal and plant life of that time. Ironically, this very catastrophe for some forms of life, also cleared the way for the rapid development of new forms on earth, including much of the plant and animal life of Africa as we know it today. Nevertheless, it was only after the recent Miocene 15 to 10 million years ago that Africa became a continent on its own, although it still had Arabia attached to it. The Red Sea opened up about 10 million years ago.

With a current land surface of 30 287 318 km², Africa is exceeded in size only by Asia. At times, seas have submerged part of it, and volcanic activity still occurs, especially along the Great Rift System. Such volcanic rifting has been ripping eastern Africa apart for millions of years. The Great Rift is an immense system of cracks that runs 5600 km across the face of Africa from the Red Sea to Mozambique. In East Africa, it divides into the Western Rift Valley which passes west of Lake Victoria through the Ruwenzori Mountains, and the Eastern Rift Valley which runs east of Lake Victoria through the Aberdares and the

Serengeti-Mara ecosystem. The two arms join again at Lake Malawi. Outside Africa, this rift continues north through the Dead Sea to Turkey. The three main branches of the Great Rift are the East African Rift, the West African Rift, and the one below the Gulf of Aden. Together they form the Afar Triangle, named after a tribe of nomads who live there. This triangle has seethed with volcanism for some 20 to 30 million years. Volcanism has also created the fertile lands which are now found along the Great Rift's shoulders, and troughs of up to 2 km deep and 90 km wide have formed there. In a lower part of the Eastern Rift Valley, the Ngorongoro Crater with its rich and varied wildlife was formed in a titanic volcanic explosion 3 million years ago, followed by a crater collapse. Despite this area of intense volcanism, however, and unlike much of the rest of the world, most of Africa's face was shaped and changed by wind and rain rather than by volcanic activity.

Africa is unique in that its surface is made up of a continuous crystalline shield which is exposed over large areas, but which in others has been partly covered by often unaltered sedimentary rocks since the Precambrian Period. During the time of Gondwana, much of Africa was smoothed to a low, flat landscape. Even in the Miocene, when most of Africa as we know it today emerged, much of the continent was still less than 300 m above sea level, and contained little animal life. When Africa became separated from the rest of the Gondwana elements, a line stretching from central Angola to eastern Sudan divided the continent into north-western, flat and mostly flooded lowlands, and south-eastern, faulted dry highlands. This division is still a fundamental feature of the African savannas. It is also reflected in their climate, vegetation, and ecosystem functioning.

The vegetation and wildlife of Africa

Africa is unique in spanning the whole climatic range from the subtropics in the north to the subtropics in the south. Its vegetation zones occur in belts which radiate north and south of the equator. Like Australia and South America, and contrary to what is found in the northern hemisphere, large parts of Africa consist of ancient land masses. These old landscapes have had a profound effect on the evolution and distribution of the African vegetation, and hence also on its animal life. Moreover, Africa has moved north over time, and southern Africa was at least 14° to 15° further south 30 million years ago than it is at present. At that time, southern Africa had a humid and tropical climate. Africa is also one of the most diverse regions in the world because it has remained biologically isolated from much of the rest of the earth. For much of its history, Africa's landscape has changed backwards and forwards. In consequence, its vegetation flourished and faltered, and its fauna changed continually. Yet Africa had few animals as little as 225 million years ago, and its recent mammals only developed after the demise of the dinosaurs 65 million years ago. About 150 million years back, Africa experienced another wet phase, and its vegetation became more modern. It was then also that the main tree families of the African savannas evolved.

Some 50 million years ago, Africa attained a shape much like that which it has today, and mammals and flowering plants were at their peak of development. Then the Great Rift started erupting volcanically, and this spread fire to vegetation not previously exposed to it, altering it in the process. This volcanic era also lifted up much of the continent, affecting wind and rainfall patterns and shaping the vegetation even further. It was a wet phase, followed by a major dry one for much of the Pliocene during which the forests shrank and many of the great lakes of Africa even dried up. Nevertheless, the hoofed creatures survived. As recently as 3,5 million years ago, much of Africa was again heaved and lifted up further. Of greater significance, however, were the vast ice sheets which then covered most of the northern regions of the world. Some 7 million years ago, Africa moved further north to enclose the Mediterranean Sea. This stopped the flow of warm sea-water into the Atlantic from the Indian Ocean, and an ice sheet spread over Greenland, which set the scene for at least four successive glacial periods, the first of which formed 2,5 million years ago. The glacial periods were, however, interrupted by warmer periods when the ice retreated. The last Ice Age reached its peak 18 000 years ago, retreating over the next 8000 years. These ice sheets caused rapid and major climatic changes in Africa, although the ice sheets themselves never extended to Africa itself. However, the consequent drop in temperature on the equator led to more humid conditions and the renewed expansion of the forests. It also caused the ocean levels to drop, creating temporary land bridges for animals to cross and colonise new areas. Many of Africa's carnivores crossed into Africa from Eurasia in this way during the most recent Ice Age. Such wet periods are invariably followed by dry ones, and the current dry phase started 10 000 years ago, at a time when the first evidence of crop agriculture in the world is found.

Africa has almost 25% of all the mammal species of the world. It also has more mammal families than any other zoogeographic region. This varied fauna is, in part, the result of its range of vegetation, but also of

5

its long history of semi-seclusion and relative geological stability, while remaining close to the other regions of the world from where it could receive new fauna from time to time. A special feature of Africa is its vast herds of herbivores which developed in the great savannas. Most of these savanna herbivores in Africa emerged from Eurasian ancestors, and with them a whole guild of large carnivores developed, whose ecology and behavioural biology are the focus of this book.

The African savannas

Broadly speaking, the African savannas are those areas of vegetation which occur between the forests and the deserts. The word savanna is said to be a derivative of an old Caribbean word, but its etymology is not clear. The French word *savane* has been known since 1529, and the English one *savanna(h)* since 1555. Originally, the term savanna was used in South America to describe land which had no trees, but which had an abundance of grasses, either tall or short. Its use has subsequently been expanded, first, to include grasslands with trees, and then to describe the mixed tree and grass woodlands which are found in all the tropical latitudes. Now a savanna is a region which is conspicuously woody. In many areas, local phrases are used to describe particular variations of savanna. For instance, the term miombo describes a particular open, woodland savanna which is found in central and southern Africa. In southern Africa, the term bushveld describes a local park-like form

The Niassa Game Reserve in northern Mozambique forms part of a huge *Brachystegia* woodland savanna stretching north into southern Tanzania.
Photo: J. du P. Bothma.

A relatively arid
Acacia woodland
savanna on the
foothills of Mount
Kenya in central
Kenya.
Photo: J. du P.
Bothma.

of savanna, which is regarded as one of its most typical forms.
Even the more northern areas of the southern Kalahari
System support an open, arid savanna with scattered large
trees. In its current usage, a savanna is a landscape with
a continuous grass layer which is occasionally interrupted by trees and shrubs, where fires occur from time to
time, and where the main patterns of vegetation growth
are closely associated with alternating wet and dry seasons. However, although the grass layer appears to be continuous, it is actually more generally clumped into individual
perennial tufts. The grass layer may also be temporarily absent
or replaced by herbs in times of drought. Savannas are not transi-
tional zones between forests and pure grasslands, but a biome
of their own.

By definition, savannas could not have existed
before the development of trees and grasses. The
main savanna tree families of Africa evolved 150
million years ago, but the main savanna grasses probably
only appeared at 60 million years, reaching a peak 30 million
years ago at a time when Africa had moved 14° to 15° north to its present position. This widened the gap between Africa and both Antarctica
and Australia, but moved it closer to Eurasia, which also established the
present oceanic circulation pattern and climate of Africa. The resultant

7

Roan antelope in a
typical bushveld
savanna in South
Africa.
Photo: J. du P.
Bothma.

increase in areas of seasonal rainfall was ideal for grasses, and they reached their peak about 38 to 26 million years ago. The large grazing animals could then develop, and the first of them appeared in the Miocene 25 to 15 million years ago. With the emergence of an annual dry season and the consequent presence of a continuous annual supply of dry fuel about 15 million years ago, regular fires were inevitable, and the savannas of Africa were born. When South and North America pushed against each other about 3,5 million years ago, the Isthmus of Panama diverted the flow of warm sea water which had flowed from the Caribbean Sea to the Pacific Ocean. This warm current was now diverted northward to where it fed the Arctic snows with moisture. A cooler, drier global climate resulted, turning much of the African forests into extensive grasslands which were roamed by our human ancestors.

Today, the savannas are one of the world's major biomes. They occupy 12% of the world's surface area, but are particularly abundant in sub-Saharan Africa where they cover 60% of the land surface. Many of Africa's game reserves and national parks are situated in its savanna regions. Savannas support an immense biomass of animal life, much of it invertebrate. This rich animal life is a source of food for many carnivores. Herbivores reach their highest densities and diversity in the savannas, especially in the wet season in the Serengeti savannas. However, not all the herbivores arrived or developed simultaneously in

Africa. The antelopes, wild pigs, giraffes and rhinoceroses probably all arrived in Africa soon after reconnecting with Eurasia, but the zebras and hippopotamuses arrived later. About 7 to 2,5 million years ago there was a massive species radiation in the antelopes and wild pigs of Africa. This radiation corresponded with a high degree of speciation in the grasses and the exploitation of the savannas as a primary herbivore habitat. While the African antelopes are still diverse and abundant, however, only a few remnants of the former rich pig fauna remain in Africa today. Because the abundance of herbivores provided a basic food resource, the carnivores of Africa also flourished. Although some of the larger African carnivores have now become extinct, the continent still has a rich complement of them.

The larger carnivores of Africa

In this context larger carnivores are loosely defined as all carnivorous mammals larger than a jackal. About 65 million years ago, mammals still rarely reached the size of a small domestic cat. Then the dinosaurs became extinct, and the absence of specialised terrestrial carnivores allowed the evolution of large, flightless birds, some of which were carnivorous and may have been competitors of the evolving mammal carnivores. The earliest known members of the Order Carnivora were small, arboreal Viverridae. The Hyaenidae and Felidae are related, but by the Miocene, the hyaenids had phenotypically become more dog-like, with large genera of hunting hyaenas in Africa, Eurasia and North America. Of all the cats, the genus *Felis,* which includes the lynx and the puma, apparently originated in North America, and the roaring cats of the genus *Panthera* in Eurasia. Three species of lion occurred earlier in Eurasia, Africa, and North and South America, while the earliest cheetahs were found in Eurasia. Leopards have a long history in Africa. The earliest canid was a small, fox-like animal of North America. The modern canids began to radiate in Asia in the late Miocene, 15 to 10 million years ago.

Carnivora started to occupy Africa in the early Miocene 30 to 25 million years ago, and South America in the late Miocene, 15 to 10 million years ago. The first true Carnivora also reached Africa from Eurasia in the Miocene. They were the ancestors of the civets, mongooses and cats. In the late Miocene and early Pliocene, they were followed by the ancestors of the bears, dogs, and other cats. Continental interchanges of fauna then led to great animal diversification. Almost all the recent Carnivora are the result of radiations which occurred in the last 7 million years. It is therefore clear that the current rich complement of large carnivores found in the African savannas is the result of a complex chain of events which, among others, can be traced first to the evolution of trees 150 million years ago, then to the evolution of grasses and the extinction of dinosaurs 65 million years ago, followed by the evolution of grazing herbivores at 25 to 15 million years ago, and eventually to the evolution of the mammal carnivores themselves about 7 million years ago. Many of the larger carnivores of the African savannas, however, only reached Africa 18 000 years ago when they crossed a land bridge which formed between Africa and Eurasia as a result of the last Ice Age. The existence of large carnivores in the African savannas is clearly still in its infancy in terms of geological time. Nevertheless, it has already led to many and varied ecological and behavioural adaptations, some of which will be discussed here.

The natural areas

For the sake of brevity, the full name of a national park or another natural area is only given when it is first mentioned in the text. Thereafter an abbreviated name as indicated in brackets below is used where applicable. Not all the names are abbreviated, however, because of possible confusion with the names of places and people, or where such a name is only used infrequently. The ecology and behaviour of large carnivores from the following natural areas in alphabetical order are discussed at some length in the text.

- **Amboseli National Park (Amboseli):** Situated on the northern foothills of Mount Kilimanjaro in south-eastern Kenya. Portions of it consist of an open *Acacia* savanna, but there are also extensive grasslands and flood plains. The annual rainfall is about 350 mm.

- **Bushmanland:** A communal, pastoral region in north-eastern Namibia. It is a woodland savanna, with an annual rainfall which varies from 400 to 500 mm.

- **Central Kalahari savanna:** An arid, open *Acacia* savanna in central Botswana, with an annual rainfall of 300 to 450 mm. This area includes the Central Kalahari Game Reserve, and the adjacent Khutse Game Reserve.

- **Comoé National Park (Comoé):** A mosaic of savanna and forest in north-eastern Ivory Coast, close to the border with Ghana and Burkina Faso. The rainfall is highly variable, with an extensive dry season.

- **Etosha National Park (Etosha):** A woodland savanna surrounding a huge prehistoric, but now ephemeral, lake of some 140 km in width and 4660 km² in extent, in northern Namibia. The annual rainfall is about 300 mm in the west and 450 mm in the east.

- **Hluhluwe-Umfolozi Park (Hluhluwe-Umfolozi):** A dense bushveld savanna in South Africa, with an annual rainfall of 500 to 600 mm.

- **Kafue National Park (Kafue):** A *Brachystegia-Julbernardia* woodland with flood plain grasslands along the Kafue River in western Zambia. The annual rainfall is about 800 mm.

- **Kaudam Game Reserve (Kaudam):** A woodland savanna in Bushmanland in north-eastern Namibia, with a rainfall of 400 to 500 mm per year.

- **Klaserie Private Nature Reserve (Klaserie):** A large, privately owned bushveld savanna reserve adjacent to the Kruger National Park in South Africa. It receives an annual rainfall of about 600 mm.

This huge prehistoric lake in the Etosha National Park in Namibia is surrounded by an arid woodland savanna.
Photo: J. du P. Bothma.

The bushveld
savanna in the
Kruger National
Park is home to
numerous
herbivores,
including the sable
antelope.
Photo: J. du P.
Bothma.

- **Kruger National Park:** A mixed bushveld savanna adjacent to Mozambique in north-eastern South Africa. It is a long park, stretching some 320 km from the south (annual rainfall: 440 mm) to the north (annual rainfall: 740 mm).

- **Lake Manyara National Park (Lake Manyara):** A mixed woodland savanna next to Lake Manyara in the Eastern Rift Valley in Tanzania. The annual rainfall is some 600 mm.

Lake Manyara
National Park lies in
the Eastern Rift
Valley in Tanzania.
Photo: J. du P.
Bothma.

- **Lichtenburg Nature Reserve:** A open, *Acacia* savanna interspersed with grasslands in north-western South Africa. The rainfall is about 650 mm per year.

- **Masai-Mara:** The northern portion of the Serengeti-Mara ecosystem in Kenya. This region includes the Masai-Mara Game Dispersal Area and the Masai-Mara National Reserve. It is a mixed woodland savanna interspersed with tall-grass plains. The drainage lines are wooded too. The annual rainfall is 1200 m.

- **Masai Steppe:** An arid, short-grass plain south-east of the Tarangire National Park in Tanzania. It forms part of the Tarangire ecosystem. The rainfall is about 400 mm per year.

- **Matobo National Park (Matobo):** This open woodland savanna in southern Zimbabwe is interspersed with grasslands and granite outcrops. It was formerly known as the Matopos National Park, and it receives about 800 mm of rain per year.

- **Mikumi National Park (Mikumi):** This national park in Tanzania lies just north of the Selous Game Reserve. It is a *Brachystegia* woodland with an annual rainfall of some 1000 mm.

- **Moremi Wildlife Reserve (Moremi):** This reserve along the north-eastern edge of the Okavango Delta in northern Botswana lies on Kalahari sands. It consists of the mopani *Colophospermum mopani* woodlands, interspersed with flood plains and islands with tall palm trees. It receives about 450 to 500 mm of rain per year.

The Masai-Mara region in southern Kenya is the northern portion of the Serengeti-Mara ecosystem which stretches south into Tanzania.
Photo: J. du P. Bothma.

13

The rim of the Ngorongoro Crater in Tanzania rises 500 m above the crater floor. Photo: J. du P. Bothma.

• **Mountain Zebra National Park:** This park in south-central South Africa consists of an arid, hilly, *Acacia* scrub woodland savanna, interspersed with grassland plateaus. The annual rainfall is about 400 mm per year.

• **Nairobi National Park:** A park adjacent to the bustling city of Nairobi in Kenya. This short grassland and open *Acacia* savanna receives about 850 mm of rain per year.

• **Namib Desert:** This desert stretches along the entire coast of Namibia in the west. It receives less than 100 mm of rain per year. It is not a savanna, but it is mentioned here for comparative reasons.

• **Ngorongoro Crater:** This caldera, with a floor surface area of about 250 km², is an open grassland savanna with scattered *Acacia* woodlands and flood plains. It occurs in the Eastern Rift Valley and is part of the Ngorongoro Conservation Area in Tanzania. This conservation area also contains the Olduvai Gorge some 30 km northwest of the Ngorongoro Crater, where numerous fossils of our human ancestors are found together with those of various other animals. The crater's rainfall is about 600 mm per year, and its rim gen-

erally rises 500 m above the floor. The Ngorongoro Crater lies at the southernmost edge of the Serengeti-Mara ecosystem.

The lakes of the Ngorongoro Crater in Tanzania are rich feeding grounds for various wading birds, and a source of water for its other wildlife.
Photo: J. du P. Bothma.

• **Rustenburg Nature Reserve:** A small *Acacia* woodland reserve with grassland plateaus in northern South Africa. It receives about 700 mm of rain per year.

• **Ruwenzori National Park (Ruwenzori):** Formerly known as the Queen Elizabeth National Park. This park lies in south-western Uganda adjacent to Lake Rutanzige (formerly Lake Edward) in the Western Rift Valley. It consists of short grasslands, with scattered thickets, undulating taller grasslands, and *Acacia* woodlands. The annual rainfall is about 1000 mm.

• **Sabi-Sand Game Reserve (Sabi-Sand):** A privately owned, mixed bushveld savanna reserve adjacent to the Kruger National Park in South Africa. The annual rainfall is about 500 mm.

• **Savuti Marsh (Savuti):** This marsh is found in the northern part of the Mababe Depression, an ancient lake in northern Botswana. It forms part of the Chobe National Park, and it is tall grassland which occasionally becomes a marsh. It is surrounded by mixed woodlands.

15

The marsh is fed by the Savuti Channel, which only flows occasionally, after exceptional rains have fallen in the catchment area of the Kavango River in Angola. This allows the water of the Okavango Delta to spill over into the Savuti Channel, which then drains into the Savuti Marsh to flood it. This marsh was dry for 100 years or so until 1957, when it filled again. It has now been dry since 1981. The Savuti Marsh receives an annual rainfall of about 500 mm.

- **Selous Game Reserve (Selous):** This is an immense natural area in southern Tanzania, stretching from just south-west of Dar-es-Salaam in the north, to just north of the Mozambique border in the south. It is a *Brachystegia* woodland, with tall inselbergs, and receives about 1000 mm of rain per year.

The Savuti Marsh in the Chobe National Park in northern Botswana is ephemeral. The last time it was wet was in 1981. Photo: J. du P. Bothma.

- **Serengeti National Park (Serengeti):** This is another huge natural area which lies in northern Tanzania with its north-western edge almost touching the Speke Gulf of Lake Victoria. It consists of open grassland plains interspersed with woodlands, especially on the hilly areas and along the drainage lines. The rainfall varies from about 400 mm in the south-east to 1000 mm in the north-west.

- **Serengeti-Mara ecosystem:** A large ecosystem characterised by its massive, annual herbivore migrations. It stretches south from the Masai-Mara Game Dispersal Area and the Masai-Mara National Reserve in Kenya, to the Serengeti National Park and the Ngorongoro Conservation Area in Tanzania. Westwards, it almost reaches Lake Victoria. The rainfall and vegetation of the above regions are discussed separately where each area is described.

The vast Serengeti Plains are interspersed with woodlands along the drainage lines, and isolated tall trees which form handy perches for birds such as the secretary bird.
Photo: J. du P. Bothma.

17

- **Southern Kalahari savanna:** The northern portion of the south-western Kalahari System. It is an arid, open *Acacia* savanna on Kalahari sands, where the normally dry Nossob River forms the boundary between the Gemsbok National Park of Botswana and the Kalahari Gemsbok National Park of South Africa. The annual rainfall varies from 240 to 300 mm.

The Tarangire National Park in Tanzania has an unusual abundance of baobab trees. It is also the southern-most distribution area for the striped hyaena in Africa. Photo: J. du P. Bothma.

- **Tarangire National Park (Tarangire):** This national park is a mixed woodland savanna south-east of Lake Manyara in Tanzania. It has an unusual abundance of baobab *Adansonia digitata* trees, and wetlands occur along the Tarangire drainage system. It forms an ecological link with the Masai Steppe to its west to form the Tarangire ecosystem, and it receives about 600 mm of rain per year.

- **Timbavati Game Reserve (Timbavati):** This is a privately owned, bushveld savanna reserve adjacent to the Kruger National Park in South Africa, with an annual rainfall of about 650 mm.

- **Tsavo National Park (Tsavo):** This national park in the southeastern corner of Kenya is divided into the Tsavo National Park East and the Tsavo National Park West by the Nairobi-Mombasa road. However, they form an ecological unit. In Tsavo East, the vegetation varies from grasslands and bush to woodlands and forests, interspersed with rocky hills. In Tsavo West, the vegetation is even more diverse. It varies from grasslands to montane forests interspersed with riverine forests and rocky hills. In the woodlands, baobab, *Commiphora* and *Acacia* trees are abundant. The rainfall varies from 250 mm in the east to 650 mm in the west.

19

The scientific nomenclature

In this text, an attempt has been made to conform to the most recent taxonomic classification of the Order Carnivora which is available. Although it is recognised that there may still be some disagreement about this classification, the system suggested by W.C. Wozencraft when he classified the Order Carnivora in the 1993 edition of the book, *Mammal species of the world,* by D.E. Wilson and D.M. Reeder (editors), is used here. The full scientific name of a given organism is used only when it is first mentioned in the text. Occasionally, however, the nature of the text might also require its subsequent use.

BIBLIOGRAPHY

Barker, J.F. 1983. Towards a biogeography of the Kalahari. Part 1: To which region does the Kalahari belong? *Botswana Notes and Records,* 15: 85–91.

Bourlière, F. & Hadley, M. 1983. Present-day savannas: an overview. In Bourlière, F. (Ed.), *Ecosystems of the world,* 13: 1–17. Amsterdam: Elsevier.

Brown, L. 1965. *Africa.* New York: Random House.

Cloudsley-Thompson, J.L. 1975. *Terrestrial environments.* London: Croom Helm.

Cole, M.M. 1986. *The savannas – biogeography and geobotany.* New York: Academic.

Delany, M.J. & Happold, D.C.D. 1979. *Ecology of African mammals.* London: Longman.

Iwago, M. 1986. The Serengeti: a portfolio. *National Geographic,* 168(5): 559–583.

Martin, L.D. 1989. Fossil history of the terrestrial Carnivora. In: Gittleman, J.L. (Ed.), *Carnivore, behavior, ecology and evolution.* London: Chapman & Hall, 536–568.

Menaut, J.C., Barbault, R., Lavalle, P. & Lepage, M. 1985. African savannas: biological systems of humification and mineralization. In: Tothill, J.C. & Mott, J.J. (Eds), *Ecology and management of the world's savannas.* London: Commonwealth Agricultural Bureau, 14–33.

Myers, N. 1972. *The long African day.* New York: Macmillan.

National Geographic. 1998. Physical earth: millennium in maps. *Supplement to National Geographic,* 193(5).

Partridge, T.C. 1997. Evolution of landscapes. In: Cowling, R.M., Richardson, D.M. & Pierce, S.M. (Eds), *Vegetation of southern Africa.* Cambridge: Cambridge University Press.

Scholes, R.J. 1997. Savanna. In: Cowling, R.M., Richardson, D.M. & Pierce, S.M. (Eds), *Vegetation of southern Africa.* Cambridge: Cambridge University Press.

Scholes, R.J. & Walker, B.H. 1993. *An African savanna.* Cambridge: Cambridge University Press.

Stager, C. 1990. The Great Rift Valley. *National Geographic,* 177(5): 2–41.

Van Rooyen, N. & Van Rooyen, M.W. 1997. Vegetation of the south-western Kalahari. Paper read at the *Kalahari Desert Colloquim,* Royal Society of South Africa, Pretoria.

2

The African lion

The lion *Panthera leo* was one of the most fearsome beasts which roamed the African and Asian plains with the early pastoralists. Although the lion has been the dominant large carnivore in Africa and south-western Asia for millennia, this may not always have been so. Paintings by Cro-Magnon man, for example, show both the lion and another large felid without a mane or a tufted tail. Along with skeletal remains, this felid has been identified as the cave lion *Panthera spelaeus* which inhabited Europe between 340 BC and 100 AD. In the fossil evidence from Africa there also are sabre-toothed cats, another large cat *Panthera crassidens,* and a lion-sized cat with a jaw like a tiger. The rise of the African lion as the dominant carnivore of Africa is therefore relatively recent, and may well have coincided with the rise of man.

The lion is Africa's largest cat, but food intake and genetics play a major role in determining the actual size of a lion, and therefore it varies in size from region to region. Big males in Etosha can weigh up to 260 kg, and females 165 kg. In southern Africa lions usually weigh in the region of 200 kg and 140 kg respectively. The lions from East Africa are smaller than those from southern Africa, and males usually weigh about 180 kg and females 120 kg, although the maximum known weight for an East African male lion is 238 kg and 182 kg for a female. The African lion has a fair degree of genetic variation as opposed to the small population of Asiatic lions which has little such variation. The African lion was first described scientifically as *Felis leo* by Linnaeus in 1758, from a specimen collected at Constantine on the Barbary coast of

In terms of size the African lion has been the dominant large mammal carnivore in Africa in recent times. Photo: J. du P. Bothma.

Algeria. It was renamed *Panthera leo* by R.I. Pocock in 1917. The generic name *Panthera* was first used by L. Oken in 1816, and Oken also created a genus *Leo* in 1816, which is no longer in use. However, it was Pocock who separated the Felidae into three subfamilies: the large or roaring cats of the subfamily Pantherinae, the cheetah of the subfamily Acinonychinae, and the small cats of the subfamily Felinae. This division of the subfamilies is based on the structure of the hyoid bones which are fully ossified in the Felinae and Acinonychinae, but imperfectly in the Pantherinae.

A lion's eyes seem to have always held a great fascination for man, and were, for example, carefully rendered in Assyrian and Ancient Egyptian sculpture. In many parts of Africa the successful initiation of young hunters also depends on a test which requires the initiate to face a lion's fierce and awesome stare directly. In ancient Egypt, the city of Leontopolis was named after a lion cult which flourished there. Moreover, the annual flooding of the Nile River which was the most important event in the Egyptian calendar was depicted hieroglyphically by a lion's head. Ramses II kept lions, as did most of the royalty of those times. Ramses II was also said to have trained a lion called *Auto-m-nekht* to run beside his chariot horses and knock down anyone approaching the chariot. The great menageries in Alexandria, which were built up by the Ptolemies, the successors to the pharaohs of ancient Egypt, were ultimately destroyed by the emperor Theodosius who banned all animal cults in the year 384 AD.

The lion's piercing eyes have long fascinated man. Photo: C.H. Walker.

The classical Phrygian goddess Cybele also became the object of a widespread lion cult called the Galli. This Asian goddess personified the earth in its primitive and savage state, and held dominion over all wild beasts. She was symbolically represented being drawn in a chariot by two lions. Some of the priests of the Corybantes, as the followers of this cult were called, travelled far and wide and were often accompa-

25

nied by a bear or a lion which was used in the exorcism of evil spirits. The Romans in turn used lions as sacrificial beasts, and Julius Caesar had 400 lions killed to consecrate his Roman Forum. When Germanicus was nominated as consul, a further 200 lions were sacrificed. In Africa there are also numerous tales of wizards with magical powers who associated with lions. Even more powerful were the secret societies that killed people at night in the guise of spirit lions or lion-men. Even outside Africa lion trophies have long been held to have powerful medicinal and magical effects. For example, in 1563 the Swiss physician Konrad Gesner described how the dried and powdered blood of a lion could be used to treat carbuncles, other growths and swollen glands. He also wrote that this powder would make blemishes and spots on the face disappear when mixed with other ointments; that eating a lion's heart could alleviate a cold, and that drinking the liquid of a pickled lion liver would relieve liver ailments.

The Shona people of Zimbabwe believe that there are three types of lion. These are the normal lion which can be hunted, and two other types that must not be harmed. One of the latter is the benign spirit of a former chieftain who comes to visit his family at times. He is a maned lion and will not harm them. The other is the embodiment of an evil person whose craving for raw flesh has caused him to transform himself into a maneless lion which must be avoided at all costs. It is interesting to note that the possession of a mane is part of lion folklore, much as it is also part of a current controversy over the relationship and existence of maned lions. In African lions, manes have developed in varying degrees. The extinct Barbary and Cape lions lived in worlds many thousands of kilometres apart, yet they both had well-developed manes which came fairly far down the body, as did other lions else-where. However, the Horn of Africa, of which Somalia forms a major portion, has a peculiar fauna, and the main characteristic of its lions, which were still relatively abundant there as late as 1984, is the absence of a mane, even in fully grown males.

Our hunting ancestors knew the lion well, and it appears in a lot of African folklore. Many parts of a lion's body are used in superstitious practices and in traditional medicines. The lion's stature among men is projected by many honorary titles and garments relating to lions. The head of the ancient dynasty of Ethiopia assumed the title The Lion of Judah. The warriors of many African tribes also use headdresses which imitate a lion's mane. This mane seems to have a special significance for them because the maneless lioness is never imitated. It has been sug-gested that the male lion's proud bearing, his thunderous roar, and per-haps even the resemblance between manes and beards, have all led to the adoption of the lion as a martial symbol for many people.

Lions can be identified individually from the pattern of their whiskers. These whiskers occur between the upper lip and the nose, and there are distinctive spots where they emerge from the skin. These spots form four to five rows above and roughly parallel to the upper lip. The shape and number of these spots, and the distribution of the rows

The male lion's proud bearing and his impressive mane may have contributed to its adoption as a martial symbol by many people in Africa. Photo: C.H. Walker.

27

varies with individual lions. Some South African lions in and around
the Kruger National Park also show a coat colour anomaly in that they
have an inherited recessive white coat. They are not albinos, however,
because the eyes of a white lion have the normal yellow pigment and
are not pink-red as in an albino. The presence of leopard-like spots on
the cubs and on some adults is a vestigial characteristic retained from an
ancestral cat which probably lived mainly in forests.

Social behaviour

With lions, the lioness and her young are the focus of the pride and
there is no consistent leader. The pride usually occupies a limited area,
but there are also nomads of both sexes who wander widely.
Nomadism and pride membership are not mutually exclusive, and a
nomad may become a resident, and vice versa, but each category
implies a vastly different way of life. A pride usually occupies a defended area of limited size, which is sometimes called a territory, while a
nomad occupies an undefended range. The size of the pride's range is
related to the size of the pride, and the ranges of various prides may
overlap. The lion's pride size varies from area to area according to the
availability of prey. In Serengeti the modal pride size in one study was 2
(mean: 2,8) and the maximum pride size 13. Elsewhere in East Africa
prides may be much larger. In the prey-rich Ngorongoro Crater the
largest lion pride studied had 30 members (mean: 8). In the Kruger
National Park prides of up to 39 individuals may be found. In Etosha
pride size ranges from 5 to 16 members, although prides of up to 30
(mean: 7,2) have been recorded there. In the southern Kalahari savanna the largest pride recorded by F.C. Eloff had 14 members (mean:
4,2).

Because lion pride size varies from area to area, so will lion density.
One lion requires at least 100 prey animals over a full year to remain
alive. In Etosha however, there seems to be more lions per unit of prey
than in most known conservation areas. Where prey is more abundant,
as in the more mesic savannas, lion density should therefore also be
higher. This is indeed so. In Serengeti, for example, the available prey
density varies markedly between a mean of 20 000 kg/km² in the wet
season when the migratory prey is present, and 1000 kg/km² in the dry
season. There the mean annual density of lions is one lion per 10 km²
(10 lions per 100 km²). By contrast, in the Ngorongoro Crater the prey
biomass is much more stable, varying from a mean of 11 693 kg/km² in
the wet season, to 12 000 kg/km² in the dry season. The mean lion den-

sity of one lion per 2,5 km² (40 lions per 100 km²) in the Ngorongoro Crater, is four times that of Serengeti. At Lake Manyara National Park conditions are probably close to a maximum sustained density of lions. There the prey biomass is 7200 kg per km² at most times, and the lion density there is around one lion per 2,6 km² (38,4 lions per 100 km²). This density is sustained over time. The Selous Game Reserve carries one lion per 12,5 km² (8 lions per 100 km²). The lion density in Etosha was estimated by some authors at one lion per 4,5 to 6,3 km² (15 to 22 lions per 100 km²), but others believe that it is as low as one lion per 35 km² (2,8 lions per 100 km²). However, it also varies according to local prey abundance, the highest being in western Etosha where prey densities are greater because of the presence of a number of artificial water points. In the Savuti Marsh prey biomass ranges from 2000 kg/km² in the dry season to 27 000 kg/km² in the wet season. The mean lion density there is one lion per 5 km² (20 lions per 100 km²). The Kruger National Park is essentially an arid savanna. Yet it has a relatively high lion density of one lion per 7,7 km² (13 lions per 100 km²) and there are 110 prey animals present for every lion. The southern Kalahari is an open, arid savanna. Consequently it has a relatively low density of one lion per 68,5 km² (1,5 lions per 100 km²). The arid Masai Steppe is known to have the lowest natural lion density in Africa at one lion per 306 km² (0,3 lions per 100 km²).

In a lion pride, the adult males are usually interrelated, as are the females, but the males are not related to the females. Female cubs born to pride lionesses usually remain in their natal pride for the life of that pride. In contrast, the male cubs are usually evicted at puberty. Any male cubs which do survive till puberty, leave the pride together, and may stay together, to become breeding adult males in a new pride. In the process of taking over a new pride, serious injuries are rare, but the conflict may be fierce and noisy. Occasionally a defending pride male may be fatally wounded or he may be disabled which will lead to a lingering death. However, an adult male is not a pride prerequisite, especially where prey is abundant and prides can easily kill food. For example, in the prey-rich Savuti 44% of all the lion prides found feeding at a kill, had no adult male lion in attendance. Large lion prides also typically dominate smaller ones in a given area.

It is often believed that lion prides are prime examples of sociability in predators. However, this is not altogether true. Although most lion prides show a fair degree of social order among the females, the Etosha lions, for example, live in prides with no social hierarchy among the lionesses. Nevertheless, sisterhood does have its advantages, because

29

pride-mates will jointly defend their cubs against invading males, and will share in raising the young. An angry group of females can ward off the attack of a lone male which is nearly twice as large as a female, and will also frequently attack and kill less powerful, trespassing females. Although some females are also nomadic, it is mainly the males who become nomadic after puberty. They then wander widely and eventually evict the resident adult male(s) from a pride. After doing so, they often also kill all the cubs present (infanticide). The pride females may respond to the death of the cubs by all coming into oestrus simultaneously and ultimately producing new young in unison. Nomadic lions travel widely. In Serengeti one nomad used an area of at least 4700 km². The range size of these nomads is at least 10 times that of prides in the same region. Nomadic lions are markedly tolerant of one another, and these lions, which have no land of their own to defend, usually accept strangers easily.

Lions have a well-developed communication system which incorporates many facets. Vocalisation, facial expressions, scents, body postures and much more, all play a role in the functioning of lion sociability. Roaring and scent-marking are usually long-range signals, while other vocalisations, facial expressions and body postures are used more for short-range communication. The acute senses of hearing, sight and smell are particularly powerful tools in such communication. Although lions also purr at times, this purr is unlike that of the domestic cat, being produced during exhalation only and not as a continuous action while breathing in and out. Purring does seem to signal contentment, but compared with cats of the *Felis* group, it appears to be unimportant in the social life of a lion.

Roaring is a characteristic of the *Panthera* group of cats to which the lion also belongs. Lions do not roar regularly, but both sexes may do so at intervals throughout the night. They often roar most at sunset and just before dawn. Roaring and scent-marking by lions in Serengeti and the Ngorongoro Crater are most frequent when prey is most abundant, a time when intruder pressure from nomadic lions is also the greatest. Lions can clearly scent-track other lions, or even their prey. As a lion moves about, it leaves tracks, urine and faeces in the environment. These may all convey messages to other lions which may pass by later, although in lions the faeces do not appear to be used for specific messages as in other carnivores. Although all cats advertise and mark their territorial boundaries, none do it on quite the same grand scale as the African lion. In combination with urine, all cats possess highly developed and usually sebaceous (fat) glands above the tail, as well as anal, praegenital, circumoral, submandibular, and interdigital glands between the footpads. In common with some other cats, lions also scrape or wipe with their hind feet before marking with urine. This leaves an olfactory and visual signal to other lions, and such behaviour complements rather than supplements the other. When scraping, a lion rakes the ground from 2 to 30 times with the claws of the hind feet, undoubtedly leaving a concentration of scent. Both males and females scrape, but lions do not defecate on their scrapes as tigers do. The frequency and intensity of scraping varies with the type of habitat. Scraping by one lion in a pride also frequently stimulates others to do so.

5 cm

Urine is used widely by lions in communication. Male, nomadic or resident lions especially, squirt urine against objects in their range. In doing so, a musk-smelling secretion from two anal glands near the base of the tail mixes with the urine. Lions often rub their faces on vegetation before spraying it with urine and scent. As the same objects may be used repeatedly for scent-marking in this way, it is possible that they receive certain chemical messages during such rubbing. The subsequent spraying may then be a reaction to this kind of message. When spraying the fluid is squirted upward at an angle of 30 to 40° for a distance of 3 to 4 m. The musky odour can be detected from as far away as 5 m. Male lions prefer bushes or tree trunks at least 1 m high against which to spray-urinate. Small squirts of urine are also used by lions to scent-mark. In doing so, the animal often wets its hindlegs. This fluid has little or no scent from the anal glands, and its flow is usually steady but weak. Lions of all ages also rake the trunks of trees with their forepaws. Although this could serve to sharpen and groom the claws, it also serves as a signpost, because some of these trees are clawed repeatedly. Lions also roll on the faeces of other animals, but the reason for this is unknown.

12 cm

Reproduction and young

Lions reproduce at rates which are in balance with the abundance of their resources, particularly food. They have no clear mating season in some areas, but in the Nairobi National Park their births show a distinct peak in December and January although they do mate throughout the year. In Serengeti lion reproductive rates are the highest in those years with relatively wet dry seasons, or with relatively dry rainy seasons. At such times, the migrating prey herds remain in the same area of the park for a greater length of time, creating more ideal conditions for cub survival. Pride size also influences reproductive success, because the females in the larger prides often breed synchronously and help to raise each other's cubs, resulting in increased cub survival.

Lions use chemical signals to display their readiness to mate as domestic cats do. Both the urine and the cheek gland secretions of a female cat appear to contain pheromones which inform the males about her hormonal phase. Males react to such messages by showing flehmen, which is a grimace following a whole array of stimuli, including a female's urine, and helps to determine the receptiveness of such a female. The age of sexual maturity in lions varies. Female lions in the Nairobi National Park first conceive when they are about 30 months old, but this could take place at a younger age. In Serengeti it is from 40 to 54 months. In the Kruger National Park female lions first conceive at the age of 43 to 66 months (median age: 48 months), and by the age of 5,5 years all females have been pregnant at least once. Pride males, and consequently reproducing males, are usually between 5 and 9 years old. Although males may be sexually mature from an age of 30 months, they are prevented from mating at that stage by social behaviour.

Pride females in the Kruger National Park tend to come into oestrus and give birth simultaneously. Oestrus in lions usually lasts a week, and recurs at 3-week intervals. Mating lions stay together for 2 to 3 days, copulating two to three times every hour. It is also possible that a lioness may produce cubs fathered by different males, in the same litter,

A male lion in the southern Kalahari savanna sniffing the urine of a receptive female to determine her reproductive status.
Photo: J. du P. Bothma.

A male lion showing flehmen in response to the pheromones in a female's urine in the southern Kalahari savanna. Photo: J. du P. Bothma.

because multiple-mate copulations do occur occasionally, although this is rare. Competing males may also fight fiercely over a receptive female. In Kenya, for example, a case is known where two males fought a raging battle for 10 hours in the presence of a receptive female, ending in the death of both combatants. Mating lions seldom attempt to hunt. Gestation lasts about 110 days, but relatively few copulations actually lead to conception. In Serengeti, for example, conception occurs in only 20% of all matings. In one study of lions in the Kruger National Park, 20% of all the parous females were pregnant, 21,7% were lactating and consequently had cubs younger than 9 months old, and 6,7% were sterile. The rest were in an interlitter phase. Females usually have a reproductive life of some 11 to 13 years.

Lionesses give birth in isolation, and keep their litters hidden for the first 6 to 7 weeks when the cubs are most vulnerable to predation. A lion cub's eyes are closed at birth, and they only really join the pride when they are 10 weeks old. In the Kruger National Park the mean litter size is 3,08 at birth dropping to 3,02 when the cubs are a year old or less, and to 2,71 when they are between 1 and 2 years old, but litters of

Young lion cubs in the southern Kalahari savanna are often left alone for extended periods, a time when they are vulnerable to various forms of mortality.
Photo: J. du P. Bothma.

up to 6 are possible. This is much the same as that found in lions in the Nairobi National Park, or in the southern Kalahari savanna. Litter size therefore does not seem to be influenced by food abundance, but litter survival definitely is.

Infanticide is a common and normal reproductive strategy in lions, although it has long been considered an aberrant form of behaviour. It usually follows the takeover of a pride by a new male or a cohort of males. In the process all the cubs already present in the pride are killed by the new males. The females then often come into oestrus synchronously and mate with the new males. This is a reproductive strategy which prevents females from investing more energy into raising progeny from males which have been displaced, and also speeds up the return of sexual receptivity in the females. However, it is clearly disadvantageous to the females who have already invested in cubs and who then adapt to it in various ways to try and minimise the loss of their existing cubs. One way in which they try to counter such a loss is to physically prevent the males from killing some or all of their cubs. A second way is to accept the inevitable and imminent loss of their cubs rapidly and without further aggression. Sometimes older cubs may not be killed by the new males. However, they will be evicted from the pride and may then be accompanied by some females resulting in only a partial pride takeover. Despite all these countermeasures, cub losses from infanticide may be considerable.

The interval between successive litters from the same female is usually 2 years, except for litters born synchronously, which can be about 43 months apart. There is some evidence suggesting that females may refuse to raise single cubs, or cubs that have become sole survivors of larger litters, when such a cub is less than 3 months old. In Etosha pregnancy control in lions was carried out successfully when there appeared to be too many lions in the area. This was done by implanting a small capsule into the neck muscles of a lioness. The capsule released a constant but minute flow of hormones into the lioness's system, simulating pregnancy and preventing ovulation for up to 5 years.

The sex ratio is usually equal in even-sized litters. However, the ratio of cubs born within the first 300 days after a male takeover of a pride favours male offspring, and it differs significantly from that of cubs born later. In large litters sex ratios also favour male cubs significantly. Lactation in lions continues for 8 to 9 months after the birth of the cubs. All female lions help to raise the young, and the young cubs are usually gathered in a crèche. Females returning from a distant hunt often drop off to sleep as soon as they return, when any cub will suckle from any lactating female. However, if a female stays awake, she will usually nurse only her own cubs, possibly allowing other cubs to suckle when she has a surplus of milk. Such generosity among female lions is therefore more a matter of indifference than one of active choice. Males are rarely affectionate to their cubs, but they do provide effective protection for them. Nomads may also breed successfully, but their cubs seldom survive the first few weeks because of poor care.

Lion cubs grow rapidly when food is abundant, but those born synchronously survive better. Cubs also eat more, relative to their size, than adult lions. When the mother returns to the den after hunting, she makes a short, deep, humming sound to call her cubs to suckle. At their den lion cubs are highly vulnerable, being attacked and killed by other predators like spotted hyaenas *Crocuta crocuta,* leopards *Panthera pardus* and black-backed jackals *Canis mesomelas,* and even in some areas by safari ants. They can also be trampled to death by big game such as buffalo *Syncerus caffer* and elephant *Loxodonta africana*. As many as 80% of all lion cubs never reach adulthood. Although well-fed cubs can survive long periods between successive sucklings because lion milk is rich and nutritious, and although cub survival is high where food is abundant, many still die of starvation and malnutrition. This happens especially in relatively prey-poor areas where the mother may be absent from her cubs for as many as 2 to 3 days at a time. In all lions, male cubs suffer higher mortality rates than females. In Serengeti and the Ngorongoro

Crater, the survival of male cubs to 1 year also depends upon the number of male cubs present in the litter, and is significantly higher when there are three or more male cubs in the litter. However, the survival of all cubs to 3 years old is more than twice as high in the Ngorongoro Crater with its more stable year-round prey base than in Serengeti with its seasonally migrating prey.

From the age of 5 months lion cubs start showing an interest in other animals, but they only start to hunt actively when about 11 months old, although they do eat meat from an earlier age. A lioness may fetch her older cubs to feed on a kill if it is close enough to them. Weaning extends over a long period, from the age of 6 to 12 months. Young lions learn to hunt by watching the adults in a pride, and leave their natal pride from the age of 24 to 42 months. However, most subadult females will remain with their natal pride. In most areas male lions which disperse become nomadic, but in the Kruger National Park such males may remain in the vicinity of their natal pride for up to 4 years. In all lions more subadults disperse when food is abundant than when it is scarce.

Range use

The general pattern of range use in lions is that a pride occupies a defended range or territory, whereas a nomad has an undefended range. Pride territories are, however, not entirely exclusive, and may show some overlapping. The territorial system in lions is dynamic because it fluctuates in response to numerous environmental factors. Pride lions patrol their territories regularly and thoroughly, often to the exclusion of almost all else and at the expense of large amounts of energy. Although neighbouring prides may occasionally meet and fight, they more often merely approach each other, and then withdraw. When a strange lion enters a pride's territory, it keeps its distance, well away from any pride members. Many prides remain resident in the same area for years.

In the Kruger National Park, females dominate the territorial segment of the lion population, and all territorial (pride) males have a high turnover rate. The territory tenure of a male lion usually only starts when he is at least 5 years old, and does not last beyond the age of 10 years. As in other cats, range use by a female lion may decrease considerably when she has small cubs to care for. In Serengeti, prides travel further and wider, and have a lower food intake than those in the more prey-rich Ngorongoro Crater. This is so because of a migrating prey

base in Serengeti. Consequently a lion pride in Ngorongoro Crater has a range in the order of 45 km^2 compared with one of 200 km^2 in Serengeti. The larger ranges of Serengeti lions place an additional burden on the young cubs who may become weak, and are then abandoned to die when they cannot keep up with the moving pride. In times of extreme hardship, the territorial system of Serengeti lions may even break up altogether.

In the more arid, open savannas, lions must occupy huge ranges to meet all their life requirements. These ranges are usually much larger than those recorded in the more mesic savannas. Moreover, they may expand considerably in times of drought, as happened in the central Kalahari savanna where a specific pride's range increased from 702 km^2 to 3900 km^2 in response to prey dispersion during a drought. In one study in Etosha, the territories of 14 prides varied from 150 to 1075 km^2. The larger the pride, the larger its territory. In the more arid, tall, deciduous woodland savanna of the Kaudam area of Namibia, two prides had ranges of 1055 and 1178 km^2 respectively, and one in the Tsumkwe area had a range of 1745 km^2. These ranges are considerably larger than what has been reported for lions before, probably in response to a prey resource that is poor in abundance and availability, but which most likely also does not reflect a natural system. In the southern Kalahari savanna with its prey-poor resources, at least three different prides of females shared the same area with a single roving male on one occasion. Six months later, seven prides shared the same

37

area, although not always at the same time. Sharing the same area could have been the only way to survive a period of prey stress in a generally inhospitable environment.

Activity and movement

Lions rest for most of the day and much of the night, but they are capable of extensive movement. In Serengeti, 88% of all lion kills are made at night. In Etosha, 98% of all the hunts occur at night, more often between 21:30 and 22:30 than at any other time. Even when hunting, lions will often stop to rest or to indulge in other activities. There is some evidence that lions will increase their hunting activity levels during storms, when the noise, wind and vegetation movement make it difficult for prey to detect them.

Lion movements can be seasonal or diurnal in nature. In Serengeti lions follow the migratory herds of large herbivores seasonally. The same phenomenon, but on a smaller scale, occurs in the Kruger National Park where lions will follow migrating blue wildebeest over distances of up to 50 km. In Etosha lions move a mean distance of 13,2 km in 24 hours. In a study in the southern Kalahari savanna, the distances moved by five prides in 24 hours varied from 11,3 to 26,3 km. Another southern Kalahari pride once moved a maximum recorded distance of 33,8 km in 24 hours, but the mean distance moved in 24 hours by all prides in the area was 15,2 km. This is close to that found in

Although lions rest for most of the day in some suitable shade, they are ever-watchful for an opportunity to kill unsuspecting prey. Photo: J. du P. Bothma.

In contrast to most other areas, the lions of the Lake Manyara National Park often rest in trees, possibly to avoid the irritation of being bitten by flies.
Photo: J. du P. Bothma.

Etosha. However, although lions may cover vast distances in a single night, they rarely seem to hurry in doing so. In Serengeti, lions may also move long distances of as much as 21,5 km in 24 hours but, probably because of greater prey abundance, the distances covered over such a period are usually less (4,5 to 6,5 km) for its various prides than elsewhere. In the Ruwenzori National Park lions are less inclined to move about when they have recently eaten than when they are hungry.

When moving about, lions in most areas seldom climb trees, except occasionally, to escape from danger. However, at Lake Manyara and Ruwenzori the lions climb trees quite often, which may be done in an attempt to escape biting flies. Lions of the southern Kalahari savanna also sometimes climb trees, possibly to escape the sand tampans *Ornithodoros savignyi* which congregate in any available shade in that hot environment.

Feeding ecology

Lions hunt mainly at night. Food is important not only for daily survival, but because reproductive success and cub survival to adulthood in cats also depend upon the quality and quantity of available food. Lions eat any suitable food that is abundant and accessible, and their diet is more varied throughout their geographic range than that of any other large cat. In areas of low food availability, environmental stress and/or a high density of lions, cannibalism may occur as a normal predatory activity on isolated occasions. Although such cannibalism has long been thought of as aberrant behaviour, it is a natural phenomenon, but one which is more often directed at juveniles by adult males as a result of infanticide, rather than as a sincere effort to procure food. Although the lion is a highly efficient hunter, it will also scavenge for food. Those lions living in the *Acacia* savanna of Serengeti, however, are hunters rather than scavengers, killing 83% of all their food while, by contrast, lions in the open plains of Serengeti scavenge 53% of their food.

Although lions eat a wide spectrum of food, they more often eat prey ranging from 20 kg in size to a buffalo of 800 kg or more. However, large lion prides may occasionally attack larger prey such as a black rhinoceros *Diceros bicornis,* hippopotamus *Hippopotamus amphibius* or even the occasional young elephant and, in the Masai-Mara National Reserve buffalo account for a large proportion of the lion's food. In some areas, small prey make up a substantial portion of a lion's diet, but in other areas such small prey is usually taken only to tide a pride over difficult times, especially in areas where the larger prey migrate seasonally. In the relatively prey-rich Serengeti, lions use only 18 types of prey in comparison with 19 in the Kafue National Park and 38 in the Kruger National Park. This variation in choice is influenced by prey size, availability and abundance, and the availability of food for scavenging. Because lions are opportunistic feeders, they will utilise whatever food is easiest to find, and they consequently scavenge readily in some areas, but rarely so in others. Other carnivores are not generally used by lions as food, even when they are hungry.

Lions eat a wide spectrum of prey varying in size from about 20 kg to a buffalo of 800 kg or more.
Photo: J. du P. Bothma.

The prey size selected by a lion appears to increase with the number of lions present. There is an optimum pride size for the type of food resource of a given area, in which the combined energy provided is more efficient for the number of lions in the pride. When the pride is too large for the size of prey captured, it leads to intense competition at the carcass, to the detriment of the survival of the group. In Serengeti, for example, large lion prides may form when the migratory herds are present, but these prides will split into smaller groups which are energetically more efficient when the prey migrates out of the area. Opportunity and physical possibility will often determine whether a lion will kill a specific prey. Opportunity requires a lion to share the same habitat and activity cycle as its potential prey. For example, in Kafue, the puku *Kobus vardonii* and lechwe *Kobus leche* are abundant, but they are hunted with great difficulty by the lions who avoid the swampy habitat used by these prey. In comparison, the buffalo there are frequently killed by lions but more in the dry season (38,4% of all lion kills) when the vegetation density is reduced by bush fires, than in the wet season (18,1% of all lion kills) when the grass is tall and the cover dense. Lions in that region also often kill warthogs *Phacochoerus africanus,* which are easy to find.

In some areas lions definitely select specific prey. In Kafue they choose prey in their prime that are consequently in good condition. However, they also kill a higher proportion of prey in poor condition than the other predators present, and they definitely take fewer juvenile

Small herbivores such as the warthog are often killed by lions.
Photo: J. du P. Bothma.

animals than the other large carnivores. In other areas there seems to be little active selection of sick and disabled prey. However, some prey age groups may be more vulnerable than others, as happens in Savuti where lions kill significantly more buffalo cows than bulls, and where the buffalo bulls killed are mostly old individuals. Despite being effective hunters, lions may be infrequent feeders. In the Kruger National Park, for example, 47% of all lion stomachs examined were empty. Although these lions were found to feed at a mean rate of once every 4 days, some do so daily. The maximum interval between successive feeds there is 13 days.

The only known area where lions feed on a large proportion of small mammal prey consistently, is the southern Kalahari savanna with its poor prey resources. Some lions also eat large quantities of green grass, as do many other carnivores for reasons still unknown. In Etosha, lions rarely scavenge, but during the occasional anthrax epidemic, these lions do not have to hunt because they can live from scavenging the abundant carcasses, although some lions may continue to hunt. The lions there are not susceptible to anthrax and therefore do not suffer from the disease. Lions do not often eat other carnivores, yet they do kill carnivores such as black-backed jackals, spotted hyaenas, brown hyaenas *Parahyaena brunnea* and leopards, for no apparent reason.

Lion behaviour changes dramatically from day to night, transforming a shy and wary daytime animal into a bold and aggressive one at night. G.B. Schaller, who studied the lions of Serengeti for many years, states

43

that the movement of a cat is never more beautiful than when a lion purposefully snakes towards its prey. That fleeting moment of pause at the end of the stalk seconds before the final explosive rush, is one of almost unbearable tension to any observer. Lions hunt mainly at night when there is a greater chance of successful stalking. In their predation, however, they show extensive variation based upon the ecological constraints of each region, because the success or failure of a hunt depends as much upon the environment and the response of the prey as on the lion itself. In Ruwenzori lions hunting by moonlight are less successful than when there is no moon, possibly because the prey can detect the lions with more ease in the moonlight.

Lions must seek every possible advantage when hunting because of the fleet-footedness and keen senses of most of their prey. A lion normally starts hunting with a systematic search which is not directed at any particular prey animal. In searching, it sits or walks around slowly, scanning the environment. When potential prey is detected, a slow and deliberate stalk follows. Stalking can occur in bouts with the lion moving slowly and crouching low over the ground, often staring intently at its prey, and freezing when the intended victim becomes restive. Yet stalking can also take place as a slow but continuous movement with the lion making use of all available cover. Such cover would include all the main environmental features of an area such as weather, vegetation height and density, wind direction and even the time of day. Most of the hunting is done by the females and in Serengeti only 3% of more than a thousand observed lion stalks involved males. The lions there also usually hunt at night and do not seem to select for wind direction when hunting. In Etosha, by contrast, they hunt significantly more often and more successfully in downwind conditions. Lions may increase their hunting activities during rainstorms when the noise, wind and vegetation movement make it difficult for prey to detect the hunting lions.

A typical lion hunt involves a stalk of varying length during which the lions orientate themselves, mainly by sight. This is followed by a final rush which may reach speeds of up to 60 km/h for a short time, resulting in the kill if successful. The lion is not built for a prolonged chase. Its heart, for example, forms only about 0,5% of its body mass as opposed to 10% in a spotted hyaena, which can sustain chases over long distances. Lions will, however, adapt their hunting technique to the prevailing circumstances, sometimes surprising a prey animal at rest and killing it by simply pouncing on it without stalking or chasing, or by hunting from ambush. In Serengeti such opportunistic hunting attempts have the highest success rate. Female lions hunt proportionately more often than the males, and ecological factors will lead to local adaptations in the hunting behaviour of male lions.

Lions are known to hunt singly or in prides. Hunting as a pride requires less cover for a given lion, and it is done most frequently under the additional cover of darkness. When hunting as a pride, the individual pride members spread out in different directions to stalk a common prey. In doing so, the prey may or may not be surrounded. Often some pride members will circle the prey, while others wait to ambush any prey that moves towards them. The circling females usually initiate the attack, causing the prey to flee into the path of the ambushing females who make the kill. Pride hunting also seems to require an optimum pride size for maximum hunting efficiency. In the dry season in Etosha the optimal size for hunting would appear to be two females, while during the wet season female prides of all sizes each obtained more than the minimum daily food requirement for survival. When hunting in a pride, each lioness in Etosha repeatedly occupies the same position in the hunting formation. This preference for a specific hunting position seems to ensure a higher degree of success than when a position is chosen at random. However, the hunting behaviour of an individual pride member will differ according to variations which may occur in the composition of the pride over time, and in response to the hunting behaviour adopted by other pride members. Whatever the case, hunting as a pride will increase the feeding efficiency of each of the members of that pride, especially during the dry season.

In Serengeti male lions do not participate in hunting as a group, and also pursue their migrating prey less frequently than females. Nevertheless, they clearly benefit from any prey which has been hunted by the female members of the pride, and can therefore be construed to be cheating. Such cheating by refraining to help in the hunt is common in lions, and some females also do it sporadically, but especially when the prey is relatively common or easy to kill. In Etosha where prey occurs at low densities in isolated pockets, the females of a pride will probably cooperate more often and cheat less frequently.

When making a kill the lion is both a stalker and a runner, and the killing method used varies with prey type and size. Even when hunting as a pride, the actual kill is usually done by a single lioness when hunting easily killed prey such as a warthog or a wildebeest *Connochaetes taurinus*. However, when the prey is more difficult to kill, several individuals may cooperate in making the kill. The prey base of a given area therefore influences the degree of cooperative hunting practised by lions. In the flat, open savanna of Etosha, for example, lions often hunt

With its long canines, a lion kills its prey easily. Photo: C.H. Walker.

the fleet-footed springbok *Antidorcas marsupialis,* which requires a great deal of teamwork. By contrast, the hunting of massed prey during migration in Serengeti can be quite opportunistic and disorganised.

A lion is extremely powerful and when making a kill even the smaller lionesses can grab and pull down large prey such as a zebra *Equus burchellii* by simply using a grip on its rump. The prey may be stunned by a blow to the head, but it is usually suffocated with a muzzle grip, although its neck may also be broken occasionally. The killing method may vary, however, as the lion may adopt a special technique to kill certain game.

In the southern Kalahari savanna the lion has developed a special technique which allows it to kill a gemsbok which could easily kill its attacker with its long, rapier-like horns.
Photo: J. du P. Bothma.

For example, the potentially lethal gemsbok *Oryx gazella* in the southern Kalahari savanna is never attacked from the front. Instead, it is attacked from behind, with the lion jumping on to the gemsbok's haunches, breaking its back at the lumbosacral joint, and then seizing it by the muzzle or throat to suffocate it or crush its neck. The back is not broken by the impact of the attack but by a deliberate, sharp upward jerk. This is an adaptation to a type of prey which has long been known to be able to kill an attacking predator with its rapier-like horns. The fact that lions which kill gemsbok in Etosha do not adopt the same approach as in the southern Kalahari, has been ascribed to the smaller occurrence and diversity of the prey base available in the Kalahari, which makes killing gemsbok a more frequent necessity there.

Elsewhere lions also adopt special killing techniques for specific prey. For example the giraffe *Giraffa camelopardalis* is killed with a specialised technique which has been developed to knock this animal off its feet, pulling it down in such a way that the hooves of its powerful front feet are avoided. A giraffe uses these feet to chop down at an attacking lion with deadly accuracy and even its hind legs can be employed to danger-ous effect in a powerful backward kick. In attacking dangerous prey, lions may be killed or injured. Although temporarily injured lions will be cared for by other pride members, they must still attempt to avoid injury at all costs. When their prey is not caught at once, lions usually do not pursue the victims for long distances, although C. McBride believes that Savuti lions are capable of sustained bursts of speed over

47

In attacking a porcupine, a lion may sustain potentially debilitating injuries, which may eventually lead to starvation and death. Photo: J. du P. Bothma.

distances of as much as 1 km. In Etosha fleet-footed prey is usually hunted cooperatively, during which 73% of the prey killed is hunted from an ambush involving a chase of less than 10 m.

The lion's killing rate varies from area to area depending upon the terrain, pride size, prey composition and abundance. In Ruwenzori, only 28,8% of all the lion hunts are successful, but hunts involving an ambush are more successful (57,1%) than others. In Serengeti opportunistic hunts without much preparation are the most successful (61%), followed by hunts involving stalking by single lions (17 to 19%), and then by those of single lions chasing prey (8%). However, almost half of all the hunts there involve two lions hunting together, with a killing success of 30%. For larger prey, the killing rate increases with increasing pride size. Single lions in Serengeti kill 15% of all the large prey they hunt, whereas prides of 6 to 8 lions kill 43% of the prey hunted. In Etosha lions kill 15% of all prey hunted, but single females are mostly unsuccessful (2,3% success) in capturing large, fleet-footed prey. Cooperative hunts in the region have a mean success rate of 27%, but this also increases with increasing pride size. Multiple kills sometimes occur too. During 12 hunts recorded in Etosha, a pride killed two prey animals in the same hunt, and three prey animals in each of three different hunts.

Lions occasionally kill unnecessarily. This happens in predators when many more prey are killed in one attack than could possibly be eaten, and may occur because of unusual circumstances when the prey is not reacting to normal stimuli, such as during a violent thunder-storm. Surplus killing in the wild is rare among lions, but a pride of lions did once kill 15 buffalo in a single attack in the Kruger National Park. Also, a severe drought in the southern Kalahari System in 1985 led to the concentration of thousands of game at waterholes where lions would lie and wait to attack the milling mass. As these lions were usually already satiated, they ate little of their kills. Once the surplus killing trigger has been released, the impulse seems to continue to operate until all vulnerable prey have been attacked, or the lions have become exhausted.

When feeding at a carcass, lions are well organised socially, although there is considerable squabbling. The larger males are dominant over the females, but in the Kruger National Park large territorial males are present with pride females for only 6,1% of the time, and at only 13% of the kills of such prides. Young cubs usually get whatever food happens to remain after the adults have fed, but they may occasionally be allowed to feed with the males. A small kill or a piece of a larger carcass can also be claimed by a single lion, especially if the lion can carry the food away on its own. Heavy carcasses are pulled backward into some shade by one or more of the lions. They feed while lying on their bellies, and are the only cats which habitually do so. Most of the others sit, crouch or stand while feeding. The prey may or may not be gutted before feeding begins. Unlike most other cats, lions seldom eat the stomach, but they do eat the intestines of their prey. The viscera are sometimes covered with soil and vegetation. The lion that made the actual kill usually rests for a while, allowing the other lions in the pride to start feeding first. When feeding, males usually start on the buttocks, while the females and cubs start on the internal organs. Porcupines are frequently hunted in the southern Kalahari savanna, and they are partially dequilled by lions and leopards before being eaten. Lions consume their large prey as completely as possible, and a pride of lions can take up to 4 days to finish a big carcass such as a buffalo.

In Savuti a lion's food intake is 1,6 times higher in the rainy season when more large prey is available than in the dry season. In Serengeti lone females may often eat more than the individual females of a pride. The main food intake per sitting for a Serengeti lion is 16 kg, but one of the males is known to have consumed an estimated 53 kg of food in one night. In Etosha, however, lions that hunt alone during the prey-poor dry season do not get the estimated minimum of 5 to 8,5 kg of food required daily for long-term survival, and experience food stress periodically as a result.

49

A porcupine is partially dequilled before a lion or leopard starts to feed on it.
Photo: J. du P. Bothma.

In the Kruger National Park lions have a slower rate of digestion, and they also eat less frequently than spotted hyaenas. Lions generally experience some degree of competition for food from spotted hyaenas and they may lose a portion of their food to these hyaenas, but this is dependent upon the lion pride size. In Serengeti lions may lose 10% of the meat from a carcass to scavenging spotted hyaenas if the pride consists of fewer than four lions. The Savuti lion prides often have a shortage of adult males and therefore prides consisting of females and subadults only, may have almost 20% of their food stolen by spotted hyaenas. In studies of animal behaviour this is known as kleptoparasitism. The losses are most frequent in small prides. In the absence of large male lions, spotted hyaenas can drive female and subadult lions away from their kills, provided that they outnumber the lions by at least 4:1. Consequently the larger the pride, the more successfully it can defend its kill. Nevertheless, even those lions which are driven off their kills have usually fed well before they are deprived of their food, although such action does constitute a constant energy drain which forces these lions to hunt more frequently than would otherwise be necessary.

When water is available, lions will drink regularly, and there is no apparent preference for water quality. However, even when water is available, they may go without drinking for up to 5 days. In the southern Kalahari savanna lions are found up to 250 km away from the nearest water and are consequently independent of free water. They make use of metabolic water, the fluids of their prey and the moisture in wild fruit, and may even lick moisture off each other's fur when it rains. In

It can take a pride of lions several days to finish a large carcass.
Photo: C.H. Walker.

Kenya they are also known to chew *Sanseviera* plants and to pull them out of the ground to get at the moisture-rich roots. In cool weather the lions of the Hluhluwe-Umfolozi Park do not obtain a significant portion of their water from drinking although it is available. However, in hot weather about 50% of their water intake is from drinking. Females with cubs have a greater need for moisture than other lions. When lions do drink water, it becomes a social event for pride members. They also pant rapidly at a rate of up to 140 pants per minute to avoid heat stress.

Relationship with other wildlife

The question of whether lions and other large predators can influence their prey negatively has often been debated. In the early years of conservation in Africa, lions were shot as a deliberate management strategy because it was believed that prey populations could be increased in this way. In the process thousands of lions were shot in the Kruger National Park alone up to 1946. From 1974 to 1979 lions and spotted hyaenas were again shot there in an attempt to stop a major decline in blue wildebeest and zebra numbers. This culling was later stopped when habitat change from years of excessive rainfall, and not predation, was found to be the significant cause of the decline in these prey animals. The lions soon restored their numbers by immigration and increased reproduction.

51

It is now generally known that predators cannot regulate their prey numbers in natural areas, unless such prey is already low in number. The prey is regulated mainly by their dry-season food supply, and to a lesser extent by parasites and disease. Where man intervenes in the system, however, by creating artificial waterholes or introducing prey strange to an area for example, lions can severely influence their prey at times. In Serengeti lions are only responsible for a small portion of all the mortalities of their most common prey, the wildebeest. In the Klaserie Private Nature Reserve, the lion population dispersed after prolonged droughts caused their prey to diminish considerably in numbers.

Although lions kill the occasional elephant, they are generally wary of these large herbivores which can easily intimidate them.
Photo: C.H. Walker.

The lion of the African savannas does not compete much with other carnivores because all the larger carnivores in these savannas are usually separated ecologically. Although the lion is the leopard's closest competitor where there is some prey overlap, the degree of competition in Serengeti is reduced because the leopard usually has a much more varied diet than the lion. Lions readily appropriate spotted hyaena kills, but the reverse is equally true. It all seems to be a matter of group size and aggression. In Savuti, for example, lion prides often suffer from a lack of large males. Consequently they may lose as much as 20% of their food when outnumbered 4:1 or more by spotted hyaenas. Even when outnumbered 2:1, the lions are mobbed and disturbed by scavenging spotted hyaenas who may often feed alongside the lions in the absence of a large pride male. Therefore prides without a large male tend to hunt in groups of females and subadults which are sufficiently large to defend a kill against spotted hyaenas for long enough to satiate themselves. Nevertheless, this competition is a constant energy drain on these lions.

Population dynamics

Lion population dynamics varies from region to region because of environmental and other variables. For example, the lions of Serengeti clearly have a harder life than those of the Ngorongoro Crater. On the Serengeti Plains the large migratory prey herds make the lion's food supply more ephemeral, water is scarcer in the dry season, and denning sites are more widely scattered than in the Ngorongoro Crater. Consequently cub mortality in Serengeti is highly seasonal, and also much higher than in the Ngorongoro Crater. In the Kruger National Park the oldest lion collected was a 16-year-old male. The oldest known female collected was 14 years old, and there are considerably more old females than males in the population. All lions older than 12 years are also in poor condition. It is believed that wild lions in Serengeti can live up to 18 years.

The sex ratio of lions also varies from region to region. In the Kruger National Park male lions were found to be vital to pride functioning, although they spend the majority of their time away from the pride females, either as male coalitions or alone. There are usually two territorial males per pride and 2,9 females per male. In the southern Kalahari savanna the sex ratio of adult lions is 1,4 to 2,1 females per male. In cubs it is 1,6 females per male. The sex ratio of adult lions in Etosha is almost equal, as it is in Selous and Serengeti. However, other authors believe the sex ratio in Etosha to be 1,4 females per male which is similar to what it seems to be in most of Africa. In a deciduous woodland elsewhere in Namibia females outnumber males by 1,4:1.

In Serengeti adult lions form 57% of the population, and in the subadults the males are almost twice as abundant as females. The annual recruitment rate there is 11%. Cubs form 17% of the population and subadults 26%. In Selous juvenile lions make up 21% of the population. By contrast, 60% of the lions in the Nairobi National Park are juveniles, possibly because of the higher reproductive rates and better cub survival. Some authors believe that cub mortality rates may be the best indicator of lion population dynamics. In Serengeti 67% of all the lion cubs die each year. In one area 28% died of starvation, but more cubs probably die of starvation when the prides follow the migrating

herds of prey than for any other reason. Of all the lions, most die of disease, starvation, abandonment, old age or violent conflict with other large predators, including other lions. In Serengeti 41% of the lions which die are adults in their prime and only 10% of all the lions born there eventually reach old age. Buffaloes and elephants occasionally trample lion cubs and some adults are crippled when they attack dangerous prey. The type of prey resource available obviously influences lion survival, because some prey are more difficult or dangerous to capture than others. Mortality rates also differ between the sexes, with males being more vulnerable as was found in the Kruger National Park. There the adult males are not necessarily territorial, and intraspecific competition is high among the males.

Lions are prone to various diseases but immune to others. In southern African lions there is widespread infection from the canine distemper virus, but there are usually no catastrophic mortalities. Nevertheless, in a recent outbreak of canine distemper in the Serengeti-Mara ecosystem 33% of its estimated 3000 lions died of this disease. In Namibia, Botswana and Zimbabwe isolated cases of rabies are found in lions, but it remains a rare and sporadic disease in the lions of the African savannas. Although lions are sometimes exposed to anthrax from affected herbivores, they are fairly resistant to this disease. A recent severe outbreak of tuberculosis amongst the African buffalo in the southern part of the Kruger National Park is now threatening the survival of some of the lions which prey on them there. Lions are also heavily parasitised by all manner of external and internal parasites.

BIBLIOGRAPHY

Aiken, B. 1987. *Nightstalk.* Jersey: Afropix.

Anderson, J.L. 1980. The re-establishment and management of a lion *Panthera leo* population in Zululand, South Africa. *Biological Conservation,* 19: 107–117.

Berry, H.H. 1981. Abnormal levels of disease and predation as limiting factors for wildebeest in the Etosha National Park. *Madoqua,* 12(4): 242–253.

Berry, H.H. 1983. First catch your lion. *Rössing Magazine,* April 1983: 1–7.

Bertram, B.C.R. 1975. The social system of lions. *Scientific American,* 232: 54–65.

Bertram, B.C.R. 1979. Serengeti predators and their social systems. In: Sinclair, A.R.E. & Norton-Griffiths, M. (Eds), *Serengeti, dynamics of an ecosystem.* Chicago: University of Chicago Press, 221–248.

Bosman, P. & Hall-Martin, A. 1997. *Cats of Africa.* Vlaeberg: Fernwood.

Bothma, J. du P. 1998. *Carnivore ecology in arid lands.* Berlin: Springer.

Bryden, B.R. 1978. *The biology of the African lion* (Panthera leo) *(Linn. 1758) in the Kruger National Park.* M.Sc. thesis. Pretoria: University of Pretoria.

Caraco, T. & Wolf, L.L. 1975. Ecological determinants of group sizes of foraging lions. *The American Naturalist,* 109(967): 343–352.

Cooper, S.M. 1991. Optimal hunting group size: the need for lions to defend their kills against loss to spotted hyaenas. *African Journal of Ecology,* 29: 130–136.

Cowie, M. 1966. *The African lion.* New York: Golden.

Cruikshank, K.M. & Robinson, T.J. 1997. Inheritance of the white coat colour phenotype in African lions *(Panthera leo).* In: Van Heerden, J. (Ed.), *Lions and leopards as game ranch animals.* The Wildlife Group. Onderstepoort: South African Veterinary Association, 92–95.

De Vos, V. & Bryden, H. 1997. The role of carnivores in the epidemiology of anthrax in the Kruger National Park. In: Van Heerden, J. (Ed.), *Lions and leopards as game ranch animals.* The Wildlife Group. Onderstepoort: South African Veterinary Association, 198–203.

Eloff, F.C. 1964. On the predatory habits of lions and hyaenas. *Koedoe,* 7: 105–112.

Eloff, F.C. 1973a. Ecology and behavior of the Kalahari lion *Panthera leo vernayi* (Roberts). In: Eaton, R.L. (Ed.), *The world's cats. Vol 1: Ecology and Conservation.* World Wildlife Safari. Oregon: Winston, 90–126.

Eloff, F.C. 1973b. Water use by the Kalahari lion *Panthera leo vernayi. Koedoe,* 16: 149–154.

Fagotto, F. 1985. The lion in Somalia. *Mammalia,* 49(4): 587–588.

Fitzsimons, W.F. 1925. *South African nature study.* Cape Town: Winderly.

Frobenius, L.E. 1954. *Kulturgeschichte Afrikas.* Zürich.

Funston, P.J. & Mills, M.G.L. 1997. Aspects of sociality in Kruger Park lions: the role of males. In: Van Heerden, J. (Ed.), *Lions and leopards as game ranch animals.* The Wildlife Group. Onderstepoort: South African Veterinary Association, 18–26.

Gesner, K. 1563. *Tierbuch.* Zürich: C. Froschoverum.

Green, B., Anderson, J. & Whateley, T. 1984. Water and sodium turnover and estimated food consumption in free-living lions *(Panthera leo)* and spotted hyaenas *(Crocuta crocuta). Journal of Mammalogy,* 65(4): 593–599.

Grobler, D.G. 1997. Lion mass capture techniques. In: Van Heerden, J. (Ed.), *Lions and leopards as game ranch animals*. The Wildlife Group. Onderstepoort: South African Veterinary Association, 112–115.

Hanby, J.P., Bygott, J.D. & Packer C. 1995. Ecology, demography and behavior of lions in two contrasting habitats: Ngorongoro Crater and the Serengeti Plains. In: Sinclair, A.R.E. & Arcese, P. (Eds), *Serengeti II: dynamics, management and conservation of an ecosystem*. Chicago: University of Chicago Press, 315–331.

Johnsingh, A.J.T. & Chellam, R. 1991. India's last lions. *Zoogoer Magazine*, September–October, 16–20

Kingdon, J. 1977. *East African mammals*. Vol. III, Part A: Carnivores. London: Academic.

Kruger, J.E. 1988. *Interrelationships between the larger carnivores of the Klaserie Private Nature Reserve, with special reference to the leopard* Panthera pardus *(Linnaeus, 1758) and the cheetah* Acinonyx jubatus *(Schreber, 1775)*. MSc thesis. Pretoria: University of Pretoria.

Kruuk, H. 1972. Surplus killing by carnivores. *Journal of the Zoological Society, London*, 166: 233–244.

Kruuk, H. & Turner, M. 1967. Comparative notes on predation by lion, leopard, cheetah and wild dog in the Serengeti area, East Africa. *Mammalia*, 31(1): 1:27.

Makacha, S. & Schaller, G.B. 1969. Observations on lions in the Lake Manyara National Park, Tanzania. *East African Wildlife Journal*, 7: 99–103.

McBride, C. 1990. *Liontide*. Johannesburg: Jonathan Ball.

Melton, D.A., Berry, H.H, Berry, C.U. & Joubert, S.M. 1987. Aspects of the blood chemistry of wild lions *Panthera leo. South African Journal of Zoology*, 22(1): 40–44.

Miller, P. 1979. *Myths and legends of southern Africa*. Cape Town: T.V. Bulpin.

Mills, M.G.L. & Shenk, T.M. 1992. Predator-prey relationships: the impact of lion predation on wildebeest and zebra populations. *Journal of Animal Ecology*, 61: 693–702.

Mills, M.G.L., Wolff, P., Le Riche, E.A.N. & Meyer, I.J. 1978. Some population characteristics of the lion *Panthera leo* in the Kalahari Gemsbok National Park. *Koedoe*, 21: 163–171.

Mitchell, B.L., Shenton, J.B. & Uys, J.C.M. 1965. Predation on large mammals in the Kafue National Park, Zambia. *Zoologica Africana*, 1(2): 297–318.

Myers, N. 1972. *The long African day*. New York: Macmillan.

Nowell, K. & Jackson, P. 1996. *Wild cats*. Cambridge: IUCN Publication Services.

Owens, M.J. & Owens, D.D. 1984. *Cry of the Kalahari*. Boston: Houghton Mifflin.

Packer, C. & Kock, R. 1995. Serengeti lions recovering from canine distemper epidemic. *Cat News*, 23: 9.

Packer, C. & Pusey, A.E. 1983. Adaptations of female lions to infanticide by incoming males. *The American Naturalist*, 121(5): 716–728.

Packer, C. & Pusey, A.E. 1987. Intrasexual cooperation and the sex ratio in African lions. *The American Naturalist*, 130(4): 636–642.

Packer, C. & Pusey, A.E. 1997. Divided we fall: cooperation among lions. *Scientific American*, May, 32–39.

Pennycuick, C.J. & Rudnai, J. 1970. A method of identifying individual lions *Panthera leo*, with an analysis of the reliability of identification. *Journal of Zoology, London*, 160: 497–508.

Pienaar, U. de V. 1969. Predator-prey relationships amongst the larger mammals of the Kruger National Park. *Koedoe,* 12: 108–184.

Pocock, R.I. 1917. The classification of the existing Felidae. *Annals and Magazine of Natural History,* 8(20): 329–350.

Polis, G.A., Myers, C.A. & Hess, W.R. 1984. A survey of intraspecific predation within the Class Mammalia. *Mammal Review,* 14(4): 187–198.

Rodgers, W.A. 1974. The lion (*Panthera leo,* Linn.) population of the eastern Selous Game Reserve. *East African Wildlife Journal,* 12: 313–317.

Roosevelt, T. & Heller, E. 1915. *Life histories of African animals.* London: John Murray.

Rudnai, J. 1973. Reproductive biology of lions (*Panthera leo massaica,* Neumann) in Nairobi National Park. *East African Wildlife Journal,* 11: 241–253.

Saba, A.R.K. 1979. Predator-prey interaction: a case study in the Masai-Mara Game Reserve, Kenya. In: Ajayi, S.S. & Halstead, L.B. (Eds), *Wildlife management in savannah woodland.* London: Taylor & Francis, 41–49.

Schaller, G.B. 1972. *The Serengeti lion.* Chicago: University of Chicago Press.

Scheel, D. & Packer, C. 1991. Group hunting behaviour of lions: a search for cooperation. *Animal Behavior,* 41: 697–709.

Scheel, D. & Packer, C. 1995. Variation in predation by lions: tracking a movable feast. In: Sinclair, A.R.E. & Arcese, P. (Eds), *Serengeti II: dynamics, management, and conservation of an ecosystem.* Chicago: University of Chicago Press.

Schenkel, R. 1966. Play, exploitation and territoriality in the wild lion. *Symposium of the Zoological Society of London,* 18: 11–22.

Scott, J. 1985. *The leopard's tale.* London: Elm Tree.

Smuts, G.L. 1978a. More sex ratio data on lions. *Carnivore,* 1(2): 1.

Smuts, G.L. 1978b. Effects of population reduction on the travels and reproduction of lions in the Kruger National Park. *Carnivore,* 1(2): 61–72.

Smuts, G.L. 1978c. Interrelations between predators, prey, and their environment. *BioScience,* 28(5): 316–320.

Smuts, G.L. 1979. Diet of lions and spotted hyaenas assessed from stomach contents. *South African Journal of Wildlife Research,* 9: 19–25.

Smuts, G.L. 1982. *Lion.* Johannesburg: Macmillan.

Smuts, G.L., Anderson, J.L. & Austin, J.C. 1978. Age determination of the African lion (*Panthera leo*). *Journal of Zoology, London,* 185: 115–146.

Smuts, G.L., Hanks, J. & Whyte, I.J. 1978. Reproduction and social organization of lions from the Kruger National Park. *Carnivore,* 1(1): 17–28.

Smuts, G.L., Robinson, G.A. & Whyte, I.J. 1980. Comparative growth of wild male and female lions (*Panthera leo*). *Journal of Zoology, London,* 190: 365–373.

Stander, P.E. 1991. Demography of lions in the Etosha National Park, Namibia. *Madoqua,* 18(1): 1–9.

Stander, P.E. 1992a. Cooperative hunting in lions: the role of the individual. *Behavioral Ecology and Sociobiology,* 29: 445–454.

Stander, P.E. 1992b. Foraging dynamics of lions in a semi-arid environment. *Canadian Journal of Zoology,* 70: 8–21.

Stander, P.E. 1997. The ecology of lions and conflict with people in north-eastern Namibia. In: Van Heerden, J. (Ed.), *Lions and leopards as game ranch animals.* The Wildlife Group. Onderstepoort: South African Veterinary Association, 10–17.

Sunquist, M.E. & Sunquist, F.C. 1989. Ecological constraints on predation by large felids. In: Gittleman, J.L. (Ed.), *Carnivore behavior, ecology and evolution.* London: Chapman & Hall.

Van Orsdol, K.G. 1984. Foraging behaviour and hunting success of lions in Queen Elizabeth National Park, Uganda. *African Journal of Ecology,* 22: 79–99.

Van Vuuren, M., Styliamides, E. & Du Rand, A. 1997. The prevalence of viral infections in lions and leopards in southern Africa. In: Van Heerden, J. (Ed.), *Lions and leopards as game ranch animals.* The Wildlife Group. Onderstepoort: South African Veterinary Association, 163–173.

Verberne, G. & De Boer, J. 1976. Chemocommunication among domestic cats, mediated by the olfactory and vomeronasal senses. *Zeitschrift für Tierpsychologie,* 42: 86–109.

Verberne, G. & Leyhausen, P. 1976. Marking behaviour of some Viverridae and Felidae: time-interval analysis of the marking pattern. *Behaviour,* 58(3–4): 192–253.

Viljoen, P.C. 1997. Ecology of lions in northern Botswana. In: Van Heerden, J. (Ed.), *Lions and leopards as game ranch animals.* The Wildlife Group. Onderstepoort: South African Veterinary Association, 37–46.

Wozencraft, W.C. 1993. Order Carnivora. In: Wilson, D.E. & Reeder, D.M. (Eds), *Mammal species of the world,* 2nd ed. Washington, DC: Smithsonian Institution Press, 279–348.

Wright, B.S. 1960. Predation on big game in East Africa. *Journal of Wildlife Management,* 24(1): 1–15.

3

The leopard

There is no large carnivore as elusive and shy as the leopard *Panthera pardus*. For many a traveller the only memory of seeing a leopard, beyond the initial shock of suddenly looking into two opalescent eyes, is an incomplete and fleeting optical image.

The leopard is more revered than the lion by many African people for whom the leopard is the ultimate symbol of power because of its courage and tenacity in attack. In these societies only people of high social standing may wear leopard-skin cloaks, and many secret societies have the leopard as their totem. The right to ownership of a leopard skin is strictly regulated and is dictated by tradition. Amongst the Karamajo and Acholi people of East Africa leopard skins are part of the warrior's regalia. Among the Buganda and Zulu people the leopard skin is the symbol of kingship and only the head of the family may sit on a leopard-skin rug. The tail fur is also burned and smoked in a pipe by the Buganda to call home a straying wife, child or other relative. It is believed that just as the leopard's tail is always restless, so will the wanderer's heart be without rest until the individual returns. A leopard's claws are widely used to promote business stability. In West Africa the leopard is the symbol of wisdom, and leopard images are frequently carved by Ife and Benin sculptors. Even in ancient Egypt the priests of some of the later dynasties wore leopard-skin vestments, as do all the images which portray Sekhanit, the goddess of writing. Moreover, when Pharoah Tutankhamun's mummy was discovered, a statue which portrayed him mounted on a realistic model of a leopard was found in his tomb with him. On a continent-wide basis it is believed that an enemy can be killed by cutting up leopard whiskers and adding them to a victim's drink and food. This apparently causes peritonitis. An angry leopard is the incarnation of ferocity. It is the perfect killing machine which can concentrate all its considerable energy into an attack at lightning speed. Secretive, silent, smooth and supple as a piece of silk, the leopard is an animal of darkness, but even in the dark it travels alone.

Although this large, roaring cat lives a solitary life, it is a highly effective killer of prey. The leopard was originally described scientifically by C. Linnaeus in 1758 as *Felis pardus* from a specimen collected in Egypt, but it was first placed in the genus *Panthera* by R.I. Pocock in 1930. It occupies more diverse habitats than any other mammal except man and some rodents, being found in regions which vary from open, arid savannas to snow-capped peaks and tropical forests. This adaptive ability explains why there are still some 27 subspecies of leopard recognised by most scientists today, although there have been recent suggestions that they should be reduced to the following eight: *Panthera pardus pardus* in Africa, *Panthera pardus saxicolor* in central Asia, *Panthera pardus fusca* in India, *Panthera pardus kotiya* in Sri Lanka, *Panthera pardus melas* in Java, *Panthera pardus delacouri* in South China, *Panthera pardus japonensis* in

The leopard varies in colour from a pale yellow to a deep gold, patterned with black rosettes. Photo: F.C. Eloff.

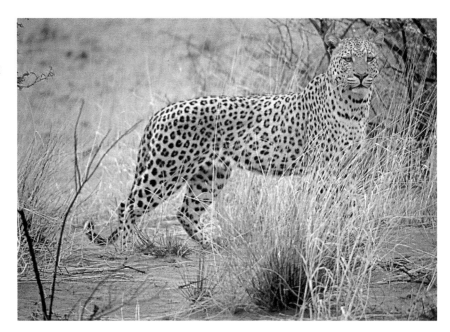

North China (which is not found in Japan as its name would suggest) and *Panthera pardus orientalis* in the Far East including Russia. The leopard's adaptiveness is further reflected by the fact that it is the most common large predator found in southern African fossil deposits which date back 1,8 to 1 million years, although this fossil leopard was larger than the modern one. Even today the leopard is the only large cat which can survive near human habitation.

The leopard varies in size and colour from region to region. Its colour ranges from a pale yellow to a deep gold, patterned with black rosettes. These rosettes or spots are spectacularly beautiful, and they allow a leopard to remain unseen in the barest of cover. The spots have been retained relatively unchanged from what was previously more of a forest life, possibly because they still help the leopard to move about undetected in other areas. Black leopards, often called black panthers, are a colour variation caused by an autosomal recessive gene, and it occurs most frequently in moist forests. Black leopards are more common in Asia than in Africa, but they are known from the forests of Mount Kenya and the foothills of the Ruwenzoris. They are also said to have been common in parts of Ethiopia. Another type of spot amalgam also occurs in the leopards of Ethiopia where the intermediate coat colour is suppressed. This closes up the margins of the rosettes to form solid black spots on the body, like those found on the legs of most leopards. Random linking of this bitonal pattern can lead to extraordinary marbling which resembles the pattern of the king cheetah. In the past there have also been reports of leopards with the spots amalgamated to form black stripes on the back, but this process differs from that causing stripes in the tiger *Panthera tigris*. Large male leopards may weigh up to 90 kg in some areas, and females up to 60 kg, but the mean weight in the Kruger National Park is 58 kg for males and 37,5 kg for females. The leopards from the coastal mountain areas of the Western Cape Province of South Africa are much smaller, the males being about 31 kg and the females 21 kg.

Leopard density varies from region to region because of prey abundance and its influence on range size. However, leopards reach their highest densities in the prey-rich tropical forests of the East. In savannas the overall leopard density is much lower than in these forests, but it can be high along riverine vegetation. In the Tsavo National Park there is a mean density of 7,6 male leopards per 100 km². In the Kruger National Park where the prey resource is adequate, the adult male leopard density varies from approximately 2 to 4 per 100 km², and from 7 to 12 per 100 km² for females. The entire population varies from approximately 9 to 16 leopards per 100 km². By contrast, the arid savannas have leopard densities as low as 1,5 adults per 100 km². In sub-Saharan Africa there seems to be a significant positive correlation between leopard density and prey biomass.

Social behaviour

Like most cats the leopard lives a solitary life, and the only groups formed are those of a female and her dependent young. Males and females associate only briefly to mate. Given the leopard's hunting behaviour, being alone is the best way for this large cat to survive. Although leopards have well-defined but partially overlapping ranges, there are also occasional nomads who wander widely through the ranges of resident leopards.

Leopards, like cats in general, use a variety of communication systems which include vocalisations, body postures and various forms of chemical communication. The female uses her tail as a visual guide when leading her cubs somewhere. When returning to her cubs, she makes a chuffing sound consisting of three or more short, sharp puffs to greet them. Leopards also emit a characteristic hoarse, rasping cough to advertise their presence when moving through their range, but they are normally silent. Females call most often when approaching oestrus, and all leopards purr loudly, especially during or after feeding. Encounters between territorial males are excessively noisy, and are punctuated by loud grunts and growls. Chemical communication is used as widely in leopards as in all cats. In scent-marking the leopard closely resembles the lion. Every potential chemical odour appears to be of use to leopards when they are scent-marking, whether employed for that purpose or not. Range boundaries are clearly marked by scent, or are proclaimed by making particular sounds. As is the case with mammals in general, it is likely that the faeces, urine and other chemical substances secreted by leopards have an individual odour which identifies the owner and allows the range to be individually marked.

A leopard's urine is mixed with glandular secretions which are used for communication in combination with the secretions of various other glands, as is the case with all cats. There was some disagreement originally about whether leopards scratched trees as a means of scent-marking, whether they were cleaning their claws by removing loose flaking strips, or whether they were simply stretching. Tree-scratching is often accompanied by spray-urination, however, and must have a chemical message function. Several authors therefore regard this action as a form of chemical communication which not only tells a given leopard where he is, but also informs other leopards of his whereabouts. Nevertheless, the degree and intensity of tree-scratching varies in leopards from different regions, and consequently must be influenced by a range of ecological conditions. In 1967 P. Turnbull-Kemp suggested that African leopards rarely claw or scratch trees, and it was indeed found that this practice occurred only rarely among the leopards of Tsavo and Serengeti. However, in the moist tropical forests of Sri Lanka tree-scratching is common among leopards and in some areas of southern Africa it also appears to be relatively prevalent. It is known to occur in the Matobo National Park, and in the southern Kalahari savanna. By contrast, tree-scratching has not been observed in the Kruger National Park leopards. Where it does occur, tree-scratching is followed by urination against the tree trunk. The same tree may be used repeatedly as a scratch post in some areas, but not in others.

Leopards also scrape over their urine when it is deposited on the ground by using each hind foot alternatively. In the Kruger National Park male leopards scrape more frequently than females, yet African leopards seem to scrape less frequently than those elsewhere. Faeces are rarely scraped over in Tsavo. The same applies to the southern Kalahari savanna where a female only once covered her faeces by scratching sand over it when she defecated close to a den containing her young cubs. Although some authors believe that the faeces have no communication function in leopards, others believe that a female leopard in the Masai Mara does use faeces to mark the boundaries of her range. It is also believed that the faeces of carnivores, which are inevitably contaminated by anal gland secretions, must have a useful scent-marking function, especially when deposited in piles on the range boundaries. Urine is the most common scent-marking agent in leopards, as it also is in the other cats. In leopards the secretions of two anal glands at the base of the tail mix with the urine to produce a scented spray which lasts for several days. When a leopard scent-marks by urination, the urine is sprayed backwards against a bush or a tree trunk, on the leaves of bushes or on other suitable objects. Both sexes scent-mark by urination, but in some regions the males do so more often than the females. Males in the southern Kalahari savanna also seem to increase their rate of scent-marking trees before mating.

Leopards rub their bodies against tree trunks as well. In the southern Kalahari savanna males do so more often than females, but such rubbing may be more for grooming than for scent-marking. However, rubbing may be combined with urination in leopards, and in the Masai Mara and the Kruger National Park female leopards rub their flanks, backs, faces, foreheads and throats along the underside of fallen branches or against bushes where another leopard has recently spray-urinated. They then spray-urinate in turn. Leopards are also known to sniff at the ground or the dung of various animals, and then roll on it. Such rolling is done even in the middle of a careful hunt, and its function is as yet unknown. Once a spotted hyaena was observed to roll on the spot where a female leopard had lain. It then devoured all the leopard droppings on the site. These events must convey a message of some kind or another.

Reproduction and young

Like in all the other cats, there is no permanent pair bonding in leopards, and mating follows the general cat pattern. Females become sexually mature when approximately 3 years old, and males probably when they are a little older. However, younger males may sometimes become sexually active when there are no older males present. There is no clear mating season. Female leopards are polyoestrous, and a female in oestrus wanders widely in her range, calling often as she does so, and leaving olfactory clues to her receptive state on the vegetation through which she passes. These clues include hormones which are mixed with her urine. Females on heat also drag their hind legs and scrape the ground, leaving visual signs of receptivity which may last for several days. In Serengeti a female who was studied when she was coming into oestrus, moved outside her normal range to find a mate, but then returned to her range with him to continue mating there. If a female has not mated, oestrus occurs again every 20 to 50 days.

A leopard's copulation is brief, but it is repeated often over a period which can vary from one to several days. When copulating, a male bites the female's neck as lions and cheetahs do. He may also emit the characteristic rasping call at that time and sometimes two males may fight fiercely over a female. In the Kruger National Park the mating success rate appears to be low, and in one study only two or 15% of 13 suspected matings resulted in the birth of cubs. This low success rate is much like that of lions (20%) in the same park. The known interval between successive litters in the same female varies from 16 to 17 months in the South African bushveld savanna where it is less than the interval of 24 to 25 months recorded in Serengeti. A leopard's gestation period is approximately 90 to 106 days and a leopard cub weighs between 500 g and 1 kg at birth. The cub's eyes are closed at birth and open for the first time after 6 to 10 days. The litter size varies from one to three cubs in most cases in the wild, although larger litters are possible.

A leopard cub is usually born in a secluded spot amongst thick vegetation, or in a suitable lair or burrow. Young cubs less than a month old are usually kept in a burrow which is often one that housed an aardvark *Orycteropus afer* or porcupine *Hystrix africaeaustralis*, and they do not follow their mother about. When a cub reaches the age of 3 months, it starts to accompany its mother when she hunts, but such cubs normally stop to take their rest for the day long before the female does. Consequently they may be left alone for up to 6 consecutive nights if the mother does not hunt successfully and this makes them highly susceptible to death from starvation and predation. When they are mobile enough, the mother returns to lead her cubs to food once she has made a kill and has fed herself for a little while. After feeding, the cubs remain near the kill, but the mother may continue to hunt.

Leopard cubs are usually born in an appropriate lair such as the burrow of another animal. Photo: J. du P. Bothma.

Suckling cubs are attended more often by their mothers than cubs which are weaned but still dependent. Leopard cubs in the bushveld savanna are totally dependent on their mother for a little more than their first year of life. They suckle for 12 weeks, but may start to eat some meat when about 8 weeks old. They begin to kill prey at 4 months, but only really start to hunt intensively with their mother at about 10 months. The cubs normally leave their mother when 12 to 18 months old, but female cubs may stay near their natal range for longer. Cub mortality is high in most areas, and even in the relatively prey-rich Masai Mara a female leopard will seldom raise all the members of a litter of three cubs successfully. In the southern Kalahari savanna cub mortality may be as high as 90%, while in the Kruger National Park at least 50% of all cubs probably die before becoming adults.

When a leopard cub is still small, it locates its den by the odour. To avoid other predators such as lions, spotted hyaenas, jackals, baboons and even male leopards being attracted to a den when the cubs are still young, its location is changed every few days over distances of up to 1,6 km at a time. Unlike the lioness, a leopard mother will bring food to her cubs at a den. When the young cubs are moved, they are carried in the mother's mouth one by one to the new den. Older and more

Young leopard cubs do not move about with their mother, but are left unattended in apparently suitable cover which does not protect them from a variety of predators.
Photo: J. du P. Bothma.

mobile cubs walk to new dens with their mother over longer distances, being carried from time to time when they tire.

Range use

The leopard's range generally excludes other animals of the same kind and sex. Although this range may be considered a territory for both sexes, its core is not so much actively defended but rather avoided by other leopards because of scented warning signals. However, male leopards may occasionally engage in fierce physical fights over a range dispute. This happens especially when two neighbouring males meet, usually by accident, and they then may engage each other and fight to the death of at least one of the combatants. The degree of overlap between adjacent ranges varies. In the savanna-forest mosaic of the Comoé National Park, female leopards apparently have widely overlapping ranges, but elsewhere they live in more discrete ranges. Despite the fact that leopard range boundaries are fuzzy in most cases, neighbours of the same sex do not use the same area at the same time. Nevertheless, male leopards may sometimes be as close as 0,5 km to each other, as happens in East Africa. In Tsavo two male leopards studied came as close as 0,8 km to each other. However, the mean spacing between neighbouring males was 2,8 km.

The degree of leopard range overlap depends largely on the prey resources and the density of other large predators in a given area. In Tsavo, the male leopards' ranges form space-efficient mosaics with little or no overlap, but in areas where prey resources are scarce, leopard ranges overlap more extensively. Both male and female leopards occasionally wander out of their ranges to explore new areas, and then return. This may be done to test the defence of an adjacent territory, or to find a mate. In the arid, savanna woodlands of Bushmanland and the Kaudam Game Reserve where prey is scarce, the mean overlap of the ranges of male leopards is 46%, and that of females 35,5%.

A male leopard has a much larger range than a female and as a result there are usually three to four females resident in each male's range. The size of a male leopard's range is determined mainly by the number of females present, but a female's range depends mainly on the number of suitable prey available. Therefore the size of a leopard's range varies extensively from region to region in the African savannas. The smallest leopard ranges are found in areas of prey abundance. In the moist, prey-rich tropical forests of Sri-Lanka, for example, leopard ranges are small, usually less than 10 km² in extent. In northern Serengeti an adult female with a young cub used a range of 15,9 km² in a 5-month period, and a young male one of 17,8 km². Elsewhere in Serengeti the ranges of two females were 40 to 60 km² in extent. In Matobo an adult female used a range of 10 to 15 km², but the leopards there generally spend most of their time in a small core area of their range where they can find abundant prey and cover. In the Kruger National Park the ranges of adult male leopards vary from 16,4 to 96,1 km², and those of adult females from 5,6 to 29,9 km². In the Sabi-Sand Game Reserve the range of one female leopard studied was 23 km².

In areas of low rainfall, prey animals are less abundant and leopard ranges are consequently large. In the arid woodland savannas of the Kaudam and the adjacent areas of Bushmanland, for example, male leopards have ranges which vary from 210 to 1164 km² (mean: 451,7 km²), and the ranges of females from 183 to 194 km² (mean: 188,4 km²). In the prey-poor southern Kalahari savanna, leopards have even larger ranges which they criss-cross extensively to obtain sufficient food to survive. There the known ranges of three adult male leopards varies from 1892,9 to 2750,0 km² (mean: 2182,2 km²), and that of five adult females from 199,7 to 908,4 km² (mean: 488,7 km²). A subadult male in the same area shared his temporary range of 1323,6 km² with an adult male, to a certain extent, for 19 months. Then the subadult leopard moved a minimum linear distance of 112,6 km away to a new area where he established a permanent range of 1905,1 km².

Activity and movement

As is the case with most animals, environmental factors influence the activity patterns of leopards. Despite being regarded by many people as strictly nocturnal animals, leopards are also quite active by day, when they will even hunt.

However, a leopard will usually rest in some convenient, elevated shade during the hotter part of the day. In the southern African bushveld savanna, dry water courses, reed beds, rocky outcrops, and trees such as leafy baobabs and evergreen wild figs where their spotted coats make them all but invisible in the dappled shade, are favourite leopard resting spots. However, in the southern Kalahari savanna the leopard usually rests under the low-growing and densely foliated shepherd's tree *Boscia albitrunca,* or underground in a cool aardvark or porcupine burrow.

In the daytime a leopard usually rests in good, elevated shade.
Photo: J. du P. Bothma.

71

In the southern Kalahari savanna where rocky lairs are absent, leopards often rest in the shade under a suitable tree by day. Photo: J. du P. Bothma.

It frequently lies down to rest again soon after being active, or just before finally going to rest for the day after a night of activity. However, even when resting a leopard remains alert. Ever the watcher, it sees all but is seldom seen.

The leopard is extremely mobile, an agile climber and immensely strong. It can drag heavy prey high up a tree with apparent ease. When bridging a gap, a leopard can easily jump distances of up to 6 m. When displaced by man, some leopards show strong homing instincts.

Cool porcupine burrows are often enlarged by leopards and are then used to lie up in during the day in the southern Kalahari savanna. Photo: J. du P. Bothma.

The leopard is an accomplished and agile climber.
Photo: J. du P. Bothma.

Normal daily movements are largely dictated by success or failure at satisfying its food and mating needs. In prey-rich areas the range size and hence the extent of a leopard's daily movements are small. In Tsavo, for example, leopards travel only 2 to 5 km per day. In the Kruger National Park most leopards also do not move more than 5 km per day, but adult males travel nearly twice as far (mean: 2,8 km) as females (mean: 1,5 km) per day. The presence of young cubs restricts their mother's movements for up to 6 months after their birth.

Rocky outcrops on the Serengeti Plains are important features of a leopard's habitat there.
Photo: J. du P. Bothma.

73

In those areas of the Kruger National Park where prey is less abundant, leopards travel further per day than elsewhere. The same applies to the prey-poor southern Kalahari savanna, where adult male leopards travel a mean distance of 14,2 km (maximum: 33 km) in 24 hours, and females 13,4 km (maximum: 27,3 km). However, a leopard's state of hunger significantly influences the daily distances moved. The leopards of the southern Kalahari savanna are compelled to hunt at every available opportunity, and can only intensify their hunting efforts as their hunger grows by increasing the distances over which they move daily. For example, male leopards that had recently eaten, travelled a mean distance of 10,1 km in 24 hours, those that had been without food for a day travelled 14,2 km, those without food for 2 days travelled 20 km, and those that had not eaten for 3 days or more, travelled 21,8 km. Ambient temperatures also influence the daily distances covered by southern Kalahari leopards. On those winter nights when the minimum air temperature is at or below freezing point, leopards with an equal degree of hunger travel a mean distance of 29 km in 24 hours. On nights of between 1 and 15 °C they do so for 19,1 km, and on warmer summer nights above 15 °C they travel 15,2 km.

A dispersing subadult male leopard may remain close to its natal range for a while before moving away to set up its own permanent range elsewhere. Female subadults more commonly stay close to their natal areas throughout life. However, dispersal is costly and many dispersing subadults die before finding a permanent range of their own. When disturbed a leopard shows little fear, and will simply sit, lie down, or move away slowly. Even in the open southern Kalahari savanna the mean flight distance of a leopard is only 91 m, with a maximum flight distance of 2,7 km. Only two of 23 leopards disturbed at a kill there did not return to the kill later. In both these cases, the kill had been largely consumed before the leopard was disturbed.

Feeding ecology

Most predators will eat whatever food is the easiest to obtain, and the leopard is no exception. In a leopard, its size and age have considerable bearing on what it eats. Although ungulates generally form the bulk of the leopard's diet, it is extremely adaptable, to the point of even eating the beetles which are present in buffalo dung in Kenya, and fish at Lake Kariba.

5 cm

Canid carnivores such as the bat-eared fox feature regularly in the leopard's diet. Photo: J. du P. Bothma.

Unlike lions, other carnivores feature regularly in the leopard's diet. These may include wild dogs *Lycaon pictus,* cheetahs *Acinonyx jubatus,* jackals and lion cubs. In some areas, leopards seem to have a definite taste for canine flesh, but this may be an acquired habit. They also sometimes become habitual killers of a single type of prey. For example, in the southern Kalahari savanna one leopard had the habit of ambushing porcupines when they emerged from their burrow, eating little else for several days at a time. Another leopard left marooned on an island when Lake Kariba was formed, learned to feed exclusively on fish and continued to catch fish even after it was relocated inland to Kafue. Leopards also readily eat carrion and they scavenge food when it is available. They are said to be both frequently or only occasionally cannibalistic depending on where they live. However, they do not attack each other as prey, but a leopard will feed off the carcass of another leopard when it finds it.

Because of their wide geographical range, leopards from different regions eat different types of prey. In some areas small prey is especially targeted, while in others leopards more often eat prey of 20 kg or larger. When feeding on smaller prey the leopard may be making use of a seasonally abundant food resource, much as it would also adapt to the abundance of larger migratory prey, provided that such prey animals were of a suitable size. Such abundance is the result of short-term envi-

75

ronmental influences. For example, in the northern woodland parts of Serengeti in the dry season, an estimated 80% of all the ungulate herbivores which are then present are too large for leopards to kill easily. While leopards in some areas readily and often eat rodents and birds like doves, the guinea-fowl *Numida meleagris* and various francolins, these types of prey are rarely taken in other areas.

Even on the individual level the leopard's diet may differ widely because the available prey base may vary from range to range. In many of the African savannas the impala *Aepyceros melampus* is an important and stable prey resource for leopards and forms their staple diet even in years of drought. Leopards will also eat wild fruit on occasion, but they possibly do so more for moisture than for nutrition.

Even the mainly arboreal genet is occasionally preyed upon by leopards in the southern Kalahari savanna. Photo: J. du P. Bothma.

When prey animals are abundant, leopards can and will hunt selectively for prey type, age, sex and even body condition. This is done to expend the least possible energy in hunting while gaining the best possible energy from their food. This situation is commonly called *energy maximisation*. However, in prey-poor environments such as the southern Kalahari savanna, leopards have to hunt every possible, available prey. Consequently they cannot afford to be selective. This is called

Hyraxes are small herbivores which are commonly used as prey by leopards in many of the African savannas. Photo: J. du P. Bothma.

77

number maximisation. It is also possible that in areas of intermediate prey abundance such as most temperate African savannas, some prey selection may exist, but its degree of occurrence will depend on the prey composition and abundance in each area.

When hunting, the leopard is a stalking specialist, although it also hunts from ambush. Its spotted coat, slow and stealthy movements, and its use of every possible scrap of cover make it difficult for any prey to detect. Even in fairly open savannas there is usually sufficient cover for a stalking leopard which is a master at concealment. In addition the leopard hunts mainly at night under cover of darkness, although late afternoon or early morning kills are also made. In the open savanna of Comoé, leopards hunt only at night during the dry season because there is not enough cover for hunting during the day as the fires which sweep through these areas at those times, leave most of the woody plants totally leafless. Prey may be watched for several hours before hunting begins, but when the prey is finally rushed, a leopard's attack is astonishingly quick. Any prey animal which unwittingly makes itself vulnerable to attack will initiate a hunting response in a leopard. Vulnerability in this sense encompasses all the physical and biological

The leopard is a master at concealment. Photo: J. du P. Bothma.

conditions that can lead to predation. Leopards will also respond to the distress calls of prey animals.

Leopards usually ambush their prey infrequently because this can only happen when there are places in the environment which prey animals will visit in a predictable way. In the Kruger National Park, however, leopards do ambush prey quite frequently, particularly near waterholes which are visited daily in a set pattern by most game animals. By contrast, most types of prey in the more arid areas are water-independent and ambushes are rare there. Contrary to popular belief, leopards rarely launch attacks from trees although such attacks do occur, and a case is known where a large leopard jumped onto a fully grown eland bull *Taurotragus oryx* from a tree. The bull promptly dashed off, stumbling twice and getting up again. On the third fall, the leopard succeeded in holding the eland down, and finally killed it by biting into its throat and suffocating it. Leopards also occasionally climb into isolated trees after monkeys or baboons, leaping from the tree to catch the fleeing animal.

When stalking dangerous or vigilant prey, a leopard may take more care and stalk over longer distances than at other times, getting as close

79

as possible to its victim before making the final rush for the kill. Optimal positioning before the final rush increases the chances of a successful hunt. Such positioning depends upon the vigilance of the prey, and on how dangerous it could be to an attacking leopard. When hunting a gemsbok calf, for example, a leopard will attempt to get as close as possible so that it can rush in, kill its prey, and retreat to a safe place before any attending cow with her lethal, long and rapier-like horns can counterattack in defence. As their hunger increases, leopards can be expected to increase their hunting rates because hunger is a primary motivation for hunting in cats. However, in prey-poor areas where all possible prey animals are hunted at every available opportunity, an increased hunting effort is possible only when a leopard travels increasingly longer distances by night as its hunger intensifies, as in the case of the leopard in the southern Kalahari savanna, where prey abundance and not hunting cover limits leopard hunting. Most hunts do not consist of the full stalk-chase-kill sequence and in the southern Kalahari savanna, for example, stalking occurs in only 35% of all leopard kills. In Serengeti only 11% of a known 9 stalks ended in a kill. When the full hunting sequence is used, however, it is one continuous, fluent action.

Cats commonly kill their prey by a throat or neck bite. Their long canine teeth penetrate between the neck vertebrae, severing or damaging the spinal cord. Leopards fit the general cat pattern when killing prey. Following an optional high-speed chase of variable distance depending upon the vulnerability of the prey, leopards either suffocate the prey with a grip on the throat, or kill it outright by a bite to the neck or base of the skull. Some prey is not chased at all, but may be surprised

Leopard spoor
and prey

when standing or lying down somewhere, and attacked instantly. Even large prey may be attacked in this way, although this technique is more commonly used for smaller prey. When killing a potentially dangerous prey such as a porcupine, warthog, baboon or gemsbok, a leopard must negotiate the defences of such prey successfully or risk lethal injury. Porcupines, for example, are harassed with great patience until the leopard succeeds in turning them over to expose their vulnerable soft underparts for the kill.

Although it is a powerful and lethal hunter, a leopard may make many unsuccessful hunting attempts in its lifetime. Once the prey has been alerted to a leopard's presence, the cat usually abandons the hunt. In the Kruger National Park only 16% of all leopard hunts are success-ful. Daytime hunts are least successful, and in Serengeti only 5% of such hunts end in a kill as opposed to an overall success rate of 11% for all hunts. Contrary to expectations the leopards of prey-poor areas such as Kaudam and the southern Kalahari savanna have a hunting success as high as 38% and 23% respectively. It may be that the very demands of survival in a prey-poor environment make these leopards more success-ful or determined hunters.

Leopards may also occasionally kill habitually which results in sur-plus killing. Surplus killing usually happens in unique circumstances when prey vigilance or the normal prey flight reactions are impaired. A leopard attacking a group of prey under such circumstances may con-tinue to kill the milling and fleeing prey instinctively and indiscrimi-nately until they have either escaped or been killed. In Serengeti prey herds milling during violent thunderstorms may elicit such a response.

Elsewhere penned stock or those hemmed in by fences may be killed in this way. Habitual killing occurs where a leopard has learned to kill a specific prey with ease and then catches that type of prey from habit. Jackals and the ostrich *Struthio camelus* are two examples of prey known to have been killed by leopards in this way.

Before starting to feed, a leopard usually eviscerates its prey at the kill site, and then carries or drags larger prey some distance away to suitable cover. Small prey may be eaten quickly and entirely where they are killed. The distance over which the prey is moved before feeding starts, varies considerably. In the southern African bushveld savanna it is seldom more than 100 to 200 m, but in the southern Kalahari savan-na it can be as much as 4,9 km. If disturbed at the feeding spot, the prey may be moved again. The leopard drags or carries its prey by grasping it by the neck and straddling it with the forelegs. In this way it can pull even large prey as high as 12 m into a tree. When the prey is eviscerated,

During unusual environmental circumstances such as violent thunderstorms, leopards, lions and spotted hyaenas may occasionally kill a surplus of prey. Photo: J. du P. Bothma.

the viscera may or may not be covered with sand or litter. Before the leopard starts to feed, the hair of furry or young prey is often removed by biting out mouthfuls with the incisors and depositing them in a neat pile. The same thing may or may not be done to other prey such as the impala. Porcupines are partially dequilled before feeding starts, and the feathers are invariably plucked before a bird is eaten. The tongue with its recurved, hair-like papillae is used to rasp off meat particles from the bones.

Feeding normally starts on the buttocks, chest or shoulders of the prey, but the muzzle, lower jaws, viscera and feet are usually not eaten. In one area of Namibia, females with cubs eat more meat (2,5 kg per day) than single females (1,6 kg per day), but less than males (3,3 kg per day). Leopards are well known for caching food in trees or in dense thickets, but contrary to popular belief this is not always a response to harassment by scavengers. However, caching is less frequent where scavengers are less abundant. For example, leopards in the South African bushveld savanna cache 31% of their kills in trees, and in Tsavo it happens in 38% of kills. By comparison only 17% of all leopard kills in the southern Kalahari savanna are cached in trees. Habitat features and the degree of interference from other predators will influence the decision to cache food, but they are not the sole reasons for food caching which may well also happen for other reasons, for example when a prey item is too large to consume entirely in one day a leopard

Before it starts to feed, a leopard often plucks out furry prey's hair with its incisors. The muzzle, lower jaws, viscera and feet of larger prey are usually not eaten. Photo: J. du P. Bothma.

will pull it into a tree and rest beside it. Despite caching food in a tree, however, lions may occasionally succeed in climbing into the tree to rob a leopard of its cache. When not robbed, a leopard may take up to 6 days to consume a large carcass in a tree.

Leopards will readily drink water when it is available, but they can survive well without free water because they use metabolic water and the moisture of fresh meat to satisfy their water needs. For leopard survival prey abundance is a more vital limiting factor than free water, even in inhospitable semi-desert areas. When wild fruit such as the tsama melon *Citrullus lanatus,* the wild cucumber *Cucumis africanus* and the gemsbok cucumber *Acanthosicyos naudianus* is available, it is used by many large carnivores including the leopard, to supplement their water supply. In the southern Kalahari savanna an adult male leopard once went for 10 consecutive days in the peak of summer without drinking water. While leopards do pant rapidly, their water loss through sweating is negligible. This enhances their survival chances in waterless areas with hot climates. When it rains leopard cubs may also obtain water by licking each other's wet fur, much as lions do.

Relationship with other wildlife

Because leopards live alone, each individual within its own range, leopard densities can never be so high in natural systems that they can have a significant impact on their prey. Similarly, the occupation of ranges in which significant portions do not overlap with those of other leopards makes intraspecific contacts rare. Nevertheless, neighbouring males do on occasion engage in fierce physical fights over range disputes. At kills there is little chance of individuals meeting, in a solitary felid such as the leopard. In one study in Matobo there was only one known instance of actual conflict between two leopards at a kill, but the intruder was repelled. In the South African bushveld savanna the only known incidences of conflict between leopards were between an adult female and her independent daughter, and between a resident adult male and a transient adult female.

In many savannas lions, leopards and other large predators inhabit the same areas, but they are usually separated ecologically by prey selection, and sometimes by their activity cycles. In most areas the lion is the leopard's closest competitor because the lion is found throughout much of the leopard's geographical range in Africa. In northern Serengeti, however, there is no relation between the boundaries of leopard ranges and those of lions. In terms of prey composition the size of 80% of the potential ungulate prey animals in Serengeti makes them unusual leopard prey. Nevertheless, the Serengeti lions will chase leopards whenever they see them, but the leopard invariably escapes safely up a tree. Yet, in the Masai Mara a leopard which was frightened by some tourist vehicles once ran into a pride of lions when fleeing. It was then attacked and killed but not eaten by the lions.

Of the other large carnivores commonly found in savannas, the spotted hyaena often deprives a leopard of at least part of its larger kills. In northern Serengeti this interference by spotted hyaenas is regarded as one of the main reasons why the leopards there kill small prey more frequently, and why the leopard most often feeds in trees when there are hyaenas in the vicinity of a kill. Such interference can be substantial. In the Kruger National Park, for example, spotted hyaenas are present at 52% of all leopard kills. However, the real impact of such interference by spotted hyaenas and other scavengers depends on the actual amount of food lost and on the frequency of such losses. In a woodland savanna in the Tsumkwe district of Namibia, for example, 12% of all leopard kills are visited by other carnivores such as wild dogs, lions and spotted hyaenas, but the leopards only lose 2% of their kills to them. The effect of spotted hyaena interference also depends upon the number of spotted hyaenas present. A single spotted hyaena is generally chased away by a leopard, but more than two hyaenas at a kill will usually cause the leopard to flee if it does not succeed in dragging its prey up a tree in time. In the savanna areas of Comoé spotted hyaenas are scarce. Where they do occur, they also often only hunt singly or at most in pairs, which reduces their competition with the leopards there.

85

Brown hyaenas in the southern Kalahari savanna often follow the tracks of hunting leopards, but they do not interfere with a kill if the leopard is still in attendance. Leopards and jackals take particular interest in each other. In the southern Kalahari savanna black-backed jackals often follow leopards about, keeping a distance of 10 to 30 m away and barking at the leopards in a peculiar way. Sometimes the leopard will suddenly turn and kill the jackal.

Black-backed jackals often follow hunting leopards about, barking at them in a peculiar way. These jackals are often set upon and killed by the leopards.
Photo: J. du P. Bothma.

A troop of baboons which encounters a leopard will usually mob it immediately, often killing or injuring it in the process. Even a warthog can be a formidable adversary and can injure an attacking leopard severely with its sharp tusks.

Population dynamics

There is only limited information available on the population dynamics of leopards, mainly because they are so secretive and difficult to study. Leopards probably do not reach an age of much more than 14 years in the wild, although in captivity they may live until they are 21 years old. Old leopard's spots are faded, their coats are scarred and their canines and incisors are sometimes missing. Because females have smaller teeth and they feed with greater precision than males, tooth wear from ageing seems to be less in females than males. It can therefore be expected that females will be able to hunt effectively to older ages than males, and hence could well live longer than the males in the wild. Female leopards are indeed slightly more abundant than males in the Kruger National Park while in Serengeti there appears to be twice as many females as males. Most older leopards die in violent conflicts or of starvation when their teeth become so worn or lost that they can no longer hunt effectively. In isolated cases, and given the correct circumstances, such old leopards may even become man-eaters. Some leopards may also be injured and die, or be killed outright when they attack prey such

The large males in a troop of baboons will readily attack and kill or injure a leopard.
Photo: J. du P. Bothma.

87

as a warthog, baboon, porcupine or gemsbok. Once a leopard loses condition it becomes prone to heavy parasite infestations which further weaken and emaciate it. Mange then becomes a common affliction.

Leopard cubs suffer high mortality rates. In the Kruger National Park it is estimated that only 50% of all cubs survive to become adults and in Serengeti cub mortality is at least 67%. In an extreme environment such as the southern Kalahari savanna cub mortality may be as high as 90%. Subadult leopards are still inexperienced hunters and many of them die of starvation. In the Kruger National Park an estimated 18,5% of all the adult leopards die annually, but the adult males have a mortality rate (25%) almost twice as high as that of the females (13,5%). In some areas of their range conflict with man becomes an additional and major mortality factor for the leopard. Leopards in the wild also suffer from various diseases including anthrax and canine distemper. Isolated cases of rabies are also known. A recent outbreak of tuberculosis is affecting some of the leopards in the southern part of the Kruger National Park. Snake bite is probably a major cause of death in adult leopards.

In most areas with a relatively stable prey base the leopard population will be stable too, with the recruitment rate equalling the mortality rate. This happens in the Kruger National Park where the leopard population seems to be self-regulated because the food resource there is adequate and the number of breeding leopard adults is stable. The loss of a female is usually compensated for by a young female produced within the same area, but the loss of a male is rectified by the influx of a young male from an adjacent area.

Being bitten by a venomous snake such as this puff-adder is probably a major cause of death for adult leopards. Photo: J. du P. Bothma.

BIBLIOGRAPHY

Anonymous 1996. Lumping leopards; should 27 subspecies be reduced to eight? *Cat News,* 25: 9.

Bailey, T.N. 1993. *The African leopard.* New York: Columbia University Press.

Bertram, B.C.R. 1974. Radio-tracking leopards in the Serengeti. *Wildlife News,* 9(2): 7–10.

Bertram, B.C.R. 1979. Serengeti predators and their social systems. In: Sinclair A.R.E. & Norton-Griffiths, M. (Eds), *Serengeti, dynamics of an ecosystem.* Chicago: University of Chicago Press, 221–248.

Bertram, B.C.R. 1982. Leopard ecology as studied by radio-tracking. *Symposiums of the Zoological Society, London,* 49: 341–352.

Bosman, P. & Hall-Martin, A. 1997. *Cats of Africa.* Vlaeberg: Fernwood.

Bothma, J. du P. 1998. *Carnivore ecology in arid lands.* Berlin: Springer.

Bothma, J. du P., Knight, M.H., Le Riche, E.A.N. & Van Hensbergen, H.J. 1997. Range size of southern Kalahari leopards. *South African Journal of Wildlife Research,* 27(3): 94–99.

Bothma, J. du P. & Le Riche, E.A.N. 1984. Aspects of the ecology and the behaviour of the leopard *Panthera pardus* in the Kalahari Desert. Supplement to *Koedoe,* 27: 259–279.

Bothma, J. du P. & Le Riche, E.A.N. 1986. Prey preference and hunting efficiency of the Kalahari Desert leopard. In: Miller, S.D. & Everett, D.D. (Eds), *Cats of the world: biology, conservation and management.* Washington, DC: National Wildlife Federation, 389–414.

Bothma, J. du P. & Le Riche, E.A.N. 1989. Evidence of a flexible hunting technique in Kalahari leopards. *South African Journal of Wildlife Research,* 19(2): 57–60.

Bothma, J. du P. & Le Riche E.A.N. 1990. The influence of increasing hunger on the hunting behaviour of southern Kalahari leopards. *Journal of Arid Environments,* 18: 79–84.

Bothma, J. du P. & Le Riche, E.A.N. 1993. Disturbance bias when tracking Kalahari leopards by spoor. *Koedoe,* 36(2): 109–112.

Bothma, J. du P. & Le Riche, E.A.N. 1994a. The relationship between minimum air temperature and daily distance moved by Kalahari leopards. *South African Journal of Wildlife Research,* 24(1/2): 18–20.

Bothma, J. du P. & Le Riche, E.A.N. 1994b. Scat analysis and aspects of defecation in northern Cape leopards. *South African Journal of Wildlife Research,* 24(1/2): 21–25.

Bothma, J. du P. & Le Riche, E.A.N. 1995. Evidence of the use of rubbing, scent-marking and scratching posts by Kalahari leopards. *Journal of Arid Environments,* 29: 511–517.

Bothma, J. du P., Van Rooyen, N. & Le Riche, E.A.N. 1997. Multivariate analysis of the hunting tactics of Kalahari leopards. *Koedoe,* 40(1): 41–56.

Bothma, J. du P., Van Rooyen, N., Theron, G.K. & Le Riche, E.A.N. 1994. Quantifying woody plants as hunting cover for southern Kalahari leopards. *Journal of Arid Environments,* 26: 273–280.

Corbett, J. 1956. *Man-eating leopard of Rudraprayag.* Oxford: Oxford University Press.

Edey, M. 1968. *The cats of Africa.* New York: Time-Life.

Eisenberg, J.F. 1970. A splendid predator does its own thing untroubled by man. *Smithsonian,* 1(6): 48–53.

Eisenberg, J.F. & Lockhart, M. 1972. An ecological reconnaissance of Wilpattu National Park, Ceylon. *Smithsonian Contributions to Zoology*, 101: 1–118.

Eltringham, S.K. 1979. *The ecology and conservation of large African mammals.* London: Macmillan.

Ewer, R.F. 1973. *The carnivores.* Ithaca: Cornell University Press.

Fey, V. 1964. The diet of leopards. *African Wildlife*, 18: 105–108.

Gorman, M.L. & Trowbridge, B.J. 1989. The role of odor in the social lives of carnivores. In: Gittleman, J.L. (Ed.), *Carnivore behavior, ecology and evolution.* London: Chapman & Hall, 57–88.

Grimbeek, A.M. 1992. *The ecology of the leopard* (Panthera pardus) *in the Waterberg.* M.Sc. thesis. Pretoria: University of Pretoria.

Grobler, J.H. & Wilson, V.J. 1972. Food of the leopard *Panthera pardus* (Linn.) in the Rhodes Matopos National Park, Rhodesia, as determined by faecal analysis. *Arnoldia*, 5(35): 1–9.

Gross, M. 1997. Leopards in Ivory Coast. *Cat News*, 27: 12–13.

Hamilton, P.H. 1976. *The movements of leopards in Tsavo National Park, Kenya, as determined by radio-tracking.* MSc thesis. Nairobi: University of Nairobi.

Hes, L. 1991. *The leopards of Londolozi.* Cape Town: Struik.

Karanth, K.N. & Sunquist, M.E. 1995. Prey selection by tiger, leopard and dhole in tropical forests. *Journal of Animal Ecology*, 64: 439–450.

Kingdon, J. 1977. *East African mammals.* Vol. III, Part A: Carnivores. London: Academic.

Kruger, J.E. 1988. *Interrelationships between the larger carnivores of the Klaserie Private Nature Reserve, with special reference to the leopard* Panthera pardus *(Linnaeus 1758) and the cheetah* Acinonyx jubatus *(Schreber, 1775).* M.Sc. thesis. Pretoria: University of Pretoria.

Kruuk, H. 1972. Surplus killing by carnivores. *Journal of Zoology, London,* 166: 233–244.

Kruuk, H. & Turner, M. 1967. Comparative notes on predation by lion, leopard, cheetah and wild dog in the Serengeti area, East Africa. *Mammalia*, 31(1): 1–27.

Le Roux, P.G. & Skinner, J.D. 1989. A note on the ecology of the leopard (*Panthera pardus* Linnaeus) in the Londolozi Game Reserve, South Africa. *African Journal of Ecology*, 27: 161–171.

Leyhausen, P. 1979. *Cat behaviour.* New York: Garland.

Leyhausen, P. 1997. How to define a subspecies? *Cat News*, 26: 23.

Mills, M.G.L. 1990. *Kalahari hyaenas.* London: Unwin Hyman.

Mitchell, B.L., Shenton, J.B. & Uys, J.C.M. 1965. Predation on large mammals in the Kafue National Park, Zambia. *Zoologica Africana*, 1(2): 297–318.

Muckenhirn, N.A. & Eisenberg, J.F. 1973. Home ranges and predation of the Ceylon leopard *(Panthera pardus fusca).* In: Eaton, R.L. (Ed.), *The world's cats.* Vol. 1: *Ecology and Conservation.* World Wildlife Safari. Oregon: Winston, 142–175.

Norton, P.M. & Henley, S.R. 1987. Home range and movements of male leopards in the Cedarberg Wilderness Area, Cape Province. *South African Journal of Wildlife Research,* 17: 41–48.

Norton, P.M., Lawson, A.B., Henley, S.R. & Avery, G. 1986. Prey of leopards in four mountainous areas of the south-western Cape Province. *South African Journal of Wildlife Research,* 16(2): 47–52.

Nowell, K. & Jackson, P. 1995. New red list categories for wild cats. *Cat News*, 23: 21–27.

Nowell, K. & Jackson, P. 1996. *Wild cats.* Cambridge: IUCN Publication Services.

Pienaar, U. de V. 1969. Predator-prey relationships amongst the larger mammals of the Kruger National Park. *Koedoe* 12: 108–184.

Pocock, R.I. 1930. The panthers and ounces of Asia. *Journal of the Bombay Natural History Society,* 34(1): 65–82.

Polis, G.A, Myers, C.A. & Hess, W.R. 1984. A survey of intraspecific predation within the Class Mammalia. *Mammal Review,* 14(4): 187–198.

Schaller, G.B. 1972. *The Serengeti lion.* Chicago: University of Chicago Press.

Scott, J. 1985. *The leopard's tale.* London: Elm Tree.

Skinner, J.D. & Smithers, R.H.N. 1990. *The mammals of the southern African subregion.* Pretoria: University of Pretoria.

Smith, R.M. 1978. Movement pattern and feeding behavior of the leopard in the Rhodes Matopos National Park, Rhodesia. *Carnivore,* 1(3/4): 58–69.

Smithers, R.H.N. 1983. *The mammals of the southern African subregion.* Pretoria: University of Pretoria.

Stander, P.E. 1997. Field age determination of leopards by tooth wear. *African Journal of Ecology,* 35: 156–161.

Stander, P.E., Haden, P.J., Kaqece // au. and Ghau //. 1997. The ecology of asociality in Namibian leopards. *Journal of Zoology, London,* 242: 343–364.

Stander, P.E., Kaqece // au., Nisa / ui., Dabe, T. & Dabe, D. 1997. Non-comsumptive utilisation of leopards: community conservation and ecotourism in practise. In: Van Heerden, J. (Ed.), *Lions and leopards as game ranch animals.* The Wildlife Group. Onderstepoort: South African Veterinary Association, 50–57.

Stuart, C.T. 1981. Notes on the mammalian carnivores of the Cape Province, South Africa. *Bontebok,* 1: 1–58.

Stuart, C.T. 1986. The incidence of surplus killing by *Panthera pardus* and *Felis caracal* in Cape Province, South Africa. *Mammalia,* 50(4): 556–558.

Sunquist, M.E. & Sunquist, F.C. 1989. Ecological constraints on predation by large felids. In: Gittleman, J.L. (Ed.), *Carnivore behavior, ecology and evolution.* London: Chapman & Hall, 283–301.

Trendler, K. 1997. Handraising techniques for large carnivores: lions and leopards. In: Van Heerden, J. (Ed.), *Lions and leopards as game ranch animals.* The Wildlife Group. Onderstepoort: South African Veterinary Association, 119–126.

Turnbull-Kemp, P. 1967. *The leopard.* Cape Town: Howard Timmins.

Turner, A. 1993. New fossil carnivore remains from Swartkrans. *Transvaal Museum Monograph,* 8: 151–165.

Turner, M. & Watson, M. 1964. A census of game in the Ngorongoro Crater. *East African Wildlife Journal,* 2: 165–168.

Van Vuuren, M., Styliamides, E. & Du Rand, A. 1997. The prevalence of viral infections in lions and leopards in southern Africa. In: Van Heerden, J. (Ed.), *Lions and leopards as game ranch animals.* The Wildlife Group. Onderstepoort: South African Veterinary Association, 168–173.

Verberne G. & Leyhausen, P. 1976. Marking behaviour of some Viverridae and Felidae: time-interval analysis of the marking pattern. *Behaviour,* 58(3/4): 192–253.

Wozencraft, W.C. 1993. Order Carnivora. In: Wilson, D.E. & Reeder, D.M. (Eds), *Mammal species of the world,* 2nd ed. Washington, DC: Smithsonian Institution Press, 279–348.

Wright, B.S. 1960. Predation on big game in East Africa. *Journal of Wildlife Management,* 24(1): 1–15.

4

The cheetah

The cheetah *Acinonyx jubatus* has had a long association with man, but its first contact with humans was actually in India and on the plains of southern Africa. Because of their speed and hunting prowess, captive cheetahs have been used by man as food hunters for many centuries. The oldest record of a captive cheetah is depicted on a decorated silver vase from a Scythian burial site at Maikop in the Caucasus Range, which shows the cheetah wearing a collar. This vase dates back to approximately 700 to 300 BC. However, it is likely that early man joined other scavengers in robbing cheetahs of their kills long before the Maikop culture. In doing so, these early hunters probably exploited the cheetah's relative timidity, daytime hunting habits, and also its open plains habitat. The Moghul Emperor Akbar the Great is also said to have kept up to 3000 cheetahs to hunt antelope, while sketches of a Dionysian procession in Alexandria during the reign of Ptolemy II from 309 to 246 BC show a cheetah on a leash. Even before the ancient Assyrian empire in Mesopotamia and during the reign of the pharaohs in Egypt, captive cheetahs were used for coursing game. During the fifth century and the early Renaissance in Italy cheetahs were also employed for this purpose. Despite its timidity, the ancient Egyptians endowed the cheetah with the spirit of courage, but today it is regarded more as a symbol of elusive grace in a declining wilderness than as a fierce hunter.

The cheetah was first described scientifically by J.C.D. von Schreber in 1775 as *Felis jubata* from a specimen collected at the Cape of Good

Hope, South Africa. The common name of this large, lanky, running cat is probably derived from Hindi in India where it is known as *chita,* which means *the spotted one.* Although the cheetah is usually associated in peoples' minds with vast, open grasslands such as the Serengeti Plains, they are actually more at home in open woodland savannas where the combination of good visibility and sufficient hunting cover yields greater hunting success and cub survival rates than on the open plains. An adult cheetah male weighs up to 65 kg and a female 55 kg. The cheetah's skull shows no post-canine gap, a unique feature in modern cats.

The cheetah has long been part of the African fauna and although it superficially resembles a dog, it is a true cat most closely related to the lion, tiger and lynx. Although it superficially appears to lack the claw sheaths commonly found in other cats, a cheetah does have at least partially retractable claws, but its sheaths are not as obvious as in other cats. Phylogenetically speaking, the cheetah developed its unique morphological characteristics rapidly in fairly recent times. Nevertheless, as recently as 10 000 years ago, several species of cheetah-like cats were widespread across Africa, Asia and North America. Of these, the modern cheetah *Acinonyx jubatus* is an eastern hemisphere (Old World) species, a region where at least two other species of cheetah also existed in the past. One of them, the large *Acinonyx pardinensis* of Europe, weighed about 95 kg and was therefore considerably heavier than a modern cheetah. *Acinonyx pardinensis* lived about 3,8 to 1,9 million years ago. A smaller cheetah *Acinonyx intermedius* existed in areas from Europe eastward to China in the mid-Pleistocene some 2,5 million years ago. Two large, extinct species of cheetah also lived in North America. These are put into a genus or subgenus *Miracinonyx* of their own, and could even be a case of parallel evolution with *Acinonyx.* They had a skull much like the modern cheetah, and were probably also closely related to the puma *Puma concolor.* The fossil evidence suggests that cheetahs may have developed in North America and not in Eurasia as was previously believed. Whatever their origin, it is clear that those features which make a cheetah such an efficient running predator have had significant advantages in many different ecosystems in the past.

There is great variation in the cheetah's coat colour and pattern. In Africa, those that live in the open, sandy Sahara tend to be pale, with ochre spots instead of black, and more diffuse tear lines and tail rings. There is also a rare local form of cheetah in the Sahara with spots so pale that it is sometimes called a white cheetah. However, those living in the black-rock areas of the Sahara mountain ranges have the more common black spots, and the Saharan cheetahs are also much smaller than those from other regions.

In the arid savannas of southern Africa there is another striking and rare coat colour variation. These cheetahs are commonly called 'king cheetahs' and their mid-dorsal spots merge to form parallel, distinct longitudinal stripes and/or transverse bars. This coat pattern generally resembles that of the serval *Leptailurus serval*. Individuals with the king cheetah coat pattern also have longer, softer and silkier hair than the more common variants. The king cheetah has been considered by various authors to be a hybrid between a leopard and a cheetah, a form of leopard known as the Mazoe leopard, or a separate species of cheetah *Acinonyx rex*. In Zimbabwe there is an old legend about a large cat or *nsuifisi* which preyed upon domestic stock at night and was neither a lion, leopard nor a cheetah. This legend possibly referred to the king cheetah. It is now known that a king cheetah is only a genetic mutation which is controlled by a single recessive coat colour gene. Although restricted mainly to the arid savannas of southern Africa, king cheetahs may also occur in the savannas of Burkina Faso.

Another rare coat colour variation is described by Jahangir, a Moghul emperor who ruled in India in the 17th century. This cheetah had blue instead of black spots on a bluish-tinted white background. It was called

In the arid regions of southern Africa there is a genetically recessive coat colour pattern known as the 'king cheetah', in which the cheetah's mid-dorsal spots merge to form parallel longitudinal stripes. Photo: J. du P. Bothma.

a white cheetah, and was not an albino but a mutant of the pigmentation gene. There is also a record of a cheetah shot in Tanzania in 1921 which had almost no spots on the neck and shoulders, and unusually small spots elsewhere on the body. From Kenya there is one reliable report of a black cheetah found in 1925.

The evidence of genetic mutation in the cheetah's coat colour and pattern is somewhat surprising because cheetahs are generally known to be remarkably homogeneous genetically. This homogeneity expresses itself in various ways. For example, a cheetah's skull has a high degree of asymmetry with the left lower jaw being longer than the right. The reasons for such a high degree of inbreeding are not yet clear. Despite their genetic poverty, however, there are still seven subspecies of modern cheetahs, but *Acinonyx jubatus velox* from west of the Kikuyu escarpment in East Africa may possibly now be extinct. It was previously known as *Acinonyx jubatus ngorongensis,* a name which also included *Acinonyx jubatus raineyii* from east of the Kikuyu escarpment in East Africa.

Social behaviour

Apart from the lion the cheetah is the only other large African cat known to form groups. Such groups consist either of a female and her dependent young or of adult sibling males.

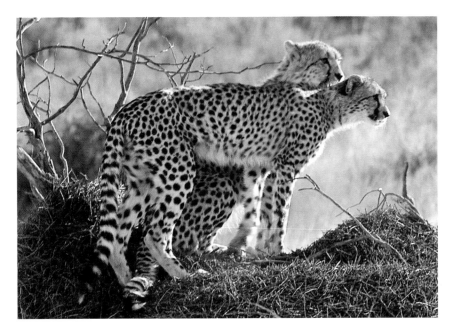

Cheetahs form groups of litter-mate males, or of adult females and their dependent young.
Photo: J. du P. Bothma.

In Serengeti most male cheetahs live singly or in related groups of two to three individuals. Unrelated males may also occasionally form groups when their superior numbers will allow them to take over a territory from a resident male or to fend off a challenge from intruders. This system of sociability in adult males and solitary life in adult females is unique in mammals. Male coalitions are stable for life and a single adult male cheetah will seldom be able to defend a territory on its own and even then not for much more than a few months at most. Single males are at a great disadvantage when attacked by a group of males. However, a male group does not have a clear or dominant leader and all the group members apparently participate in mating. In Serengeti cheetah male groups are usually larger in areas of higher prey density and smaller where prey is less abundant. This happens because cub survival is higher when prey is more abundant, and because male groups usually consist of litter mates.

The individual members of a group of male cheetahs maintain close contact, and although they are usually silent, they do have an extensive array of calls which are used to locate and communicate with each other. Cheetah calls resemble high-pitched bird calls and the most striking is an explosive yelp which can be heard as far as 2 km away. Chirping sounds are used for closer communication when two chee-tahs meet. Cheetahs also purr. Cheetah densities vary from region to region and high numbers of females gather near abundant prey

97

resources. This contributes to group formation in males in combination with overlaps in range use. In Tarangire cheetah density is only 0,25 cheetah per 100 km². However, in Serengeti it may be as high as 40 per 100 km² in areas where prey is abundant, although the long-term density is more in the order of 0,8 to 1 cheetah per 100 km². High local concentrations of cheetah are also known from the Nairobi National Park, where it is estimated that there are 20 cheetahs per 100 km². In most other savanna systems the relatively low cheetah density when compared with other large carnivores, is possibly the result of high cheetah cub mortalities, mainly from lion predation.

Territorial male cheetahs scent-mark their ranges extensively and much more frequently than non-territorial, nomadic males, which usually do not remain in a given area for more than a few days. These nomadic cheetahs travel widely and are usually in poor condition. A cheetah follows the typical cat pattern when scent-marking, depositing its marks in those areas in which these signals are most likely to be discovered. Scent marks have a pungent odour and although they do not seem to deter intruders, they may intimidate them for some 24 hours after the marking. Male cheetahs are as capable as lions and leopards of directing a jet of urine at a bush or tree trunk when scent-marking. In the southern Kalahari savanna both urine and faeces are used by cheetahs in this process. Although it is an open savanna, trees are still scent-marked there at a mean frequency of once every 1,6 km. The same tree or object may also be scent-marked repeatedly, as happens elsewhere. Cheetahs do not often scratch trees when scent-marking. They do, however, mark repeatedly over the scent marks of other cheetahs.

Reproduction and young

Adult, female cheetahs have little contact with males and even courting and mating is brief, seldom lasting for more than 24 hours. Nevertheless, females are highly selective of their mates. A female cheetah first gives birth when she is older than 3 years. Individual males in a group may share in any available opportunities for mating, but the males may also fight fiercely with strange males for possession of a female in oestrus. The cheetah is an induced ovulator. Consequently there are only slight peaks in breeding. A female in oestrus passes hormones in her urine that attract male interest and a male cheetah reacts with flehmen when smelling such urine. Tree-clawing by females is mainly associated with courtship. A high percentage of all cheetah spermatozoa show abnormalities, but the effect of this on their natural fertility is still largely unknown. Although mating cheetahs may spend as many as 3 days together, they seem to copulate solely at night. Actual copulation takes only a few minutes, and successive copulations are up to 8 hours apart. When copulating the male bites the female's neck as lions and leopards do. Gestation lasts for 90 to 95 days, and in the wild one to six cubs are born with their eyes closed, opening when about 10 days old. The interbirth interval is approximately 19 months.

Most adult, female cheetahs in the wild give birth. In the Nairobi National Park cheetah females with cubs avoid areas of high lion density and for 5 to 8 weeks after birth cheetah cubs are hidden in a den which is usually close to abundant prey. These lairs are either in tall vegetation, marshes or rocky outcrops. Male cheetahs play no role in raising the cubs which are moved frequently by their mothers to new dens in order to get them closer to prey, to avoid detection from predators and also to prevent infestation from parasites such as fleas. A female will stay close to her cubs, even when hunting, and young cheetahs remain dependent on their mother for more than a year.

Cheetah cubs in the wild weigh from 150 to 300 g at birth. They have a thick mantle of long, bluish to smoky-grey hair along the nape, shoulders and back. This mantle disappears after about 3 months when the cubs become mobile, and its purpose is probably to act as camouflage for the small cubs. Young cheetahs are especially susceptible to high mortality rates. In Serengeti 72% of all cheetah cubs die before they emerge from the den at about 6 to 8 weeks. Females who lose unweaned cubs, rapidly conceive again. Of those cubs that do survive to emerge from the den in Serengeti, 83% die before the age of 14 months. These data all translate into a low survival rate for cheetah cubs, and only 4,8% of all cheetah cubs born in Serengeti will reach independence. Elsewhere litter losses of cheetah cubs are equally high.

On the Serengeti Plains lion predation is the main cause of mortality for cheetah cubs in the den, although some cubs are also abandoned and starve to death when their mothers follow the migrating Thomson's gazelles *Gazella thomsonii*. Certain abandoned cubs may, however, join other unwilling cheetah families and steal food from them to survive. Once a cub has emerged from its lair, lions and spotted hyaenas kill about equal proportions of them (lions: 33,3%; spotted hyaenas: 41,7%). Of all the cheetah cubs killed by predators in Serengeti, lions will eventually kill 78,6% and spotted hyaenas 12,2%. In the Nairobi National Park 50% of all cheetah cubs are killed by lions, leopards and spotted hyaenas before reaching 8 months of age. Predators and starvation are also the major cub mortality factors in the southern Kalahari savanna where 50% of all cheetah cubs die in the first 6 months of their life. In that region, black-backed jackals and the occasional brown hyaena may also kill these cubs. Because female cheetahs in the harsh southern Kalahari savanna have to keep themselves alive by hunting, they may be forced to leave their young cubs unattended for long periods. At such times the cubs are vulnerable to attack from other predators, or they die because of poor nourishment. Cheetah cubs do not recognise predators and are slow to respond to this danger which makes them especially vulnerable to predation. The influence of predation on these cubs becomes clear from the much higher cub survival rates found in regions where large predators are absent. On cattle ranches in Namibia, for example, where there are few large predators, as many as four members of each cheetah litter born reach independence. Even in Serengeti cheetah cub survival in the woodland areas is much higher than on the open plains because there is much more protection for cheetah females with cubs in the woodlands where they are less visible and more difficult to detect.

During times of abundant food availability, reproductive success and cheetah cub survival increase. In Serengeti conception taking place at the time of peak food abundance when the Thomson's gazelles give birth to their lambs, have a greater success rate than at other times, although there is no clear seasonal peak in breeding. The existence of abundant food also increases cub survival because a lactating female cheetah needs to almost double her normal food intake to be able to nourish her cubs. An abundance of food in the environment may also make other predators less likely to prey on cheetah cubs. It is clear that cheetahs have extremely high cub mortality rates, and they compensate for this problem by reaching sexual maturity relatively earlier, and by having larger litters than other wild cats. By producing cubs with low birth weights, cheetah females also avoid investing too much energy in young that have a low chance of survival.

Cheetahs start weaning their cubs at about 6 weeks and it is usually completed by 3 months, although it may extend to 4 months of age. However, the cubs remain with their mother until they are about 18 months old, after which they can survive alone. There is no gradual transition to independence and the break with the mother is abrupt and rapid, taking place in a few days. Regurgitation of food from the mother to her cubs has been observed in a captive female, but it is not known to occur in the wild. Cubs start to hunt actively when about 7 months old, and although natural predatory behaviour is found in young cheetahs, the hunting training given by the mother to her cubs is critical for the development of the complete hunting behaviour sequence. This training allows the cubs to adapt their natural hunting abilities to local prey behaviour. In Serengeti young cheetahs become independent in the wet season when food is most abundant. This ensures that even if they had not yet totally mastered their hunting skills, there would still be enough food for them to survive their first few months of independence. Litter mates of the same sex may stay together for several months after independence, and some of the male litter mates form life-long groups.

Range use

Cheetah females do not defend their large ranges actively, but they do have loosely defined range boundaries while resident male cheetahs stay in small defended territories. In the Nairobi National Park two groups of females with young each used ranges of 76 and 82 km² respectively. In Serengeti female cheetahs use considerably overlapping ranges with a mean size of 833 km², but the territorial or resident males stay in small discrete ranges with a mean size of only 37,4 km². These ranges are scent-marked to keep intruders away. This is quite different from the situation found with most large cats where the male ranges are usually much larger than those of the female. Non-territorial, nomadic or 'floating' males have much larger ranges (mean: 777,2 km²) than territorial males which may occasionally make excursions of 1 to 2 days outside their range for a mean distance of up to 20 km away before they return to their own range. This may be an attempt to find mates. In the Nairobi National Park a female cheetah with cubs uses a smaller and more distinct range (mean: 58 km²) than other female cheetahs, and makes use of a small section of the range intensively for 2 to 3 days, before moving to another part of her range.

9 cm

   In the prey-poor areas inhabited by cheetahs, such as the southern Kalahari savanna, the male cheetah ranges are larger (mean: 300 km²) than elsewhere. In essence, a cheetah defends its space while moving around by scent-marking. In Serengeti cheetah territories are usually centred on areas that provide vital resources such as cover and prey. Migrating herds of prey cause resident male cheetahs in Serengeti either to vacate or occupy some of their ranges as they follow the movements of their main prey source, the Thomson's gazelle. Large areas between adjacent ranges may also be left vacant because they are temporarily or permanently low in prey. Although it was previously believed that the larger the male cheetah group, the longer it would hold a territory, it has now been established that the duration of territory tenure is unrelated to the size of the group.

Territorial males are not more likely to encounter females than roaming males. However, because nomadic males are usually alone, they are at a disadvantage when competing for a female in oestrus. These nomadic males are usually also in poorer condition, have less chance of survival and are lighter in weight than resident males. Of all the cheetah males resident in Serengeti 41% live alone, 40% live in pairs and the rest live in larger groups. Yet only 4% of the single males ever hold a territory. Young males are never territorial because body size and age are important criteria which determine whether a male cheetah will become territorial or not. Consequently a young adult male will only be able to hold a territory when he is unusually large for his age group.

In scent-marking their range, cheetahs often urinate against objects, even in arid savannas where a scent mark may possibly be less effective than in those which are more humid. Such marking locations are well known by resident cheetahs. When scent-marking, male cheetahs most commonly direct either a jet or spray of urine mixed with glandular secretions against prominent landmarks such as a vertical tree trunk, the rock face or a termite mound. The hind feet are usually used to scrape or tread at the same time as scent-marking, but males may also urinate close to the ground in a half-squatting posture, and follow this up by repeatedly raking the hind feet over and around the urine. Cheetahs also use tree-scratching to scent-mark their range, although much less frequently than urination. Even in the southern Kalahari savanna male cheetahs scent-mark trees repeatedly. They may also defecate near the trees which are urine-marked. Such faeces may be mixed with anal gland secretions which possibly also conveys a range use message to other cheetahs.

|_____| 5 cm

Female cheetahs seldom jet-urinate, but they do spray-urinate widely and frequently. In the Nairobi and Amboseli National Parks marking locations vary with the density of the woody vegetation. The marking could occur every 30 to 50 m in dense cover, but on the more open plains scent marks are usually from 50 to 100 m apart. By contrast, such marks are separated by a mean distance of 1,6 km in the southern Kalahari savanna. Non-resident males also scent-mark, but rarely. While scent-marking may not actually deter intruders, it is likely to intimidate them. Therefore scent-marking by cheetahs probably serves as a means of conveying signals that an area is occupied and that all the cheetahs within it should best be avoided unless a female in oestrus is involved.

Activity and movement

Cheetahs in Serengeti spend most of the day resting, and hunt mainly during the early morning and afternoon. They are more active by day than other cats, possibly because they rely greatly on sight when hunting.

Cheetahs are more active during the day than the other large carnivores of the African savannas. Photo: J. du P. Bothma.

By hunting during the day they may also avoid undue competition with the other large predators of the savannas who hunt mainly at night. Nevertheless, cheetahs are adaptable and may hunt by moonlight when circumstances allow. Those that live in the Sahara mountains are also mainly active at night, when it is cool. On hot days in the South African bushveld savanna, cheetahs spend up to 90% of their time resting in the shade, with most activity taking place early and late in the day and at night, but with a definite peak of activity in the late afternoon and early morning, as in Serengeti. Cheetah movements in Serengeti are affected by the activity of the Thomson's gazelles which are its main prey. Some cheetahs are more resident than others. In the Nairobi National Park a cheetah male travels about 7,1 km per day and a female 3,7 km. In the southern Kalahari savanna two adult male cheetahs once moved 252 km in 20 days, or a mean daily distance of 12,6 km. There is some evidence to suggest that translocated cheetahs will attempt to return to their region of origin.

Feeding ecology

A cheetah requires some 3 to 4 kg of meat per day to remain in excellent health. It eats different prey in different areas as most cats do, but it seldom tackles prey larger than 60 kg. A cheetah rarely eats food that it did not kill itself. On those infrequent occasions when a cheetah does

Cheetahs hunt their prey opportunistically. In the Etosha National Park the dik-dik is an abundant small herbivore prey. Photo: J. du P. Bothma.

eat carrion, it must be fresh. In the prey-rich Serengeti different types of prey are of varied importance to cheetahs because of varying abundance and availability. In all localities young prey are preferred to adults, but sick prey are not selected. However, in the prey-poor southern Kalahari savanna, all possible prey weighing from 1 to 200 kg is hunted opportunistically and there is no clear preference for prey type, age or condition.

Local habitat conditions will influence a cheetah's diet, as happens in Kafue where both the cheetah and puku prefer the open grasslands and tree savannas. Consequently more than 50% of the cheetah kills there are pukus. In Serengeti the Thomson's gazelle abounds and it forms 91% of all the cheetah kills. Likewise in the Kruger National Park, where impalas form 68% of all cheetah kills. Cannibalism is rare among cheetahs, but it may occur in exceptional cases.

A cheetah hunts in three basic ways: by chance, by a purposeful search from elevated positions, or from ambush. Because it is anatomically designed for high-speed chases, a cheetah hunt usually involves a short, extremely fast chase followed by slaps to the hind legs, shoulder, rump or thigh of the prey to trip and overpower it, and culminating in death by strangulation. Hunting often starts in the early morning, but the daytime heat of the Sahara mountains forces the cheetahs to hunt at night when it is cool.

A cheetah usually first locates its prey from some vantage point such

Cheetahs often detect prey from a convenient vantage point.
Photo: J. du P. Bothma.

as a rock or termite mound. The prey is then watched intently and a given individual is selected before stalking begins. When stalking a cheetah uses a slow walk and not a crouch as is common in other cats. When the prey becomes aware of a hunting cheetah, all prey in the area may react by snorting and mobbing the cheetah. They may even actively search the cheetah out and follow it noisily as it moves away, alerting all other potential prey to the cheetah's presence, and continuing to do

Termite mounds are favoured sites for cheetahs to lie-up on, and to survey their range for possible prey.
Photo: J. du P. Bothma.

so until the cheetah is out of range. Where prey is abundant, a cheetah may select a single victim from a herd on the basis of sex, age or condition and it then uses all the available cover in its slow stalk, often freezing in position for up to 10 minutes when the prey becomes nervous, which encourages it to relax again. However, a cheetah may also sometimes merely saunter up casually to its intended prey. The chase is usually triggered when the prey starts to move off.

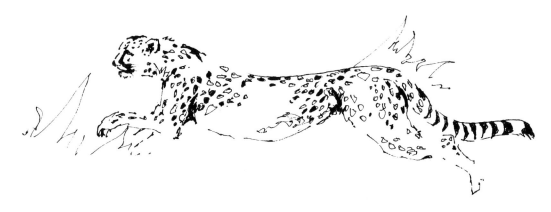

Much has been made of a cheetah's speed when running. It is commonly said to be able to reach speeds of up to 110 km/h, but in reality such sustained speeds are seldom reached in the savannas because of various obstacles and the swerving and jinking of the prey. Of 78 chases measured in Serengeti the maximum speed attained by an attacking cheetah was 87 km/h, a speed which an antelope can equal when in full flight. When running at full speed a cheetah has a stride of up to 9 m, and all four of its feet are airborne at the same time at least twice in each stride. The tail is used as a balance when making abrupt turns.

Although it was previously believed that cheetahs do not hunt in groups, it is now known that male cheetah groups may hunt cooperatively. However, no division of labour seems to occur as it does in lions. In the Nairobi National Park small groups of prey numbering from one to five individuals are targeted most often by hunting cheetahs. When the chase starts a cheetah hunts by overtaking its prey, but unless it has been caught within the first 300 m or so, the chase may be aborted, partly because a cheetah cannot tolerate its body temperature to increase beyond a given threshold as a result of the huge amount of energy expended. During or just after a chase a cheetah's breathing rate may increase ten-fold from what it is when at rest. Such high-speed chases require good visibility and relative freedom from obstructions. Consequently cheetahs usually hunt by day, and they do so more effectively in the open savannas.

In Serengeti they usually stalk to some 40 m from their prey before starting the chase. However, smaller prey such as gazelle lambs are pursued in a more leisurely way from a greater distance, presumably because they cannot run as well as larger prey. In the southern Kalahari savanna the mean chase distance of successful hunts is 218 m, and 122 m in unsuccessful ones. There the cheetahs approach their prey up to 23 m before starting the chase in unsuccessful hunts, and up to 32 m in successful ones. A close approach does not therefore guarantee success. The longest known successful chase in the Kalahari was 550 m and the longest unsuccessful one 650 m.

Once the prey has been overtaken, it is usually caught with a slap to the shoulder, rump or thighs by using the claws of the forefeet. In this action the long dew claw of the cheetah is of vital importance and sometimes the dew claw is the only means by which a prey animal is secured and held. The claw can also inflict a severe wound. Alternatively the prey can be tripped up by slapping the hindlegs. The slap often leaves a deep gash, and it weakens and unbalances the prey. The prey is suffocated by a throat or a muzzle bite, or killed by a bite to the vertebrae. A cheetah is not able to knock over a large, standing prey, and will seldom attack such a prey unless it starts to flee. Cheetah canines are rather short, only just piercing the skin when it bites, which is why it usually suffocates its prey. A cheetah also has exceptionally large nasal apertures and passages which allow it to recoup oxygen deficiencies resulting from its chase quickly, even when holding the prey firmly with clamped jaws. When large cubs accompany their mother on a hunt, they may help by holding down the prey with their paws, or with a bite to the flank. Small prey may simply be pounced upon and pinned to the ground with the forepaws before being killed. Sometimes a prey animal which is being suffocated may escape temporarily, usually only to be grabbed again and killed.

The ideal cheetah prey size seems to be around 30 kg. Like African wild dogs, cheetahs must also have a high hunting success because they both expend so much energy as coursing hunters. Nevertheless, hunting success in cheetahs varies according to the type of prey hunted, and the conditions of the hunt. Generally adult females with cubs are the more successful hunters. There is also some indication that a cheetah's hunting success increases with age, and consequently with hunting experience. In the Nairobi National Park cheetahs kill all their prey with a success rate of 37%. However, juvenile prey are killed more successfully at a rate of 76%. In the southern Kalahari savanna some prey are clearly hunted more successfully than others, and for all prey hunted there, a female with young cubs has a hunting success rate of 41%.

For all cheetahs, springbok (58,5% success rate) are clearly hunted more successfully than, for example, adult gemsbok (14,3%). Single cheetahs in that area have a hunting success rate of 32,4%, adult pairs 25,0%, and females with young cubs 71,4%. Single cheetahs also kill different proportions of the available prey base than adult pairs do, the pair being able to catch larger prey more successfully.

A cheetah eats hurriedly when feeding to avoid losing its food to other predators, consuming up to 14 kg of food in one sitting. A group of four cheetahs can consume an entire impala in only 15 minutes. Nevertheless, a cheetah may spend as much as 11 hours at a kill if undisturbed. In the Nairobi National Park cheetahs sometimes eat part of their prey, then cover it with grass, and return later. Female cheetahs with large cubs also occasionally make a kill, and then cover the carcass with leaves, grass or soil to protect it from scavengers while fetching the cubs to join in feeding. But larger cheetah cubs usually accompany their mother on her hunt, and are concealed near the prey before the hunt begins. Having made the kill, the female will then guard it while calling the cubs to the kill. Fatal fights may occasionally erupt between males over a kill, even leading to the death of one of the combatants.

The prey may or may not be dragged to suitable shade or cover before feeding starts. A cheetah does not use its forepaws to help it feed as lions and spotted hyaenas do. When several cheetahs feed together, they form a characteristic star shape around the kill. They usually feed in an orderly way, but may threaten each other as the food supply dwindles. The thighs, buttocks and ribs are normally eaten first, but like other cats the intestines, heart, and liver are usually not eaten. Blood that accumulates in the body cavity is lapped up as a source of nutrition and water, but the skin is seldom eaten. Although even young cheetahs over 6 months of age will crush and eat most of the bones of young prey, the larger bones, skin and head of large prey are usually not eaten. In Etosha when female cheetahs with cubs feed on larger prey, they do so in bouts lasting about 82 minutes, resting and grooming themselves in between for some 15 minutes. Cubs may feed up to six times at the same carcass, resting in between as well. Feeding cheetahs seldom pay attention to scavenging jackals, but they are wary of, and may lose much of their prey to other scavengers. In Serengeti they lose 12,7% of their kills to spotted hyaenas. This is equivalent to 9,2% of their meat. In this same area a group of male cheetahs is less likely to be harassed by spotted hyaenas at a kill because they consume it more quickly than single cheetahs. However, once a kill has been located by a scavenger, group size has no influence on its defence and such kills are appropriated with almost no exception. Male cheetahs may also occasionally scavenge food from the females.

Cheetahs are independent of free water as other cats are, but they do drink water when it is available. Other sources of water such as the body fluids of their prey and moisture-rich wild fruit are used to supplement their water needs allowing cheetahs to inhabit relatively waterless savannas successfully. In the southern Kalahari savanna, for example, two adult male cheetahs that travelled together, once covered 252 km in 20 days without drinking water, but they did make two kills in that time.

Relationship with other wildlife

Most predators will take at least some food away from a cheetah, but cheetahs feeding in a group, such as a female and her young or a group of males, are less likely to be harassed at a kill by spotted hyaenas or other male cheetahs than single cheetahs, because they consume the food relatively quickly. For example, in one study in Serengeti an adult female cheetah and her subadult cubs were chased away by a single adult spotted hyaena, from the carcass of an adult wildebeest bull which had died of unknown causes. Even vultures will effectively drive a cheetah off its kill. In the South African bushveld savanna, the cheetah and the leopard take much the same prey, although the leopard's is more varied. However, cheetahs are more diurnal and the leopards more nocturnal, separating them in time if not in space, and reducing the level of competition somewhat. The spotted hyaena is mainly a scavenger, and competes with the cheetah only on that level. Although they are both diurnal, African wild dogs are so rare today that they do not really compete with the cheetah or with any of the other large carnivores. In Serengeti the spotted hyaena can easily chase a cheetah off its prey but, because the cheetah is much more active by day than the spotted hyaena, the degree of actual competition is reduced. Consequently the cheetahs there hunt mainly when the spotted hyaenas are inactive.

Aggression between cheetahs is rare, but it does occur occasionally when it may lead to the death of one of the combatants. When this happens, cannibalism may occur. Other large predators are well-known killers of cheetah cubs. Even adult cheetahs may be at similar risk, particularly because they stay in one place at night where they may be attacked. In Amboseli, for example, a leopard is known to have attacked and killed a young cheetah, yet where other large predators are virtually absent, cheetah survival rates are high.

Population dynamics

The principle threats to free-living cheetahs are those of loss of habitat and prey, and the genetic poverty which reduces the viability of the population. However, some authors still doubt the influence of genetics on long-term cheetah survival. In recent years there has been a major increase in the number of prey available to large carnivores in the Serengeti-Mara ecosystem. This has come about because of disease control among the ungulates, and several years of high rainfall. The resultant increase in the number of other large predators such as the lion and spotted hyaena may have affected the cheetah population adversely, but these are only secondary factors because disease, starvation and injuries are the main causes of death for these cheetahs. Young females in Serengeti die at a rate of 0,153 per year, prime females at a rate of 0,227 per year, and half of all the old females die each year. Once a female cheetah has reached an age of 3 years in Serengeti, she has a further mean life expectancy of only 11 months, although the occasional cheetah will live to an age of 11 to 12 years in the wild. The sex ratio of the cubs is equal in cheetahs, but in adults it is heavily in favour of females. The mortality rate in the males is so great that only some 50% of all young males survive to old age, and this rate is especially severe when they are young and fight aggressively to obtain territories. In Serengeti the high densities and localised distribution of cheetah females also create ideal conditions for intense competition among the males.

There is no evidence that prey availability limits cheetahs in any way in the Serengeti-Mara ecosystem, because high cub mortality is a major problem for cheetahs in all natural systems. In Serengeti cub production is not enough to maintain the present cheetah population. However, the fact that these cheetahs have survived to date suggests that there will be other periods of sufficiently high cub production and survival to sustain the population. Such periods may be linked to periods of lower numbers of the other large predators, as happens in the Nairobi National Park. During periods of relative prey abundance in Serengeti, both the lion and the spotted hyaena population increase sharply. Following a recent similar increase, cheetah cub survival to 18 months of age decreased sharply, and recruitment of young probably also dropped. It seems likely that cheetah cub mortality in Serengeti is a major factor affecting the size of the cheetah population there, and lion predation is a major cause of this cub mortality taking 73% of all cubs between birth and independence. The recent drastic reduction of the lion population in Serengeti because of an epizootic of canine distemper will no doubt reduce cheetah cub mortality. It may also well be an example of one of the factors which creates a fluctuation in cheetah survival and mortality rates and hence of long-term population size. More evidence for the role of other large carnivores in controlling cheetah numbers comes from Namibia, where the cheetah population is considered to be the most viable of any in Africa. Yet, less than 10% of this population occurs in formally protected areas where there are also other large carnivores. Instead, most of it occurs on cattle ranches where other large carnivores are scarce or absent. Several diseases such as anthrax, tick fever, feline enteritis and *Babesia canis* are known to affect cheetahs, and they carry a variety of parasites.

BIBLIOGRAPHY

Bertram, B.C.R. 1979. Serengeti predators and their social systems. In: Sinclair, A.R.E. & Norton-Griffiths, M. (Eds), *Serengeti, dynamics of an ecosystem.* Chicago: University of Chicago Press, 221–248.

Bosman, P. & Hall-Martin, A. 1997. *Cats of Africa.* Vlaeberg: Fernwood.

Bothma, J. du P. 1998. *Carnivore ecology in arid lands.* Berlin: Springer.

Burney, D.A. 1980. *The effects of human activities on cheetah* Acinonyx jubatus *in the Mara region of Kenya.* M.Sc. thesis. Nairobi: University of Nairobi.

Caro, T.M. 1982. A record of cheetah scavenging in the Serengeti. *African Journal of Ecology,* 20: 213–214.

Caro, T.M. 1994. *Cheetahs of the Serengeti Plains.* Chicago: University of Chicago Press.

Caro, T.M. & Collins, D.A. 1987a. Male cheetah social organization and territoriality. *Ethology,* 74: 52–64.

Caro, T.M. & Collins, D.A. 1987b. Ecological characteristics of the territories of male cheetah *(Acinonyx jubatus). Journal of Zoology, London,* 211: 89–105.

Caro, T.M. & Laurenson, M.K. 1994. Ecological and genetic factors in conservation: a cautionary tale. *Science,* 263: 485–486.

Durant, S. 1998. Is bush country the key to the cheetah's survival in Africa? *Cat News,* 28: 14–15.

Eaton, R.L. 1969. The cheetah: beautiful and efficient predator. *Africana,* 10(3): 19–23.

Eaton, R.L. 1970a. Group interaction, spacing and territoriality in cheetahs. *Zeitschrift für Tierpsychologie,* 27(4): 461–491.

Eaton, R.L. 1970b. The predatory sequence, with emphasis on killing behavior and its ontogeny, in the cheetah *Acinonyx jubatus* (Schreber). *Zeitschrift für Tierpsychologie,* 27(4): 492–504.

Eaton, R.L. 1970c. Hunting behavior of the cheetah. *Journal of Wildlife Management,* 34(1): 56–67.

FitzGibbon, C.D. & Fanshawe, J.H. 1989. The condition and age of Thomson's gazelles killed by cheetahs and wild dogs. *Journal of Zoology, London,* 218: 99–107.

Florio, P. & Spinelli, L. 1967. Successful breeding of a cheetah in a private zoo. *International Zoo Yearbook,* 7: 150–152.

Frame, G.W. 1992. First record of the king cheetah in West Africa. *Cat News,* 17:2–3.

Frame, G.W. & Frame, L.H. 1981. *Swift and enduring: cheetahs and wild dogs of the Serengeti.* New York: Dutton.

Garland, T. 1983. The relation between maximal running speed and body mass in terrestrial mammals. *Journal of Zoology, London,* 199: 157–170.

Grobler, J.H., Hall-Martin, A. & Walker, C. 1984. *Predators of southern Africa.* Johannesburg: Macmillan.

Hanby, J.P. & Bygott, J.D. 1979. Population changes in lions and other predators. In: Sinclair, A.R.E. & Norton-Griffiths, M. (Eds), *Serengeti, dynamics of an ecosystem.* Chicago: University of Chicago Press, 249–262.

Hills, D.M. & Smithers, R.H.N. 1980. The "King Cheetah". *Arnoldia,* 9(1): 1–23.

Hunter, M.L. 1996. *Fundamentals of conservation biology.* USA: Blackwell Science.

Hunter, L.T.B. & Skinner, J.D. 1995. Cannibalism in male cheetah. *Cat News,* 23: 13–14.

Kingdon, J. 1977. *East African mammals.* Vol. III, Part A: Carnivores. London: Academic.

Kruger, J.E. 1988. *Interrelationships between the larger carnivores of the Klaserie Private Nature Reserve, with special reference to the leopard* Panthera pardus *(Linnaeus 1758) and the cheetah* Acinonyx jubatus *(Schreber, 1775).* M.Sc. thesis. Pretoria: University of Pretoria.

Kruuk, H. & Turner, M. 1967. Comparative notes on predation by lion, leopard, cheetah and wild dog in the Serengeti area, East Africa. *Mammalia,* 31(1): 1–27.

Labuschagne, W. 1979. *'n Bio-ekologiese en gedragstudie van die jagluiperd* Acinonyx jubatus jubatus *(Schreber, 1775).* M.Sc. thesis. Pretoria: University of Pretoria.

Lamprey, H.F. 1964. Estimation of the large mammal densities, biomass and energy exchange in the Tarangire Game Reserve and the Masai steppe in Tanganyika. *East African Wildlife Journal,* 2: 1–46.

Laurenson, M.K. 1995. Implications of high offspring mortality for cheetah population dynamics. In: Sinclair, A.R.E. & Arcese, P. (Eds), *Serengeti II: dynamics, management and conservation of an ecosystem.* Chicago: University of Chicago Press, 385–399.

Lindburg, D.G. 1989. When cheetahs are kings. *Zoonoz,* 62(3): 5–10.

McLaughlin, R.T. 1970. *Aspects of the biology of the cheetahs* (Acinonyx jubatus Schreber) *in the Nairobi National Park.* M.Sc. thesis. Nairobi: University of Nairobi.

Mitchell, B.L., Shenton, J.B. & Uys, J.C.M. 1965. Predation on large mammals in the Kafue National Park, Zambia. *Zoologica Africana,* 1(2): 297–318.

Murray, M. 1967. The pathology of some diseases found in wild animals in East Africa. *East African Wildlife Journal,* 5: 37–45.

Nowell, K. & Jackson, P. 1996. *Wild cats.* Cambridge: IUCN Publication Services.

O'Brien, S.J. 1994. The cheetah's conservation controversy. *Conservation Biology,* 8(4): 1153–1155.

Philips, J.A. 1993. Bone consumption by cheetahs at undisturbed kills: evidence for a lack of focal-pallatine erosion. *Journal of Mammalogy,* 74(2): 487–492.

Pienaar, U. de V. 1969. Predator-prey relationships amongst the larger mammals of the Kruger National Park. *Koedoe,* 12: 108–184.

Schaller, G.B. 1972. *The Serengeti lion.* Chicago: Chicago University Press.

Stevenson-Hamilton, J. 1954. *Wild life in South Africa.* London: Cassell.

Van Aarde, R.J. & Van Dyk, A. 1986. Inheritance of the king coat colour pattern in cheetahs *Acinonyx jubatus. Journal of Zoology, London,* (A) 209: 573–578.

Van Valkenburgh, B. 1996. Feeding behavior in free-ranging African carnivores. *Journal of Mammalogy,* 77(1): 240–254.

Verberne, G. & De Boer, J. 1976. Chemocommunication among domestic cats, mediated by the olfactory and vomeronasal senses. *Zeitschrift für Tierpsychologie,* 42: 86–109.

Wozencraft, W.C. 1993. Order Carnivora. In: Wilson, D.E. & Reeder, D.M. (Eds), *Mammal species of the world,* 2nd ed. Washington, DC: Smithsonian Institution Press.

5

The caracal

In Africa the caracal *Caracal caracal* is typically an inhabitant of the more open, arid savannas and their associated rocky hills, although in South Africa it also occurs in the evergreen and montane forests of the southern provinces. In Ethiopia caracals also range up to 2500 m high into the Bale and Simien Mountains. Outside Africa the caracal's range extends as far east as India. Although it is one of the larger and more abundant cats, it has been inadequately studied to date. The few studies that are available also do not refer to the more mesic savannas of Africa, possibly because the caracal is less abundant there. Consequently all the available information will be used here as a general guide to the ecology of this beautiful cat with its characteristic black-tufted ears.

In the Russian language the caracal is indeed called the *karakal,* although it does not really occur there, as its most northern distribution in Asia is Kazakhstan of the former Soviet Union. One of its other interesting descriptive names is *harnotro,* which means "killer of the black buck" in the Kutchi dialect of Gujarati, in India. The back of the caracal's ear is black, and the name caracal is believed to have originally come from the Turkish and Uzbek names *karakulak* which means *black ear.* Also the appearance of the caracals' ears, with their stiff black tufts of hair of about 45 mm long, is similar to those of the European and New World lynxes.

Consequently the caracal is often also erroneously called a lynx, although there is no close relationship between caracals and lynxes. Moreover, the lynx is anatomically and morphologically quite different

The black-tufted ear of the caracal is a characteristic feature, but caracals are not closely related to the spotted lynxes who also have such ears. Photo: J. du P. Bothma.

from the caracal, for example in having a spotted and barred coat as opposed to the unicoloured reddish coat of the caracal.

The caracal was first described scientifically by J.C.D. von Schreber in 1776 as *Felis caracal* from a specimen collected near Table Mountain in South Africa. Caracals from North Africa and Southwest Asia are generally smaller and paler than those of sub-Saharan Africa. In central Israel, about 5 to 10% of the adult caracals are grey, although their kittens are almost black. In the Karakum Desert of Turkmenistan, the caracal also has tufts of stiff hair on the paws like the sand cat *Felis margarita* in which these hairs insulate the paws from the extremes of surface heat experienced in the Sahara Desert. Like the cheetah, the caracal used to be trained to hunt for the nobility in ancient India. It is also portrayed in ancient Egyptian paintings. Embalmed caracals have been found in Egypt where they were also modelled in bronze which was valuable at that time. Gilded or bronze sculptures of sitting caracals and other cats were also used as guardians of the tombs of the pharaohs. In East Africa the Karamajong greatly admire the caracal's ears, likening them to the feathers which they wear when dancing.

Social behaviour

The caracal is a solitary cat of medium build with the males weighing in the region of 15 kg and the females 12 kg. The only social contact between adult caracals is the brief period of mating, although occasionally a female with one or two dependent young may move around together.

Caracals are said to reach their highest densities in mountainous areas, but reliable data on caracal densities are rare. In the arid, montane, scrub savanna and grassland areas of the Mountain Zebra National Park of South Africa, a probable maximum of 26 caracals in an area of 6500 ha was calculated on the basis of range use.

The caracal is generally silent, but its kittens and subadults do communicate with bird-like, chirping calls much like those of a cheetah. In addition, they are said to make a loud, coughing call occasionally which is similar to that of the leopard. Like the other cats, the caracal also uses

scent-marking, especially to advertise its range boundaries. Their conspicuous ears are believed to play some role in communication between caracals, as ears do in all the cats. However, their ears may also have become a highly mobile and extraordinary decorative signalling apparatus.

In the Mountain Zebra National Park caracals share their habitat with the Cape mountain zebra.
Photo: J. du P. Bothma.

119

Reproduction and young

Caracals probably reproduce throughout the year, but there may be regional peaks in some areas, especially in the wet season when some types of prey are presumably more abundant. In captivity, a young caracal male becomes sexually active when 12 to 14 months old, and a female may conceive when 14 months old. However, in the wild the age of sexual activity will probably be delayed by the restrictions of social behaviour, with serious sexual activity starting only at 18 to 20 months old. Oestrus lasts from 1 to 3 days, recurring every 14 days, if conception does not take place. Copulation is brief, lasting from 1,5 to 8 minutes (mean: 3,8 minutes). The gestation period lasts from 78 to 81 days (mean: 79 days), and the interbirth interval is 10 months.

In the Mountain Zebra National Park female caracals with kittens prefer to live at the base of the more densely wooded valleys and riverine thickets where there is an abundant supply of smaller prey, especially rodents, birds and small game. Litters are also born in these areas because they generally have plenty of suitable cover for lairs and dens. In other areas of the park, caracal litters may also be born in lairs under dense cover, or amongst rocks, but particularly in disused aardvark burrows. The den or lair is usually lined with hair or feathers. The kittens' eyes are closed at birth and open when they are 9 to 10 days old. Also, their ears are not fully erect when they are born, although the characteristic ear tufts develop rather early. At 21 days, the ear tufts may already be 10 mm long, and at 30 days, the kittens' ears are fully erect. Although captive caracals have litter sizes of up to six young, they more often have one to three (mean: 2,2) in the wild. Caracals probably only have one litter per year, and a female can still reproduce when she is as old as 18 years. Caracal kittens remain with their mothers until they are about 7 to 12 months, but they are weaned when about 4 months old. Once a kitten becomes mobile, it moves about with its mother, resting in any suitable cover when it becomes tired. At these times a kitten is especially vulnerable to predation, especially from jackals. When independent, a young caracal moves out of its natal range for distances of up to 42 km before settling into its own range as an adult.

Range use

The range-use pattern of the caracal is typical of that of most larger cats, with males having large territories, each one including all or portions of the ranges of several females. The male territories may overlap widely, but those of the females overlap less extensively. Although no data on range size exist specifically for the more typical savanna areas, the male caracal ranges will probably be of the same order as those of 12,2 to 16,7 km² (mean: 15,2 km²) found in the scrub savanna of the Mountain Zebra National Park, where there is a fairly high prey biomass. In the more arid areas, such as in the southern Kalahari savanna, caracals will have much larger ranges. In that region one young male caracal is known to have had a range of 308,4 km² of which it used a core area of 93,2 km² extensively. Female caracals of the more typical savannas will probably have ranges similar to those of 3,9 to 6,5 km² (mean 5,5 km²) found in the Mountain Zebra National Park. From the little that is known, a male caracal seems to have a range size which is three to four times greater than a female's. Nevertheless, caracals spend much of their time in the smaller core areas of their range.

5–6 cm

Caracal males are known to scent-mark their range boundaries with faeces, often marking the same site repeatedly. They probably also use urine scented with glandular secretions for this purpose. Caracals move

5 cm

Caracals rarely move about by day, preferring to rest in some suitable cover. Photo: J. du P. Bothma.

along a set of regularly used paths throughout their range. In male caracals these paths usually include the boundaries of their range. When a range becomes vacant, a young adult caracal will establish itself there, and the boundaries of existing neighbouring ranges may well be adjusted in the process.

Activity and movement

The caracal is predominantly nocturnal, and it will move about in daylight only under exceptional circumstances such as cold days in winter, or on cool, cloudy days in summer when it may hunt in daylight.

Caracals are not overly active and will only travel distances of some 1 to 2 km in 24 hours, with the males moving significantly further than the females. Resting caracals keep well apart. In the Mountain Zebra National Park resting adult males maintain a mean linear distance of 4 km from each other, and females 2,2 km. This means that the females are significantly closer to each other when resting than the males, a fact which is reflected in the different range sizes used by the two sexes. The caracal is much more agile than the cheetah, and it makes faster dashes from a standing start to catch its prey. It is also a great leaper as is explained below.

Feeding ecology

Because they prey on small domestic stock in farming areas, much of what is known about the ecology of
caracals concerns their diet. As in other carnivores their
diet varies from region to region depending upon the
nature of the habitat, and the type and abundance of prey
available. Like most cats the caracal is an opportunistic feeder, but its
main food is smaller mammals. In some areas rodents are especially targeted when they are abundant and in others rock hyraxes *Procavia capensis,* hares and small to medium-sized antelopes are often preyed upon.

Caracals also readily hunt and eat smaller carnivores such as the
African wild cat *Felis silvestris,* the Cape grey mongoose *Galerella pulveru-
lenta,* the yellow mongoose *Cynictis penicilata,* the genets of the genus
Genetta, the otter *Atilax paludinosus,* the polecat *Ictonyx striatus* and the
suricate *Suricata suricatta*. In many farming areas where other natural
prey has largely been exterminated, caracals prey heavily on rock hyraxes, but they also readily attack and eat smaller domestic stock.
However, not nearly all the caracals present on farmland will kill small
livestock, nor will this occur with equal regularity. Caracals also readily
eat birds.

123

A caracal is an expert at concealment when resting or ambushing its prey. Photo: J. du P. Bothma.

The caracal only eats fresh meat. Consequently it is often believed that it will not scavenge. Some authors believe that the caracal is so selective of its food that it will not even return to its own kill once it has been disturbed there. However, it is now known that a caracal will scavenge on rare occasions. In fact, fresh meat has been used successfully to trap caracals in at least one study. There are also records of caracals preying on caracal kittens, which makes them cannibalistic on occasion.

The caracal is a hunter-killer, and its speed in attack surpasses that of most of the other cats. It hunts its prey by stalking, or from ambush. The stalk is followed by a short rush, ending in a lunge or leap to catch the prey. Birds such as doves, francolins and sand grouse are plucked deftly from the air as they rise from the ground. Birds are also often stalked and batted out of the air at waterholes during the day, or are killed while they sleep at night. A caracal crouching on the ground can easily jump up to a height of 2 m to get at a bird on the wing. In feudal India there was a sport where bets were placed on how many birds a captive caracal could knock down in one rush. When the prey is caught, it is usually swiped sideways with the front paws. It is then killed by a bite to the throat, or occasionally to the neck.

A caracal's lower incisors are not well developed. This, coupled with a large diastema, which is the gap between the canines and the molar teeth, allows the canines to penetrate the prey for almost their full length. Therefore a caracal can deliver deep, lethal bites. When the prey still shows signs of life after being bitten, the caracal may throw itself on it and rake it repeatedly with the hind feet until it ceases to struggle. Caracals will occasionally kill a surplus of prey in a frenzy under conditions which make the prey mill around. This usually involves small livestock which are prevented from escaping by some obstacle or environmental circumstances. Such surplus killing is rare amongst the smaller cats.

Before starting to feed on the kill, the caracal may jerk it around with all four of its paws for 5 to 20 minutes. Small prey may also be tossed up into the air repeatedly and caught again in mid-air. The reason for such behaviour remains unknown. A caracal starts to feed on the buttocks, the area around the anus, or the ribs and breast. The stomach,

125

intestines, feathers and pieces of skin are not eaten and hair is not removed from the prey before the caracal starts to feed as happens with the leopard. The caracal does not bury the remains of its prey, but it may pull the victim up into a tree for feeding. As long as the carcass is fresh, a caracal may feed on it in separate bouts, resting in between.

Although there is no reliable scientific information on caracals' water use, their distribution, which includes arid areas and deserts, must mean that they are as independent of free water as most of the wild cats. No evidence has yet been found of caracals eating wild fruit for moisture in arid areas, but one stomach collected in the wild in South Africa did contain cultivated grapes. This seems to indicate that the caracal may occasionally eat moisture-rich fruit.

Dynamics and relationship with other wildlife

The caracal is a shy creature which will readily flee and hide when it feels threatened. Little is known about its relationship with wildlife other than its prey, and nothing is known about its population dynamics. This is surprising for a cat so widely distributed, and with such a major impact on small livestock. There is some evidence that caracals in the southern Kalahari savanna occasionally provide brown hyaenas with small but high-quality carcasses for scavenging. In all eight such cases recorded there by M.G.L. Mills, the carcass involved still contained a large proportion of meat, yet as the brown hyaena approached, the caracal withdrew without putting up any resistance.

Although once again no scientific data exists on the matter, it has also been the experience of many farmers in South Africa that when black-backed jackals are abundant, few caracals are around and vice versa. This must indicate some relationship, most probably that of the jackals competing for the same food resource as the caracals, and even the possibility of jackals actually killing caracal kittens which are left to the mercy of any likely predator at the lair, or when the kittens stop to rest when moving about. In some arid areas the caracal is also considered to be the main regulator of rock hyrax and rodent populations. In the wild a caracal probably lives for about 14 to 17 years.

BIBLIOGRAPHY

Avenant, N.L. 1993. *The caracal* Felis caracal *Schreber 1776, as predator in the West Coast National Park.* M.Sc. thesis. Stellenbosch: University of Stellenbosch.

Bernard, R.T.F. & Stuart, C.T. 1987. Reproduction of the caracal *Felis caracal* from the Cape Province of South Africa. *South African Journal of Zoology,* 22: 177–182.

Bosman, P. & Hall-Martin, A. 1997. *Cats of Africa.* Vlaeberg: Fernwood.

Bothma, J. du P. 1965. Random observations on the food habits of certain Carnivora (Mammalia) in southern Africa. *Fauna and Flora,* 16: 16–39.

Bothma, J. du P. 1998. *Carnivore ecology in arid lands.* Berlin: Springer.

Bothma, J. du P. & Le Riche, E.A.N. 1994. Range use by an adult male caracal in the southern Kalahari. *Koedoe,* 37(2): 105–108.

Caro, T.M. 1994. *Cheetahs of the Serengeti Plains.* Chicago: University of Chicago Press.

Grobler, J.H. 1981. Feeding behaviour of the caracal *Felis caracal* in the Mountain Zebra National Park. *South African Journal of Zoology,* 16: 259–262.

Grobler, J.H., Hall-Martin, A. & Walker, C. 1984. *Predators of southern Africa.* Johannesburg: Macmillan.

Kingdon, J. 1977. *East African mammals.* Vol. III, Part A: Carnivores. London: Academic.

Mendelsohn, H. 1989. Felids in Israel. *Cat News,* 10: 2–4.

Mills, M.G.L. 1990. *Kalahari hyaenas.* London: Unwin Hyman.

Mills, M.G.L., Nel, J.A.J. & Bothma, J. du P. 1984. Notes on some smaller carnivores from the Kalahari Gemsbok National Park. Supplement to *Koedoe,* 27: 221–227.

Moolman, L.C. 1984. There's a trick to catching a caracal. *Custos,* 13(8): 42–43.

Moolman, L.C. 1986a. *Aspekte van die ekologie en gedrag van die rooikat* Felis caracal *Schreber, 1776 in die Bergkwagga Nasionale Park en op die omliggende plase.* M.Sc. thesis. Pretoria: University of Pretoria.

Moolman, L.C. 1986b. Aspekte van die ekologie en gedrag van die rooikat *Felis caracal* Schreber, 1776 in die Bergkwagga Nasionale Park, en op plase daaromheen. *Pelea,* 5: 8–21.

Nowell, K. & Jackson, P. 1996. *Wild cats.* Cambridge: IUCN Publication Services.

Palmer, R. & Fairall, N. 1988. Caracal and African wild cat diet in the Karoo National Park, and the implications thereof for hyrax. *South African Journal of Wildlife Research,* 18(1): 30–34.

Pocock, R.I. 1939. *The fauna of British India. Mammalia, Vol. I: Primates and carnivora,* 2nd ed. London: Taylor & Francis.

Pringle, J.A. & Pringle, V.L. 1979. Observations on the lynx *Felis caracal* in the Bedford district. *South African Journal of Zoology,* 14: 1–14.

Rosevear, D.R. 1974. *The carnivores of West Africa.* London: Trustees of the British Museum of Natural History.

Shortridge, G.C. 1934. *The mammals of South West Africa.* London: Heinemann.

Skinner, J.D. 1979. Feeding behaviour in caracal *(Felis caracal). Journal of Zoology,* London, 189: 523–525.

Skinner, J.D. & Smithers, R.H.N. 1990. *The mammals of the southern African subregion.* Pretoria: University of Pretoria.

Smithers, R.H.N. 1971. The mammals of Botswana. *Museum Memoirs of the National Museums and Monuments of Rhodesia,* 4: 1–340.

Smithers, R.H.N. 1983. *The mammals of the southern African subregion.* Pretoria: University of Pretoria.

Sterndale, R.A. 1884. *Natural history of the Mammalia of India and Ceylon.* Reprinted 1982. New Delhi: Himalayan Books.

Stuart, C.T. 1982. *Aspects of the biology of the caracal* (Felis caracal) *Schreber 1776, in the Cape Province, South Africa.* M.Sc. thesis. Pietermaritzburg: University of Natal.

Stuart, C.T. 1986. The incidence of surplus killing by *Panthera pardus* and *Felis caracal* in Cape Province, South Africa. *Mammalia,* 50(4): 556–558.

Stuart, C.T. & Wilson, V.J. 1988. *The cats of southern Africa.* Bulawayo: Chipangali Trust.

Wozencraft, W.C. 1993. Order Carnivora. In: Wilson, D.E. & Reeder, D.M. (Eds), *Mammal species of the world,* 2nd ed. Washington, DC: Smithsonian Institution Press, 279–348.

6

The African wild dog

The African wild dog *Lycaon pictus* was originally described by C.J. Temminck in 1820 from a specimen collected on the Mozambique coast. He called it a form of hyaena *Hyaena picta,* but it was soon recognised as one of the canids, and was first renamed *Lycaon tricolor* by Brookes in 1827. The name *Lycaon* is derived from the Greek word *lykaios* which means wolfish. It was then given the specific epithet *pictus,* which is derived from the original *picta* and which is the Latin word for spotted, as directed by the International Rules on Taxonomic Nomenclature. The African wild dog is today also sometimes called the Cape hunting dog, or the painted dog. The latter name refers to the wild dog's varied coat colour with its blotched patches of white, black and yellow, which led to the use of the name *tricolor* by Brookes. Although all wild dogs have this patchy coat colour, those of the southern savannas have a bit more white in their coat than their northern counterparts.

Like all the canids, a wild dog is a lithe and muscular animal which can run at speeds of up to 30 km/h for extended periods. Canids are also a remarkably successful carnivore family which has existed in many parts of the earth, but are especially abundant in the savannas. Consequently various species of canid may occupy similar niches in different parts of the world. Of these, the grey wolf and the African wild dog are direct ecological counterparts with the wolf solving the same ecological problems in the North Frigid Zones of North America and Eurasia in a remarkably similar way to the African wild dog in the

Torrid and South Temperate Zones of Africa. The latter zone includes the African savannas.

Both the African wild dog and the Asiatic red dog or dhole are highly specialised members of the wolf-jackal canid group. In appearance the wolf and the African wild dog are quite similar, although the wild dog is smaller at 25 to 35 kg than the wolf whose weight ranges from 45 to as much as 80 kg.

Licking nose after feeding

132

The wolf also has a much longer nose than the wild dog, but the wild dog in turn has larger ears. Like the spotted hyaena and the grey wolf, the African wild dog has suffered from the prejudice of man for many years, primarily because of its hunting technique. In 1914, for example, R.C.F. Maugham, in his book, *Wild game in Zambezia,* called the wild dog an abomination and a blot upon the many interesting things of that region. He also referred to it as a murderous wild dog, and concluded by stating that it would be an excellent day for African game and its conservation when means could be found to exterminate this unnecessary creature completely. In its history the African wild dog has been the subject of many such ignorant comments, but today it is regarded by most people in a much more favourable light and as an integral part of the guild of large carnivores in the African savannas. Much has also been made of wild dogs attacking people, but there are few authentic records of such events and even those are extremely rare.

Because African wild dogs are highly mobile, they occur at low densities over extremely large ranges. This creates immense conservation problems, because few protected areas are large enough today to sustain viable populations of 200 to 300 wild dogs in a given area. Consequently the wild dog is now the most endangered canid in the world. It has already suffered a nearly fatal Pan-African population decline and there are only three substantial populations left, all of which occur in the African savannas. Currently, Selous has the largest known population of about 700 to 900 wild dogs, followed by northern Botswana with about 700 dogs, and the Kruger National Park with some 400 dogs. Although relict populations of the wild dog are still found in many countries today, viable populations are found only in Kenya, Tanzania, Zambia, Zimbabwe, Botswana and South Africa. There are probably no more than 3000 to 5000 wild dogs left in the world. However, the recent development of the concept of large conservation areas or 'peace parks', which stretch across international boundaries may well benefit the future survival of the African wild dog.

Social behaviour

In their social behaviour the canids generally show a high degree of adaptability and non-specialisation, and this has allowed them to be successful in various habitats. The various species of the Canidae show a remarkably similar pattern of social behaviour, however, despite being ecologically and morphologically diverse. In those canids living in

The African wild dog pack is a closely knit and cohesive family group that hunts and travels together.
Photo: J. du P. Bothma.

packs, some of the specialisations which have occurred are probably related to particular ecological conditions. These specialisations serve to maintain group cohesion and to reduce aggression within a species, but they are variations of degree rather than of kind. Canids are also unusual in that the family members share food and care for sick adults and dependent young. The African wild dog is specifically adapted to living in highly social packs, each of which has a primary function to obtain sufficient food for the survival of all the pack members. African wild dogs are apparently the only canids to specialise in killing large prey for food throughout the year. They are also the only canids for whom cooperative hunting has been the primary evolutionary force, which has led to the formation of their large packs.

In the African wild dog the pack is usually a cohesive, extended family group which hunts and travels together. The dominant pair determine the movements of the pack by direct leadership or by refusing to follow the lead of subordinate dogs. The degree of relatedness among dogs of the same sex within the pack is much higher than that in a lion pride. All packs have a dominant male and female who are usually the only ones to mate and reproduce. The other pack members feed and care for the pups. The pack functions primarily as a hunting unit, and its members cooperate closely in hunting and mutual defence. In the process, individual benefits are subordinated to pack benefits. There is also a strict division of labour within the pack. The typical pack consists of a dominant breeding pair, their young and the non-breeding adults who are litter mates of one of the breeding pair members, or are their offspring. The dominant pair is not related, but all the other pack members are related to the dominant pair. Pups older than 4 months usually form 25 to 50% of all the pack members, and yearlings 25%.

Pack size varies from area to area, and also from time to time within the same area. For example, near Aitong in south-western Kenya one pack ranged from 17 to 43 members in size, over an 18-month period. In the Mikumi National Park a pack of 40 wild dogs once split into three subpacks. In Moremi wild dog packs vary from 2 to 50 individuals, depending on the area and time of the year. The mean pack there has close to eight members, and packs of fewer than four dogs are rare. The larger packs occur where prey is more abundant. All the packs in Moremi, however, lead an insecure life which varies from being highly successful to experiencing various degrees of failure. In the Kruger National Park wild dog packs varied from 3 to 28 members in one study, with a mean pack size close to 13. Earlier, when much of Africa's savannas were still intact, there may have been much larger packs. Unconfirmed reports from that time mentioned packs of many hundreds of wild dogs in East and South Africa. In South Africa such large packs were believed to have been associated with previous massive

The typical wild dog pack is led by a dominant male and female pair.
Photo: J. du P. Bothma.

135

springbok migrations from that region which involved thousands of springbok moving as one huge wave, possibly in search of food. It is also possible that several wild dog packs may have congregated on these herds, creating huge temporary aggregations.

The wild dog pack maintains a clear and strict social dominance hierarchy. New packs form by the fusion of male or female groups of litter mates originating from different packs. In Serengeti young males are only recruited into the natal pack when pup survival is low or when the dominant male dies, but in the Kruger National Park male offspring often remain with their natal pack. Sometimes a pack will split into two new packs which include subordinate dogs of both sexes. The dispersal of young adult dogs usually involves a sibling female group (litter mates) who move away to form new packs with a similar but unrelated group of males. Dispersal frequently coincides with a change in the natal pack's dominance hierarchy, and the dispersing animals often move to areas with a high proportion of relatives. Because of litter size restrictions, dispersing groups of litter mates usually have only six or even fewer members. Nevertheless, some packs may retain their composition and structure for long periods.

The African wild dog varies in density from about 2 to 35 dogs per 100 km². Generally their density appears to be related to that of their prey, except in the Kruger National Park where it has been found that wild dogs are at their lowest densities in areas which have high prey densities, and which consequently also have high numbers of lions and spotted hyaenas. The lions of the Kruger National Park are a major mortality factor for its wild dogs, while its spotted hyaenas also impact significantly on the wild dogs by appropriating a proportion of the wild dog kills (kleptoparasitism). This forces the dogs to expend unrealistically high levels of energy to maintain their own basic energy requirements. This negative relationship between wild dog and spotted hyaena densities is found across a range of habitats. In the Kruger National Park wild dogs consequently live at a low minimum density of 1,7 dogs per 100 km^2 as opposed to 10 individuals per 100 km^2 for both lions and spotted hyaenas in the same area. This same negative relationship between the density of lions and spotted hyaenas and that of wild dogs also requires that efforts at wild dog conservation must focus on areas of low spotted hyaena and lion density.

There is little aggression within the wild dog pack because of the highly ritualised social behaviour of the dogs. There is a clear dominance hierarchy in a pack, but the pups have priority at the food. In Serengeti the composition of the various wild dog packs varies from time to time, and small packs never have large young with them, but the larger packs may contain individuals from at least three generations. Unlike lions and some other carnivores, wild dogs cannot function as individuals and as a result single nomads are rare. However, the packs themselves are nomadic for much of the time, except during the 3-month denning period.

The wild dog uses a variety of ways to communicate. When the dogs meet, they have a distinctive greeting ceremony with the various pack members running around, twittering and whining. Wild dogs are highly vocal, but the sounds which they emit are largely discrete. Their most distinctive call is a bell-like hoot which is used mainly when a dog becomes separated from the rest of the pack. This call consists of a series of 8 to 10 wailing hoots which are audible for up to 4 km on a still night and are heard most frequently on moonlit nights when the wild dogs may hunt at night. In response to this call the entire pack usually comes running over to the stray within a few minutes. Spontaneous communal hooting akin to the howling of a wolf pack does not seem to occur among wild dogs. In response to potential danger the dogs bark as domestic dogs do, and some dogs may also growl, with or without barking. Pups will whine when they become separated from the pack, when they are otherwise distressed, or when greeting adults and begging for food. Adults whine at the den entrance to induce the

When wild dogs become excited, they raise their white-tipped tails as a form of communication. Photo: J. du P. Bothma.

pups to come out. When wild dogs are excited they raise their tails, and the more excited they become, the higher the tail is raised. The white-tipped tail is also used to help keep other pack members in sight when hunting.

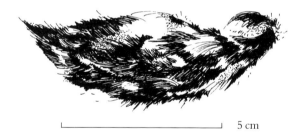

5 cm

Canids generally use urine to scent-mark their territory. The wolf's faeces are also known to emit volatile components which could be used for scent-marking. G.B. Schaller did not find any positive proof that wild dogs scent-mark, but later studies have shown that it may occur in much the same way as in wolves, where urine is used primarily to scent-mark the periphery of the range, and faeces the more central areas. Although there is no tail gland in the wild dog, it uses urine extensively in scent-marking, and anal dragging, body rolling and body rubbing also occur. Both their urine and faeces are deposited repeatedly in the same spot, although their use as scent markers seems to be con-

139

fined to the dominant pair. African wild dogs are believed to have sebaceous glands all over the body, and their consequently strong body odour must therefore also leave scented messages to other dogs when they roll on the ground, rub themselves against objects, or merely rub on the vegetation through which they pass. When lingering at a kill longer than other pack members, an individual wild dog may possibly use interdigital gland secretions or traditional pathways to relocate the pack, as is known to occur in the Asiatic red dog or dhole.

Reproduction and young

Reproduction in the canids is greatly affected by variations in the availability and abundance of their major food items. Canids in general breed seasonally, and both sexes increase their frequency of scent-marking and vocalisation during pre-oestrus periods. Although the reproductive system in canids is usually one of obligatory monogamy, in the case of the wild dog it is one of modified monogamy tending towards polyandry, with a sex ratio favouring males in the adults, and with male helpers and mainly female emigration. The dominant male and female do most of the mating, but a subordinate male may also occasionally mate with various subordinate females. When subordinate females do produce young, however, the pups are usually born several weeks after those of the dominant female. The pups of subordinate females also apparently receive less care than those of the dominant pair, and rarely survive beyond their first year of life. In the Kruger National Park only 3 of 29 (10%) of the pups from two different packs studied were not sired by the dominant male, and only 4 of 51 (8%) of the pups born were not produced by the dominant female. In Selous, which harbours the largest known population of African wild dogs in the world, the dominant females produce 76% of all the pups and in the wild dog packs of the Kruger National Park they produce 81% of all pups. Only 6 to 17% of all subordinate female dogs in both locations give birth each year, compared with 82% of all the dominant females. This pattern of limited reproduction has a profound influence on the conservation status of wild dogs. For example, of the 700 or so wild dogs present in Botswana, there are only some 70 to 80 breeding pairs. This is a small and fragile gene pool.

A wild dog pack typically produces one litter of pups per breeding season, and false pregnancies are known to occur from time to time, as in other canids. Parturition appears to coincide with periods of abundant prey. In the northern Serengeti-Mara ecosystem, the birth of pups coincides with the arrival of the annual prey migration. In the Kruger National Park it coincides with the end of the impala rut when the rams are out of condition and more vulnerable to predation. At this time all the game concentrate around the dwindling water resources. It is a time when the savanna is more open and visibility is best for hunting. The general mating behaviour of the African wild dog is typical of that of all canids. Actual mating lasts only from 3 to 7 days, but oestrus builds up slowly over several weeks before mating. A female in oestrus scent-marks frequently and several males may copulate with the same female. Before copulation the male strokes or scratches the female with a paw, and she then rises to be mounted. The copulatory or mating tie is a special feature of canid mating, and is caused by swelling of the base of the penis. When the penis is then gripped by the vaginal sphincter muscle, the mating pair becomes tied for a time that may vary. The purpose of this is as yet unclear, but it may possibly serve to increase the chances of successful fertilisation. Although it was earlier believed that the African wild dog was the one canid exception to this rule, it has now been shown that a copulatory tie also occurs in the wild dog when mating. However, it is unlike that of other canids, because it is of short duration, lasting no more than 50 to 112 seconds. Gestation lasts for some 70 days in the African wild dog, and the interbirth interval is a year. Litter size usually varies from 6 to 12 pups, but occasionally more. The sex ratio of the pups at birth is normally equal, but males can sometimes be in the majority. A wild dog pup is born in a den which is usually a burrow in the ground. In the Kruger National Park disused aardvark, warthog or spotted hyaena burrows are often used for this purpose. The actual breeding chamber is usually lined with grass and/or leaves.

All members of the wild dog pack care for and help to raise the young, and the adult males often carry the small puppies around. Pup survival is correlated directly with the number of females in the pack. Some females may even have minor confrontations over who will be allowed to care for the pups. Each female in the pack will nurse all the young present. The pups suckle for about 3 months, but they already start to eat meat when 14 days old, begging for food from the older members of the pack who will regurgitate food for them. Suckling is done in bouts of 3 minutes or so in an upper chamber of the den near the entrance, with the female either standing or lying down. Weaning is usually complete when the pups are 2 months old. When the pups are disturbed at a den, their mother will move them to a new one by carrying them singly in her mouth, gripping them in a haphazard fashion by the head, back, tail, leg, or in any other suitable way. There is also a report of a pack consisting of one adult female, five adult males, and nine 5-week-old pups. When the only female in the pack died, the five adult males fed and reared the pups themselves.

An African wild dog pup is small and utterly dependent at birth. Its eyes are closed when it is born, opening in about 10 days. It is also hairless, and requires a considerable amount of care. Helpers are therefore essential in raising the pups which are restricted to the den for the first 3 months of life. At the den the pups are usually guarded by females because adult males rarely do so. In Serengeti one adult female stayed with her pups on 72% of all pack hunts. The necessity of having helpers to raise the young can become a serious constraint to wild dog survival when pack size is reduced below the required minimum threshold. A lone wild dog pair are in effect incapable of reproducing and raising their young successfully. When a pack is killing prey regularly, three adult dogs are needed to regurgitate sufficient food for the pups normally present in a pack. When food becomes scarce, the adults will continue to feed the pups until they are themselves threatened with starvation. Only then will they abandon them. Sometimes the yearlings will also steal regurgitated food from the pups, which places additional stress on the adults.

In the South African bushveld savanna pup mortality between the ages of 4 and 10 months is 44%. In the Kruger National Park lions are a major predator of wild dog pups, and in one instance a pair of lionesses killed 12 of a group of 26 wild dog pups in a single morning. The chances of pup survival increase with pack size, and therefore with the number of females and helpers available to raise the pups. In Serengeti there is an impermeable calcium carbonate hardpan layer about 1 m below the surface of the shortgrass plains. This hardpan forms the floor on which the pups lie within the den. During the rains these plains are often quite wet. Consequently the den floor may be damp or even become flooded, killing some pups as a result of hypothermia and drowning others.

Range use

The size of their food supply and its availability in time and space can greatly influence the range-use patterns of canids. The African wild dog has solved this problem by living in packs. Each pack is a nomadic unit which moves to new rest sites every day in response to the movements of its prey, except during the breeding season when the pack occupies a smaller range centred around the den containing the pups. Where more than one pack occurs in large conservation areas, there may be range overlaps of up to 80%, but the packs seldom actually meet. When wild dog densities are low in Serengeti and the Kruger National Park, their range sizes are large because of a lack of competition between the various packs. In Serengeti, with its migratory herds of larger prey, the wild dog pack ranges are larger where the prey is seasonally scarce, but smaller where the prey offer a year-round food supply. Wild dog packs are not territorial for most of the year, and they do not actively defend a range. Consequently the large range overlaps. However, they do become territorial during the denning time when the territory centres around the den containing the pups. Despite their range overlaps, however, each individual pack has a preferred core area of use in its range which the other packs rarely enter.

In the Serengeti and Kruger National Park wild dog packs normally range over areas varying in size from 260 to 3800 km², depending upon prey abundance and availability. However, during the 3 months of denning, a pack in Serengeti hunts in an area of only 100 to 200 km², and of 50 to 170 km² in the Kruger National Park. A pack will remain in the same area as long as there is sufficient food. When two packs do meet, one usually chases the other away. The whole range is searched extensively for food, and when food is scarce, even large ranges may be traversed in 2 to 3 days. These movements are more restricted when the pups are small. In the Ngorongoro Crater one pack of 21 wild dogs stayed in the crater for only 4 months, reappearing at irregular intervals.

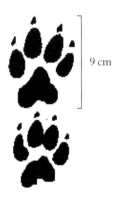

9 cm

In an area in south-western Kenya a pack of 17 to 43 wild dogs was able to use a relatively small range of some 660 km² because of a high year-round prey abundance. In the Kruger National Park wild dog packs have ranges varying from 357 to 930 km². These packs seldom meet, although they are closer than 5 km to each other in at most 8% of all occasions. However, the packs are often at least 10 km, but usually 25 km or more apart. The ranges of large wild dog packs in the Kruger National Park contain significantly more kudus *Tragelaphus strepsiceros* than the smaller ones. However, there is no such relationship with the impala which is the major wild dog food source there. In a recent study in Hluhluwe-Umfolozi a single wild dog pack used a range of 218 to 242 km² which is also relatively small. The ecological factors involved here are not known, but it is known that this pack also avoided areas of high lion and spotted hyaena density. In a relatively small park, this avoidance must lead to the use of a small range.

Wild dogs are mostly active at dawn and dusk. Photo: C.H. Walker.

Activity and movement

The African wild dog is a crepuscular predator because it is most active at dawn and dusk. As it hunts primarily by sight, it obviously needs some degree of light when hunting. It was earlier believed that wild dogs only hunt in daylight, but more recent evidence suggests that they may hunt at any time in a given 24-hour period if the need arises, and there is sufficient light to see their prey. In Serengeti and the Ngorongoro Crater where prey is numerous, however, the wild dogs only hunt when the sun is close to the horizon in the early morning or late afternoon. Most of the day is spent in a suitable cool resting place.

Being highly mobile, wild dogs can move considerable distances. The mean daily distances moved during normal activities are about 10 km, but a pack can move as far as 20 km during a single morning. When wild dogs are 1 year to 30 months old, same-sex groups of litter mates disperse together. The dispersal rate is affected by the availability of food, and possibly also by the composition of the natal pack. However, the females seem to start dispersing at an earlier age than the males. Dispersing groups of wild dogs either join unrelated sibling groups of the opposite sex to form new packs, or they join established packs. Dispersal distances can be as much as 200 km or more, but they are usually less. Such occasional, long-distance dispersals infuse new genetic material into the larger population and increase its genetic diversity. In Moremi, the wild dog displays an interesting dispersal anomaly because, in contrast to most other areas, it is the male sibling groups that disperse over long distances of up to 150 km, while the dispersing females establish themselves close to their natal range, as is the case with most other mammals. There is no clear reason for this difference within the same species in different parts of its range. In the Kruger National Park local males are indeed usually recruited into the natal pack as they are in East Africa, but female dispersal there is in turn less common than in Serengeti. It seems therefore that the dispersal pattern in the different sexes may vary in response to different ecological conditions.

The African wild dog drinks water regularly. Photo: C.H. Walker.

Feeding ecology

In general the canids are not as strictly carnivorous as the cats. Consequently they are greater opportunists in selecting food, and eat almost everything available to them. Although the African wild dog will sometimes hunt small prey in the absence of a sufficient supply of large ungulates, the main prey throughout their range consists of ungulates weighing between 15 and 100 kg. Under normal circumstances the wild dog is the only canid which consistently takes large prey as food throughout the year. Wild dogs will also scavenge for fresh food when it is available, as they do in Serengeti and south-western Kenya, but they generally do not eat carrion. There is a case on record of a wild dog pack which scavenged from an elephant carcass shot by man. Such scavenging requires the ability to travel long distances with a low energy expenditure.

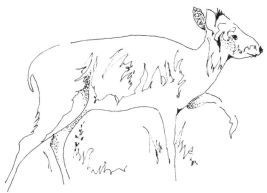

145

In the Masai-Mara, the wild dogs use male Thomson's gazelles and young wildebeest as their main prey. This is similar to the type of prey selected in the Ngorongoro Crater. Of the Thomson's gazelles killed in Serengeti, males are selected in preference to females because of their shorter flight distances, and this in turn is linked to the territoriality of these gazelles. During the gazelle breeding season the territorial males are also usually in poorer condition than the females because of breeding stress and are consequently more subject to sarcoptic mange than the females. However, they are not selected as a primary food source because of their poorer condition, but mainly because their flight distances are shorter than that of the females. There is still no clear evidence that these wild dogs select old or sick prey, as has been suggested by some authors. When hunting Burchell's zebras, the wild dogs of Serengeti usually kill the mares which tire more quickly than the stallions when fleeing.

In one study in Kafue, wild dogs killed 15 types of prey, concentrating on the common duiker *Sylvicapra grimmia* (26%), the reedbuck *Redunca arundinum* (25%) and Lichtenstein's hartebeest *Sigmoceros lichtensteinii* (15,6%). The influence of prey availability on prey choice is clear from the seasonal differences in prey killed in that area. The duiker is present at the same rate throughout the year, but the reedbuck inhabits a locality which is largely inundated and inaccessible to predators for most of the rainy season. Consequently it is killed by the wild dogs mainly during the dry season when it is more vulnerable. In Hluhluwe-Umfolozi a pack of wild dogs preferred the adult nyalas *Tragelaphus angasii* and juvenile impalas for food because they were abundant and easy to capture, compared with the other available prey.

146

Their prey preference also did not follow the prey distribution during the year.

Wild dogs in Etosha also target those prey animals which are most abundant. There the main prey includes the springbok, Burchell's zebra and even the smaller springhare *Pedetes capensis*. In Moremi impalas (85%) are the staple wild dog food, but they also eat a variety of other ungulates. This is similar to observations in the Kruger National Park where impalas are also plentiful and form 73% of the wild dog's food. Kudus (5%) are used as prey all year round in the Kruger National Park as well, but the relative proportions of kudu and impala taken, vary regionally within the park. Other carnivores are also eaten occasionally by wild dogs. Even lions may be chased, killed, and eaten at times, as is known to have happened in the Masai-Mara and Kafue. Smaller prey such as hares, rodents and birds are usually taken by wild dogs which are hunting alone.

As a pack-hunting predator, the African wild dog has attained the unenviable reputation of being a cruel animal. Nevertheless, it is an apparently tireless and efficient hunter. Of all the canids, cooperative hunting is most important and ritualised in the African wild dog, and leads to a high hunting success rate. The wild dog is a running or coursing predator as most canids are, because it does not possess the necessary morphological specialisations which would allow it to bring down large prey as quickly and efficiently as a large cat. It also cannot use cover to camouflage its presence as effectively as a cat can. Nevertheless, in areas of dense vegetation such as Hluhluwe-Umfolozi, wild dogs are believed to flush and ambush prey opportunistically and frequently. This is an acquired behaviour pattern adapted to local circumstances. As a further consequence of the dense vegetation there, prey chases seldom exceed 1 km.

While moving through its range, a wild dog pack on the hunt usually locates a potential herd of prey by sight during daylight. The pack then moves slowly closer over a wide front, and when they get close enough, all the dogs in the pack charge the herd which starts to flee. Prey animals can clearly detect the intentions of a wild dog pack and react to it, however, and when a pack is merely walking through an area, the prey may allow the dogs to come as close as 50 m before they flee. However, when the intention of the pack is clearly to hunt, the prey may start to run when the pack is still as far as 2 km away. When the herd begins its flight, an individual prey target is selected visually by one of the pack leaders after the chase has begun. The chase is usually not excessively long, but it can last for several kilometres at maximum speeds of up to

66 km/h. When chasing prey, the dogs do not run in relays as has often been suggested in the past. Once a target has been chosen, all the other potential prey victims are ignored. Larger prey animals are attacked on the run by any pack member which catches up with them. Flanking dogs will remain behind the pack leader to intercept the prey if it dodges or circles back. The hunt ends when the victim falters, stops and is killed. Smaller prey is often caught and killed without an extended chase. Wild dogs in Moremi use an interesting variation of the hunting approach commonly adopted by most wild dogs. There the pack may chase several prey targets at once, splitting up to do so, but regrouping later at the starting point, to find out whether a kill has been made by any of the other pack members. Those dogs that killed prey, also return to the starting point to collect the other pack members. Smaller prey, which is usually hunted by solitary dogs, is located in the tall grass by hearing rather than by scent. Such prey may be batted down with a front paw before being snapped up and eaten. Other prey such as the cane rat *Thryonomys swinderianus* and porcupines are killed with a quick but well-directed bite.

During the hunt the experience of the older pack members is vital. Adults 2 to 6 years old do most of the hunting in Serengeti. When a pack of wild dogs was reintroduced into Etosha in 1978, the absence of experienced hunters was probably one of the main reasons for its failure. In addition, the dogs were released into suboptimal areas with low prey density, and they were also vulnerable to lion predation. This pattern was repeated during further reintroductions in 1989 and 1990. When wild dogs hunt, they must invest a substantial amount of energy. The usual chase lasts for 10 to 60 minutes, and it has been estimated that African wild dogs normally hunt for 3,5 hours per day. If only 25% of their food is stolen by spotted hyaenas, they must increase their hunting time to 12 hours per day to maintain the correct balance between energy gained and energy expended. This is an impossible requirement and explains why the wild dogs in the Kruger National Park and Hluhluwe-Umfolozi occur at low densities in areas of high spotted hyaena density, where the risk of losing a kill is great despite the apparent abundance of prey. As is the case with other pack-hunting canids, when a wild dog pack goes on a kill it is often a protracted affair. Any dogs which catch up with the prey while it is still being chased, will begin to tear out lumps of flesh or even the intestines, weakening it until it falters or stops. The actual kill is then usually made by the older and more experienced members of the pack.

Although African wild dogs hunt in packs, they do not hunt cooperatively in the sense of coordinating the movements and actions of the pack, as a pride of lions would do. However, they are highly successful hunters. Certain prey types and age groups are hunted more successfully than others. Smaller packs are less successful hunters than larger ones, and may also lose a significant portion of their kills to other predators as is the case in south-western Kenya. In the northern Serengeti-Mara ecosystem impalas (80% success) and Thomson's gazelles (68%) are hunted most successfully, but wildebeest (31%) and warthogs (14%) less successfully. Other potential prey such as the topi *Damaliscus lunatus korrigum* and Burchell's zebra were rarely hunted in that area by wild dogs. However, in other parts of Serengeti zebras are killed regularly and even habitually by some wild dog packs. In Hluhluwe-Umfolozi the nyala is hunted most successfully (67%), followed by the blue wildebeest (50%), and the impala (33%). By comparison, in one particular study the kudu, warthog and buffalo were never killed.

The size of a wild dog pack is important in determining its hunting success, but its effect seems to be most profound when the pack approaches a certain minimum size. For example, in one study in south-western Kenya, the hunting success of a known pack was not affected when its size was suddenly reduced from 29 to 19 members because of the dispersal of six young dogs and the death of four old dogs. In this instance the pack probably retained sufficient adult and experienced hunters to remain an efficient hunting unit, and kept on hunting at an overall success rate of 51%. In the Ngorongoro Crater, with its abundant and relatively stable prey base, wild dogs have a high hunting success rate of more than 85% with Thomson's gazelles (54%) and young wildebeest (36%) forming most of the prey. There is as yet no documented evidence that a wild dog pack will perform surplus killing, which is known to occur in other large African savanna predators.

A wild dog pack feeds rapidly, usually consuming everything but the head, some skin, the larger bones and the hooves of its prey. Nevertheless, smaller packs may be driven off their prey by scavengers such as spotted hyaenas before they can finish feeding. When feeding a wild dog uses its front paws as an aid in more than 50% of all cases. Although they do eat some bones, wild dogs have a low incidence of tooth fractures compared with spotted hyaenas. Except when it feeds on skin, a wild dog also chews its food much more thoroughly than any of the other large predators such as the lion, spotted hyaena or cheetah. Its small body mass and low mechanical advantage because of its small skull size, do not allow it to crush bone effectively. The long snout also precludes effective and strong jaw-closing bites when compared with some of the other large carnivores of the savannas.

Because the canids are not as strictly carnivorous as the cats, peaceful feeding is much more common in them than in the cats. A pack of wild dogs feeds quietly and in an orderly manner with a definite hierarchy of access to the kill. This hierarchy is generally the opposite to that which is found in most of the other large carnivores. In the wild dog, the young pups have clear overall priority when feeding, but the dominant pair has priority over the preferred food parts. In feeding priority, the pups are followed by the yearlings, then by the dominant pair, and only then by the subordinate adults. Smaller kills may even be consumed entirely by the young pups, leaving nothing for the rest of the pack.

In the Masai-Mara the wild dog's mean daily consumption varies from 80 to 200 g of meat per kg of dog per day. All the edible portions of the kill are consumed in the feeding process. Elsewhere in Kenya an adult wild dog eats an estimated 1,2 to 5,9 kg of meat per day, of which about 1 kg is regurgitated to the pups after every full meal. These consumption rates are similar to those of other pack-hunting carnivores. It was previously thought that the African wild dog was one of a few canids which did not cache food, mainly because its large range size and mobility would make it impossible for it to return to the cache site soon enough to make effective use of the food stored there. However, it is now known that wild dogs of both sexes in Serengeti will occasionally cache food near the den when there are small pups. These caches are not shared with the other pack members, and are eaten by the dogs who make them. In some cases the cached food may be covered with loose vegetation or soil. A wild dog also seems to know exactly where its cache is, moving directly to the site.

The African wild dog drinks water regularly.

Relationship with other wildlife

The prey population in the Ngorongoro Crater is not unduly diminished by wild dog hunting. However, they may have the effect of limiting the overall number of some of the smaller prey there. Nevertheless, most kills focus on the more abundant prey such as Thomson's gazelles and young wildebeest which can absorb considerable predation pressure. This is probably true for most large conservation areas. Even in the smaller Hluhluwe-Umfolozi a pack of wild dogs had no significant impact on numbers in their main prey, the nyala. There is considerable interaction between African wild dogs and some of the other members of the large carnivore guild in African savannas, but the main competition is not so much for prey type (exploitation competition), as for actual kills (interference competition). Wherever they occur together, spotted hyaenas seem to be a major threat to wild dogs, driving them off from a considerable proportion of their prey, especially when the wild dog pack is small. This pressure varies from region to region and with pack size. In one study in south-western Kenya spotted hyaenas were absent from 59% of all the wild dog hunts and kills. In that region the hyaenas never appropriated the wild dog kills, but the wild dog pack was large, and the dogs even attacked the hyaenas and chased them away. The hyaenas there also do not usually harass the wild dogs because their own prey is normally abundant. However, when prey becomes scarce, the spotted hyaenas severely threaten the wild dogs, even to the extent of killing their pups. In the Ngorongoro Crater the spotted hyaena is the wild dog's greatest competitor, despite the presence of a varied and abundant prey resource. In the Kruger National Park and Hluhluwe-Umfolozi the wild dog clearly avoids areas of high spotted hyaena density because even a small loss of food to the spotted hyaenas has a major impact on the dog's energy budget.

The lion is a major wild dog competitor throughout its range, occasionally taking over its kills and even killing wild dogs themselves at times. Although the dogs will chase and even kill lions on occasion, they are more commonly harassed or killed by the lions. As with spotted hyaenas, the smaller the wild dog pack, the more vulnerable it is to such competition. In the Kruger National Park lions are the major

cause of wild dog deaths, killing 39% of all the pups born and 43% of all the adults present. Areas of high lion density in the region are avoided by the wild dogs which means that it has to live in areas of low prey abundance not favoured by the lions. Much the same situation occurs in Hluhluwe-Umfolozi. In Etosha three attempts at reintroducing wild dogs in 1978, 1989 and 1990 all failed partly because of lion predation. Conservation attempts for wild dogs must therefore focus on areas of low lion and spotted hyaena density. Apart from lions and spotted hyaenas, wild dogs are also known to chase cheetahs and leopards, and even to steal fresh food from jackals. Black-backed jackals, the tawny eagles *Aquila rapax* and vultures are often present at wild dog kills in the Masai-Mara, but they do not take over these kills. Wild dogs may also be attacked and killed by leopards.

Population dynamics

There are only about 3000 to 5000 wild dogs left in Africa today, and this carnivore has undergone extensive reduction in numbers and range because of its conflict with man. Large reserves are essential for the survival of the African wild dog, and the minimum viable population in any given area is 25 dogs. The modern trend of creating large parks and reserves which cross international boundaries may well be a major conservation factor for the wild dog in the future. This is underscored by the fact that all the wild dogs present in the huge Serengeti-Mara ecosystem form one breeding population and are not genetically isolated. In terms of pack size, a minimum of at least four to six dogs seems to be required for effective functioning. Although a pair of wild dogs will reproduce, they cannot raise their pups successfully without the aid of helpers. In the Kruger National Park there is a high population turnover rate among the wild dogs. Nevertheless, the overall wild dog population in this large park and its adjacent conservation areas seems to have been stable for many years, probably because of a low incidence of disease and poaching.

Although many wild dog litters have equal numbers of male and female pups, some appear to contain more males. Some older groups of wild dog also seem to possess more males than females, probably because it is mainly the females who disperse. When dispersing and joining new packs, these females are highly susceptible to mortality. Nevertheless, in the Kruger National Park such dispersal, especially over the occasional long distances, infuses new genetic material into the population and is essential to help maintain high levels of genetic diversity. It has recently been suggested that a major population decline in the wild dogs of Serengeti from 1965 to 1991 can be linked mainly to diseases which were induced by stress which resulted from intensive handling and vaccinating against canine distemper which they experienced. However, in other studies this did not occur and it is not considered likely by these authors to have occurred in Serengeti. Nevertheless, this is a serious matter which merits close analysis and care, taking alternative causes into consideration. The world's wild dog population is so small that it may be better to be conservative and pay attention to the possibility that in studying them by using methods which involve capture and handling, we may possibly be contributing to their demise rather than their survival.

Wild dogs are susceptible to various forms of mortality, including predation, fighting when dispersing, and disease. They are known to be a potential reservoir of *Babesia canis*. However, they seem to be highly resistant to anthrax in the Kruger National Park where disease does not seem to be a major cause of wild dog mortality. Elsewhere some diseases do occur in wild dogs. Across their range, the annual survival of adults varies from 65 to 85%. Pup survival rates usually vary from 14 to 73%, and are clearly influenced by food availability and the number of adults in the pack that can hunt and care for the pups. In some areas pup survival can be as low as 10%. When there is a high rate of pup and dominant male mortality, more young males gain breeding opportunities in their natal packs, and they are then less likely to disperse.

BIBLIOGRAPHY

Andreka, G., Linn, I.J., Perrin, M.R. & Maddock, A.H. 1999. Range use by the wild dog in the Hluhluwe-Umfolozi Park, South Africa. *South African Journal of Wildlife Research* 29(1): 1-9.

Asa, C.S., Mech, L.D. & Seal, U.S. 1985. The use of urine, faeces, and anal gland secretions in scent-marking by a captive wolf *(Canis lupus)* pack. *Animal Behaviour,* 33(3): 1034–1036.

Bailey, T.N. 1993. *The African leopard.* New York: Columbia University Press.

Barrett, A. 1994. Africa's wild dogs pussyfoot around the big cats. *New Scientist,* April, 30: 17.

Bertram, B.C.R. 1979. Serengeti predators and their social systems. In: Sinclair, A.R.E. & Norton-Griffiths, M. (Eds), *Serengeti, dynamics of an ecosystem.* Chicago: University of Chicago Press, 221–248.

Boggs, L.P. & McNutt, J.W. 1994. Running wild. *Africa,* 2(5): 28–36.

Burrows, R. 1995. Demographic changes and social consequences in wild dogs, 1964–1992. In: Sinclair, A.R.E. & Norton-Griffiths, M. (Eds), *Serengeti II, dynamics, management and conservation of an ecosystem.* Chicago: University of Chicago Press, 400–420.

Burrows, R., Hofer, H. & East, M.L. 1994. Demography, extinction and intervention in a small population: the case of the Serengeti wild dogs. *Proceedings of the Royal Society of London,* Series B, 256: 281–292.

Childes, S.L. 1988. The past history, present status and distribution of the hunting dog *Lycaon pictus* in Zimbabwe. *Biological Conservation,* 44: 301–316.

Creel, S. 1992. Causes of wild dog deaths. *Nature,* 360: 633.

Creel, S., Creel, N.M., Mills, M.G.L. & Monfort, S.L. 1997. Rank and reproduction in cooperatively breeding African wild dog: behavioural and endocrine correlates. *Behavioral Ecology,* 8(3): 298–306.

Cumming, R.G. 1850. *Five years of a hunter's life.* London: Murray.

De Vos, V. & Bryden, H. 1997. The role of carnivores in the epidemiology of anthrax in the Kruger National Park. In: Van Heerden, J. (Ed.), *Lions and leopards as game ranch animals.* The Wildlife Group. Onderstepoort: South African Veterinary Association, 198–203.

Dye, C. 1996. Serengeti wild dogs: what really happened? *Tree,* 11: 188–189.

Eltringham, S.K. 1979. *The ecology and conservation of large African mammals.* London: Macmillan.

Estes, R.D. & Goddard, J.D. 1967. Prey selection and hunting behaviour of the African wild dog. *Journal of Wildlife Management,* 31(1): 52–70.

Fanshawe, J.H., Frame, L.H. & Ginsberg, J.R. 1991. The wild dog – Africa's vanishing carnivore. *Oryx,* 25(3): 137–146.

FitzGibbon, C.D. & Fanshawe, J.H. 1989. The condition and age of Thomson's gazelles killed by cheetahs and wild dogs. *Journal of Zoology, London,* 218: 99–107.

Frame, L.H., Malcolm, J.R., Frame, G.W. & Van Lawick, H. 1979. Social organization of African wild dogs *(Lycaon pictus)* on the Serengeti Plains, Tanzania: 1967–1978. *Zeitschrift für Tierpsychologie,* 50(3): 225–249.

Fuller, T.K. & Kat, P.W. 1990. Movements, activity and prey relationships of African wild dogs *(Lycaon pictus)* near Aitong, south-western Kenya. *African Journal of Ecology,* 28: 330–350.

Fuller, T.K. & Kat, P.W. 1993. Hunting success of African wild dogs in south-western Kenya. *Journal of Mammalogy,* 74(2): 464–467.

Fuller, T.K., Kat, P.W., Bulger, J.G., Maddock, A.H., Ginsberg, J.R., Burrows, R., McNutt, J.W. & Mills, M.G.L. 1992. Population dynamics of African wild dogs. In: McCullough, D.R. & Barrett, R.H. (Eds), *Wildlife 2001: populations.* London: Elsevier, 1125–1139.

Fuller, T.K., Nicholls, T.H. & Kat, P.W. 1995. Prey and estimated food consumption of African wild dogs in Kenya. *South African Journal of Wildlife Research,* 25(3): 106–110.

Ginsberg, J.R., Mace, G.M. & Albon, S. 1995. Local extinction in a small and declining population: wild dogs in the Serengeti. *Proceedings of the Royal Society of London,* Series B, 262: 221–228.

Girman, D.L., Mills, M.G.L., Geffen, E. & Wayne, R.K. 1997. A molecular genetic analysis of social structure, dispersal and interpack relationships of the African wild dog *(Lycaon pictus). Ecology and Sociobiology,* 40: 187–198.

Gorman, M.L., Mills, M.G.L., Raath, J.P. & Speakman, J.R. 1998. High hunting costs make African wild dogs vulnerable to kleptoparasitism by hyaenas. *Nature,* 391: 479–481.

Grobler, J.H., Hall-Martin, A. & Walker, C. 1984. *Predators of southern Africa.* Johannesburg: Macmillan.

Grzimek, B.B. 1975. The African wild dog. In: Grzimek, B. (Ed.), *Grzimek's animal life encyclopedia.* New York: Van Nostrand Reinhold, 254–264.

Hines, C.J.H. 1990. Past and present distribution and status of the wild dog *Lycaon pictus* in Namibia. *Madoqua,* 17(1): 31–36.

Jennions, M.D & Macdonald, D.W. 1994. Cooperative breeding in mammals. *Tree,* 9(3): 89–93.

Johnsingh, A.J.T. 1982. Reproductive and social behaviour of the dhole, *Cuon alpinus* (Canidae). *Journal of Zoology, London,* 198: 443–463.

Kat, P.W., Alexander, K.A., Smith, J.S. & Munson, L. 1995. Rabies and African wild dogs in Kenya. *Proceedings of the Royal Society of London,* Series B, 262: 229–233.

Kingdon, J. 1977. *East African mammals.* Vol. III, Part A: Carnivores. London: Academic.

Kleiman, D.G. 1967. Some aspects of social behaviour in the Canidae. *American Zoologist,* 7: 365–372.

Kleiman, D.G. 1968. Reproduction in the Canidae. *International Zoo Yearbook,* 8: 3–8.

Kleiman, D.G. & Eisenberg, J.F. 1973. Comparisons of canid and felid social systems from an evolutionary perspective. *Animal Behaviour,* 21: 637–659.

Kruger, S. 1996. The feeding ecology of the African wild dog *Lycaon pictus* in Hluhluwe-Umfolozi Park. MSc thesis. Pietermaritzburg: University of Natal.

Kruuk, H. 1972. Surplus killing by carnivores. *Journal of Zoology, London,* 166: 233–244.

Kühme, W. 1965. Communal food distribution and division of labour in African hunting dogs. *Nature,* 205: 443–444.

Macdonald, D.W. 1992. Cause of wild dog deaths. *Nature,* 360: 633–634.

Maddock, A.H. 1989. The wild dog photographic project: final report. *Quagga,* 28: 18–20.

Maddock, A.H. & Mills, M.G.L. 1994. Population characteristics of African wild dogs *Lycaon pictus* in the Eastern Transvaal Lowveld, South Africa as revealed through photographic records. *Biological Conservation,* 67: 57–62.

Malcolm, J.R. 1980. Food caching by African wild dogs *(Lycaon pictus). Journal of Mammalogy,* 61(4): 743–744.

Malcolm, J.R. & Marten, K. 1982. Natural selection and the communal rearing of pups in African wild dogs *(Lycaon pictus). Behavioural Ecology and Sociobiology,* 10: 1–13.

Maugham, R.C.F. 1914. *Wild game in Zambezia.* London: John Murray.

Mech, L.D. 1975. Hunting behavior in two similar species of social canids. In: Fox, M.W. (Ed.), *The wild canids.* New York: Van Nostrand Reinhold, 363–369.

Mills, M.G.L. 1985. Wild dogs: victims of man's prejudice. *Custos,* 13: 4–7.

Mills, M.G.L. 1990. *Kalahari hyaenas.* London: Unwin Hyman.

Mills, M.G.L. & Gorman, M.L. 1997. Factors affecting the density and distribution of wild dogs in the Kruger National Park. *Conservation Biology,* 11(6): 1397–1406.

Mitchell, B.L., Shenton, J.B. & Uys, J.C.M. 1965. Predation on large mammals in the Kafue National Park, Zambia. *Zoologica Africana,* 1(2): 297–318.

Moehlman, P.D. 1989. Intraspecific variation in canid social systems. In: Gittleman, J.L. (Ed.), *Carnivore behavior, ecology and evolution.* London: Chapman & Hall.

Paquet, P.C. 1991. Scent-marking behavior of sympatric wolves *(Canis lupus)* and coyotes *(Canis latrans)* in Riding Mountain National Park. *Canadian Journal of Zoology,* 69: 1721–1727.

Schaller, G.B. 1972. *The Serengeti lion.* Chicago: University of Chicago Press.

Scheepers, J.L. & Venzke, K.A.E. 1995. Attempts to reintroduce African wild dogs *Lycaon pictus* into Etosha National Park, Namibia. *South African Journal of Wildlife Research,* 25(4): 138–140.

Skinner, J.D. & Smithers, R.H.N. 1990. *The mammals of the southern African subregion.* Pretoria: University of Pretoria.

Van Heerden, J. 1980. The transmission of *Babesia canis* to the wild dog *Lycaon pictus* (Temminck) and the black-backed jackal *Canis mesomelas* Schreber. *Journal of the South African Veterinary Association,* 51(2): 119–120.

Van Heerden, J. 1981. The role of integumental glands in the social and mating behaviour of the hunting dog *Lycaon pictus* (Temminck, 1820). *Onderstepoort Journal of Veterinary Research,* 48: 19–21.

Van Heerden, J., Mills, M.G.L., Van Vuuren, M.J., Kelly, P.J. & Dreyer, M.J. 1995. An investigation into the health status and diseases of wild dogs *(Lycaon pictus)* in the Kruger National Park. *Journal of the South African Veterinary Association,* 66(1): 18–27.

Van Valkenburgh, B. 1996. Feeding behavior in free-ranging African carnivores. *Journal of Mammalogy,* 77(1): 240–254.

Walker, E.P. 1983. *Walker's mammals of the world,* Vol. 2, 4th ed. Baltimore: Johns Hopkins University Press.

Wozencraft, W.C. 1993. Order Carnivora. In: Wilson, D.E. & Reeder, D.M. (Eds), *Mammal species of the world,* 2nd ed. Washington, DC: Smithsonian Institution.

Wright, B.S. 1960. Predation on big game in East Africa. *Journal of Wildlife Management,* 24(1): 1–15.

7

The spotted hyaena

To many people the whooping call of the spotted hyaena is as much a symbol of the African night as the haunting call of the fish eagle symbolises the day. Yet, this most abundant large carnivore of the African savannas is often maligned and persecuted because of human prejudices based on ignorance. When the spotted hyaena was originally described scientifically, the error made with the identification of the African wild dog was reversed. Whereas the wild dog was originally described as a form of hyaena, the spotted hyaena was first characterised as a new species of dog, *Canis crocuta,* from a specimen collected in Senegambia by J.C.P. Erxleben in 1777. It was, however, recognised as a form of hyaena when it was renamed *Crocuta crocuta* by Kaup in 1828. The name *Crocuta* itself was not originally used as the generic name for a hyaena, because it was first used by Meigen in 1800 for an insect. This use of *Crocuta* for an insect classification was suppressed in 1962 in favour of the spotted hyaena in accordance with the International Rules on Zoological Nomenclature.

The spotted hyaena is widely distributed in Africa, but it does not occur in forests. It is the largest of all the living hyaenas, with a male weighing up to 80 kg and a female 86 kg. It is a true savanna carnivore, although it also enters those desert regions which have a permanent supply of water. The spotted hyaena is one of only four species of hyaenid in existence today. However, the Hyaenidae was once a much larger family. Fossil evidence contains nearly 100 hyaenid species. One of these was the cave hyaena *Crocuta crocuta spelea* which, like the great cave bear *Ursus spelaeus,* also lived and possibly hibernated in caves in what is now Great Britain. In these caves there are vast accumulations of bone in the narrow, underground tunnels which were used by this hyaena. The cave hyaena was larger, with an especially long humerus and femur and greatly thickened and shortened metacarpals. Of the fossil hyaenids some species possibly lived as far back as 25 million years ago.

All three of South Africa's modern hyaenids, the spotted hyaena, brown hyaena and the aardwolf, already existed in the Pleistocene at Swartkrans, Sterkfontein and Kromdraai some 1,8 to 1 million years ago where they kept company with other large carnivores some of which are still alive today and some extinct. These include the modern leopard, modern cheetah, the extinct hunting hyaena *Chasmaporthetes nitidula* which was as large as a living lion, and the dirk-toothed cat *Megantereon cultridens.* Large modern and ancient predators, and many extinct and living prey species therefore coexisted for a considerable time in the African savannas. Although the hyaenids reached their peak in Africa in the early Pleistocene, the spotted hyaena originally invaded Africa from Eurasia fairly late in geological time, as was the case with most of the other large carnivores present in Africa today. The hyaenids are more closely related to the cats than to the dogs, both having originated from an ancient weasel- or civet-like ancestor.

The phylogenetic origins of the spotted hyaena genus *Crocuta* are not known exactly, but this genus contains several fossil species from Eurasia. Some of these species were larger and some smaller than the living spotted hyaena. The *Crocuta* species were the world's dominant carnivores throughout the second half of the Pleistocene, but the reasons for the extinction of the genus outside Africa are not clear. Today the spotted hyaena is exclusive to Africa. Spotted hyaenas are massively built with particularly strongly developed forequarters and neck muscles which make it easy for them to carry heavy pieces of food high off the ground. The females are heavier and more stout than the males. Spotted hyaenas grow slowly, however, and only reach their ultimate adult weight when about 10 years old, compared with 7 to 8 years in a lion.

Many people still loathe spotted hyaenas because of three ancient myths. One myth is the belief that a spotted hyaena will deliberately search for a grave to dig up and eat the corpse. Another holds that the spotted hyaena is a hybrid which originated from an unnatural union between a dog and a cat after the Great Flood. Consequently it was not part of the animal complement of Noah's Ark and therefore it is not pure. The last myth is that the spotted hyaena is a hermaphrodite which can change its sex at will. Many people in Africa still regard the spotted hyaena with great awe, and it plays a part in many African tales of sorcery. In parts of East Africa a spotted hyaena's nose is used as a cure for blindness, and their faeces are burned to allay the spirits or *amayembe*. The older Zulu people believed in the existence of a dreaded fraternity of secret assassins who dealt in human fats and body parts. These people or *inswelaboya*, which means 'those without hair', were reputed to ride about on monstrous spotted hyaenas. In East Africa too, female witches are believed to ride about on spotted hyaenas, while the wizard or *ekapalan* is reputed to ride a hyaena to any village which death approaches. In many parts of Africa it is still believed that the spotted hyaena can transform itself into either a familiar form or into a ferocious and supernaturally cunning one. In ancient Egypt spotted hyaenas were believed to be a cure for barrenness and in Uganda they are regarded with awe because they are known to have become man-eaters. This happened during the severe trypanosomiasis epidemics of 1908 and 1909 when the spotted hyaenas became so bold that they seized their victims from special sleeping sickness camps protected by armed sentries. The same thing happened in 1950 to 1951 in Manyani, Kenya. When a person is eaten by a spotted hyaena, it is treated like any other food source. In turn, the starving people of Turkana, in Kenya, speared and ate spotted hyaenas which attacked their cattle and villages during a severe drought in 1967. The practice of eating hyaenas also dates very far back because they were domesticated, fattened and eaten by the people of ancient Egypt.

Although a female spotted hyaena's external sexual features are difficult to distinguish from a male's, the spotted hyaena is by no means a hermaphrodite. This sexual mimicry of the male by the female is related to the dominant position of the female in the spotted hyaena's social structure. The belief that the spotted hyaena was a hermaphrodite was recorded and refuted by Aristotle as early as 384 to 322 BC. Pliny the Elder (AD 23 to 79) repeats the myth, although he also mentions that Aristotle disagreed with him. Claudius Aelianus, who lived in about AD 160 to 220, not only repeated the myth, but added that the spotted hyaena changes its sex in alternate years. Even as recently as 1936 Hemingway still believed that the spotted hyaena was a hermaphrodite.

The sheer size of the female spotted hyaena and the remarkable maleness of her external genitalia make the origins of the hermaphrodite myth obvious. A male and female spotted hyaena are impossible to distinguish in the field. Except for the larger nipples of a pregnant female, the sexes are externally identical in all respects. The clitoris is large and capable of erection, and the female also has a large, false scrotum. Internally, however, the anatomical differences between the sexes become clear. The main reasons for the female sexual mimicry of the male lie in her larger size, her dominant position in the clan, and her high foetal levels of androgen, all of which lead to the overdevelopment of her sexual organs through their effect on embryonic development. However, there does not seem to be a clear adaptive advantage in having such an outwardly male appearance. The female's social dominance is probably the result of a translocation of genetic material from the Y to the X chromosome, which exposes the female foetus to high testosterone levels. High plasma androgen levels are still present in an adult female spotted hyaena, and they may also play a role in shaping her aggression and social dominance over the males.

Social behaviour

The spotted hyaena is a highly social carnivore which lives in large groups or clans. The communal den is the centre of spotted hyaena activity and plays a vital role in the life of the clan. The term clan for a group of spotted hyaenas was first used by H. Kruuk. It is derived from the Scottish social system with its hierarchical clan lineages, although those are more patrilineal than the matrilineal lines which are found in the spotted hyaena. The word clan itself is derived from the Middle English word *clann*, which in turn has its origins in the Latin word *planta*, meaning sprout. The spotted hyaena clan is a complete society in which various individuals play different roles. Such an intricate social system consisting of numerous members is common amongst the primates, but it was only when Kruuk studied the spotted hyaenas of Serengeti and the Ngorongoro Crater that it was also used with reference to a large carnivore. The spotted hyaena clan consists of females, dependent cubs less than 2 years old, and three social classes of male hyaenas: resident natal males, central immigrant males, and peripheral immigrant males. The dynamics of the clan operate on a system of male dispersal, closely related females, and a strong linear dominance hierarchy. The division of the clan into cooperative relatives and subordinate immigrants ensures optimal use of the available resources. The size, distribution and stability of a spotted hyaena clan varies from area to area depending on the nature and distribution of the vital natural resources such as cover, food and water. In the northern part of the Serengeti-Mara ecosystem, local prey abundance determines the distribution of the clans. Within each clan the adult females dominate all clan members, but there are also dominance hierarchies within each sex. The female aggressiveness and dominance is associated with a syndrome of masculinisation of the female which includes a larger body size than the males, elevated androgen levels, and the masculinisation of the external genitalia.

In Serengeti and the Ngorongoro Crater spotted hyaena clans vary greatly in size from as few as 10 to as many as 100 members, or possibly even more. Stability in the Serengeti clans is greater, however, because of their habit of commuting to the migratory herds which provide them with a larger and more stable food resource than those in Ngorongoro. It also allows them to maintain larger clans than would be possible if they relied on the resident prey only. The concept of commuting will be discussed in greater depth under range use and feeding ecology later. Spotted hyaena clans in Serengeti and the Ngorongoro Crater vary in size between 30 and 80 members. In the more southern savannas the clans are usually smaller because of lower prey densities. However, the southern savanna clans are more stable because their prey often does not migrate as much as in some parts of East Africa, and water is usually available. In Savuti clans of 56 to 62 members exist, each containing 22 to 24 adult females. However, when they forage, the clans split into smaller groups of two to four hyaenas. In Etosha clan sizes are smaller than in East Africa. There, clans of 15 to 23 are the norm, but they also split into smaller groups to forage. In the southern Kalahari savanna, with its more limited prey and permanent water resources, spotted hyaenas live in small clans of 3 to 13 members, with four to six adults each. Although a clan of 50 has been found there in the past, this is rare. Normally, the smallest spotted hyaena clan in the Ngorongoro Crater is still 2,5 times larger than the largest one in the southern Kalahari savanna. This is mainly because of food abundance and prey distribution.

Habitat conditions clearly influence the density of spotted hyaenas in any given area. Although it is the most abundant large carnivore of the African savannas, its highest density is found in flat, open savannas with abundant water and prey. For this reason, Serengeti and the Ngorongoro Crater are ideal spotted hyaena habitats. In the Masai-Mara the spotted hyaena density of 12 per 100 km² is still lower than that of the Ngorongoro Crater which has a staggering 170 spotted hyaenas per 100 km². By contrast, one of the lowest densities of spotted hyaenas is found in Comoé. This savanna and forest mosaic has a highly variable annual rainfall and prey base. The spotted hyaenas there usually hunt singly, or at most in pairs. In the Kruger National Park there are some 10 spotted hyaenas per 100 km². In the more arid savannas it is much lower. For example, Etosha as a whole has some 5 spotted hyaenas per 100 km², with the highest local densities in areas occupied by the migratory springbok, blue wildebeest and zebras. In the more arid and

The spotted hyaena is the dominant African savanna predator by sheer numbers. Its highest density is reached in flat, open savannas with abundant water and game. Photo: J. du P. Bothma.

prey-poor southern Kalahari savanna, spotted hyaenas occur at an even lower density of just less than one hyaena per 100 km².

A spotted hyaena clan has a complex social organisation. However, an individual hyaena can rapidly change from being a solitary nomad to a highly social member of a clan. No other hyaenid has such a wide range of social behaviour patterns. Consequently most clans are quite stable social units. The spotted hyaena clan is a matriarchal society, with clear dominance hierarchies. The adult females form the social nucleus of the clan. They are all related and form a close and dominant sisterhood. The adult females also usually outnumber the adult males in a clan. Although they can be highly aggressive, the clan's adult females usually maintain amicable relationships with each other, and with their young. The dominance and aggressiveness of the adult females are partly a consequence of their larger body size and elevated levels of androgen hormones. Within the female sector there is also a dominance hierarchy, with the dominant female and her descendants ruling all the other females and their young. Such matrilineal rankings continue to be stable because maternal rank is inherited. The dominant female's male offspring are the only males which are able to dominate some of the adult females.

Despite the high degree of clan sociality, the nomadic male spotted hyaenas which emigrate to a new clan play a vital role in the survival of the population, because they do most of the mating. Once assimilated into a new clan, these males also often lead the foraging groups. Young

Nomadic males which become immigrant males in new clans, play a vital role in the survival of the spotted hyaena population. Photo: C.H. Walker.

165

male spotted hyaenas usually leave their natal clans around puberty when they are 24 to 30 months old, joining a population of nomadic males and wandering widely before settling in with a new clan. However, they may again leave their adopted clan after a variable period of residence, although many of these males do become permanent members of new clans. Nomadic males travel through the ranges of various clans with apparent disregard for territorial borders. While nomadic, they have no lasting relationships with other spotted hyaenas. Apart from young males, the nomads may also include a few old males and possibly a few females.

The assimilation of a nomadic male as an immigrant into a new clan is a slow process. When he first approaches a new clan, a nomadic male will stay around its periphery, occasionally joining in at the feed. At first he is treated as an intruder. If the nomad persists in visiting the clan, he may eventually be accepted into it, but this may take several months. Once accepted, the immigrant male is subordinate to all the other residents. He also has the lowest feeding priority and a generally precarious social relationship. Later, however, he may become a more important member of the clan who stays in close attendance on the females. He then has an unrivalled breeding status and also plays an important role in foraging expeditions.

The spotted hyaena has an intricate system of communication which is used to maintain its range integrity and complex social organisation. The need for clear communication is imperative because several spotted hyaenas, or even the whole clan, will forage and feed together. They use body postures, calls and scent signals extensively when communicating. Unlike the other social carnivores such as lions, which frequently call as a group, spotted hyaenas usually call as individuals in order to advertise themselves. The whooping call of the spotted hyaena is used primarily to advertise the identity of various individuals within the clan, but it is also used to request support and to convey information about the location of the caller. Whooping calls made by spotted hyaenas therefore differ by influencing factors such as sex, age and the reason for calling. In adult male spotted hyaenas, the whooping call is used mainly for sexual display and to advertise their space use. When doing so, they whoop more often than the females. Adult females whoop primarily during disputes with other clan members and in clashes between neighbouring clans. They also whoop to locate their offspring, to rally clan members to the defence of communal resources, and to deter potentially infanticidal immigrant male hyaenas from approaching and killing the cubs at the den. The cubs whoop mainly to provide other clan members with information on their whereabouts, and to request support. They chuckle like the adults when excited, but in a cub the chuckle is sharper and of a higher pitch than in an adult. When the clans are small, such as those in the more arid savannas which may often have only one adult male, the need for sexual advertising may possibly become so reduced that whooping is then used only to discourage a nomadic male from joining the clan.

Spotted hyaenas also communicate by way of a whole range of intricate body postures. Such postures usually convey information on sexual receptivity, are an invitation to play, indicate aggression, or act as a greeting. The spotted hyaena's greeting ceremony is quite elaborate, and when two of them meet, their greeting ritual involves much sniffing, leg-raising, and even licking of the sexual organs. At the same time the hyaenas may emit a lowing call or whine while adopting an appeasement posture. Muzzling-wrestling, which is an important intragroup interaction in the brown hyaena, does not appear to occur in the spotted hyaena.

Scent-marking is another highly developed system of communication in the hyaenids, all of which have an extrudable anal pouch whose secretions are used in such marking. Scent-marking involves the pasting of anal secretions and the use of faecal latrines which all convey specific messages. A spotted hyaena's paste is a long-lived, lipid-rich, creamy-white secretion which has a pungent smell. The paste is commonly deposited on grass stalks, in a conspicuous ritual.

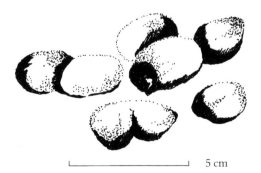

5 cm

Most of the pasting is done either at a latrine or at some other specific environmental feature, but subadult spotted hyaenas paste conspicuously more often near the den than elsewhere. Scent-marking in spotted hyaenas does not follow the same pattern in all the clans, but it is a response to those local ecological pressures which act upon a particular clan. For example, spotted hyaenas in the southern Kalahari savanna have large ranges because of the prey-poor nature of the region. Consequently they cannot use pasting to mark the boundary of their whole range effectively, given their limited time and supply of scent available. Instead, they mark over their whole range, and more frequently in the range centres along the normally dry Nossob river-bed. It is in this river-bed that these hyaenas spend most of their time, and where most of their food occurs. By contrast, the spotted hyaenas of the Kruger National Park and the Ngorongoro Crater paste more frequently near a latrine on the boundary of their range. In the southern Kalahari savanna any particular spotted hyaena is usually within 500 m of a scent mark in the interior of its territory, and within 1 to 2 km from one over the entire extent of it. Individual spotted hyaenas also do not paste at a set frequency. When adult male and female hyaenas in the southern Kalahari savanna move long distances to their range periphery, they paste much more frequently than at other times, although they do not seem to paste more often than elsewhere in the range per unit of distance covered, once they are at their range boundary. Adult males also paste more frequently than adult females, but the immigrant males paste most frequently, probably to advertise vigorously their intention to join a clan. When foraging or hunting, the pasting frequency increases considerably. This may be, in part, an advertisement indicating that a particular section of the range has been recently used by a specific individual, either for itself or to alert other hyaenas, because spotted hyaenas are believed to be able to distinguish individual members of the clan from the odour of their pastes. In the southern Kalahari savanna they paste at a mean frequency of 13 pastes per 100 km moved. This rate is about 20 times less frequent than that of brown hyaenas in the same region.

Spotted hyaenas also commonly defecate in selected spots where a considerable accumulation of faeces may develop over time. These faecal accumulations are called latrines, and they also have a scent-marking function. In some areas the latrines are found along the range boundaries, and the hyaenas often paste near them too. However, in the southern Kalahari savanna latrines are more often found in the centre of the range. These ranges are so large as a result of the prey-poor nature of the region, that the latrines are made mainly in the centre of the range near the river-beds where most of the prey is found, and consequently where most spotted hyaena activity occurs. The spacing of the latrines over the range is also often influenced by the features of the environment such as pathways, river-beds, dens or water. This spacing is usually at fairly regular intervals, and a specific latrine may be used for many months or even years. However, spotted hyaenas do not only defecate at their latrines, but may also do so elsewhere while moving about.

A spotted hyaena does not only visit its latrines for the purpose of defecation, but also sometimes pastes near the latrine to leave an additional scent mark. Although most spotted hyaena populations use latrines regularly, those at Savuti seldom do. The reason for this difference is not clear. They also use scrapes to scent-mark their range, often near their latrines. When scraping, a spotted hyaena scrapes or paws the ground with its front feet, depositing secretions from its interdigital glands in the process. They also roll on, or rub against, rotten carcasses to communicate the presence and state of this food to their companions during normal greeting ceremonies. In addition spotted hyaenas follow the scent trails left by other members of their own clan as they move about. These scents are deposited from their interdigital glands. Damp soil increases the efficiency and possible detection of such a trail.

Reproduction and young

Initial attempts to study reproduction in the spotted hyaena were hampered by the lack of knowledge of the nature and extent of the female's true sexual anatomy and morphology. However, in 1939 the pioneering work of L.H. Matthews concerning the reproductive anatomy and physiology of the spotted hyaena solved many of the former riddles. This work was followed by the more detailed studies of various authors. It is now known that a female spotted hyaena's reproductive tract is morphologically quite different from that of the other living hyaenas. Also, as is the case in the brown and striped hyaena, the spotted hyaena's penis has no baculum, a bone which commonly occurs in the penis of other carnivores such as the dog, bear and weasel.

There is no clear breeding season for the spotted hyaena, but there may be smaller local peaks of conception and consequently of births in response to local seasonal prey abundances. Clear seasonal breeding peaks cannot really develop in the spotted hyaena because the complete, normal female cycle lasts for little more than a year. As a result, it is a different group of spotted hyaenas every year which takes reproductive advantage of seasonal prey abundance peaks such as the birth of impala lambs in the Kruger National Park. The spotted hyaenas of Savuti seem to be something of an exception. There, all the births occur in the extended dry season from May to November, with a clear birth-peak in

June when 66% of all the cubs are born. This phenomenon is linked to the synchronised weaning of most of the dependent yearling cubs some 4 to 6 months earlier, during a time of abundant food when migrating zebras foal there. Such a seasonal abundance of food may cause the suckling and dependent yearlings to be weaned earlier than usual, and to take place over a short time, allowing the females to conceive again after 3 to 8 weeks once they have regained their physical condition. In the Kruger National Park dependent yearling spotted hyaenas also appear to be weaned somewhat earlier than elsewhere in response to a local abundance of impala lambs, which allows the females to conceive again. In this instance it causes a slight peak in the late-summer births, which clearly differs from the timing of the peak observed in Savuti. However, the mechanism of reproductive activity remains the same, and this variation in reproductive activity again emphasises the influence of fluctuations in food abundance on spotted hyaena reproduction.

The spotted hyaena's mating system is polygamous. Consequently various litters have various parents. Although the dominant male usually does most of the mating, all the resident males also court the females regularly. A male spotted hyaena becomes sexually mature when he is about 2 years old, and a female at about 3 years. A female has a reproductive life of about 13 years. Reproductive success among the females is not influenced by age, size or social rank, and both the male and female spotted hyaena seem to have three reproductive options. A male can either remain with his natal clan, become a nomad, or migrate to another clan. A female can either remain with her natal clan, form a new clan, or migrate to another clan. The female has an oestrus cycle of 14 days. She advertises her condition by emitting a smell, and may also walk around with her tail erect to signal her receptivity. Oestrus recurs after 14 days if fertilisation has not occurred, making the spotted hyaena polyoestrous. Copulation appears to be a difficult feat because of the male-like external genitalia of a female spotted hyaena. This physical difficulty is compounded by the male's fear of the female, the lack of cooperation from a female when mating, and the lack of overall aggression between competing males. When a male mounts a female successfully, his whole underside rests on the female's back, and his chin lies on her shoulder. Only his back toes are on the ground. Copulation lasts for about 5 minutes, and may be repeated several times. Both partners remain silent when copulating. Gestation lasts approximately 110 days, and the interval between successive litters is usually some 14 to 16 months.

In contrast to the African wild dog, another pack-living large carnivore of the African savannas, litters in the spotted hyaena are small. The usual litter size is about two cubs, but they can be as few as one and as many as four. At birth a spotted hyaena cub is born in an advanced stage of development, with its eyes open. The coat colour at birth is a deep chocolate brown. A female spotted hyaena is thought to be able to adjust the sex ratio of her litter in response to the current population levels of hyaenas. When the population is below the ecological capacity of the area, she may possibly produce more female cubs than males, yet all-female litters are rare.

In the Masai-Mara, where the spotted hyaena clans are relatively large and stable, there is some evidence that a high-ranking female in the clan tends to produce more male than female cubs, thus increasing her genetic representation in the clan progressively during her life. In a spotted hyaena clan the reproductive success of the dominant female is indeed measured in terms of the number of male offspring which she produces. The dominant female's sons behave differently from those of all the other females, in that they are less submissive to other dominant females later in their life. They also leave their natal clan later than the other young males do. This may give them greater survival and reproductive chances in life, and consequently ensures the long-term propagation of their mother's genetic material in the population.

The cubs are born in a birth den which soon becomes the centre of social activity for the whole clan. A birth den consists of an enlarged entrance cavity which tapers off into a narrow tunnel of about 200 mm in diameter. A female crouching in the entrance cavity is well hidden from the surface, and is provided with enough shelter from the sun during the day. The tunnel then spirals down, being enlarged along the bends to form bigger spherical chambers where the cubs can pass each other. About 1,2 to 1,5 m below the surface, there is a large resting chamber in which the cubs spend much of their time. It is only the cubs which can access this chamber through the narrow tunnel, allowing them to evade a large predator such as a lion, when the adults move away from this kind of danger. Despite being born in a relatively advanced state of physical development, spotted hyaena cubs have poor coordination for the first 2 weeks of their life, and therefore rarely venture outside the birth den. After this period they are carried by their mother to a communal den which is used by all the clan members and which is also a centre of social activity. In smaller clans such as those found in the southern Kalahari savanna, this cub isolation for the first 2 weeks of life may not occur. A typical communal den consists of several cavities which are clustered in one area. When the clan members leave to forage, the cubs are usually left unguarded. Therefore the primary function of the communal den is to offer protection to the cubs when the adults are absent. Small spotted hyaena cubs emerge only when an adult is present. However, a large clan's communal den may contain cubs of all ages.

Because a spotted hyaena cub is largely dependent on its mother for food and requires a diet supplemented by milk for at least a year, lactation extends over a year or more. Moreover, its permanent canines only appear when it is 12 to 15 months old. At the communal den in Serengeti a spotted hyaena mother will visit her cubs almost every morning and evening until they are about 4 weeks old, after which the frequency of her visits declines. A cub's weight doubles in its first 25 days of life, and triples in the first 37 days. When 100 days old, a cub will weigh about 9 times its mean birthweight of 1,5 kg. The juvenile coat is gradually replaced from the age of 7 weeks, but the change to the adult coat may only be completed by 9 months of age, the young hyaena retaining a mid-dorsal stripe over the back, neck and top of the head until that age.

In the Kruger National Park an adult female may lactate for 75% of her life which requires a high-protein diet. Because the spotted hyaena feeds opportunistically, it may well be able to exploit periods of food

A juvenile spotted hyaena only attains a fully adult coat when 9 months old. Photo: J. du P. Bothma.

abundance to increase its reproductive success. Such periods will ease the energy burden on the lactating female, either through a more efficient replacement of her own energy supplies, which will allow her to conceive again, or through more rapid weaning of existing litters. Unlike brown hyaenas, a female spotted hyaena seldom suckles cubs other than her own, and spotted hyaenas rarely bring food to the cubs at the den. Spotted hyaena cubs suckle for 12 to 18 months, remaining at the den for most of that time. Females with single cubs attend them with the same frequency as those with twins, but single cubs grow more rapidly than twins and have greater survival rates.

In Serengeti some spotted hyaenas are compelled to commute (see Range use, below) great distances to access migratory prey during certain times of the year. Commuting means that a female with young cubs may be absent from her cubs for several days. When their mother commutes to obtain food, the body weight and growth rate of her cubs will decline. When she returns, however, the cubs drink great quantities of milk to compensate for their weight losses in the days when she was absent.

In Savuti spotted hyaenas also commute occasionally to reach water supplies in the dry season or during droughts. Whether they do so to obtain food or water, large but still dependent cubs may accompany their mothers when commuting. In this way they become familiar with these vital routes. Also in Savuti communal dens are not used to feed mobile cubs of 3 months or older. Instead, the main function of the communal den is to assimilate the cubs into the social system of the clan. There, the spotted hyaenas bring all the mobile cubs from the communal den, which is usually in the woodlands, to disused aardvark burrows in the more open, sandy marsh areas, every evening. The cubs are protected in these temporary night dens by a few adults or subadults while the rest of the clan hunts. At dawn the cubs are led back to the communal den by their mothers. Spotted hyaena cubs gradually start to eat solid food as they grow older, but they are dependent on a milk-supplemented diet until they start to forage with the clan when about 12 months old. The spotted hyaena does not usually supply its cubs at the den with solid food. Most authors believe that they never do so, but it did seem to occur on one occasion in Amboseli. The high-ranking female's larger cubs are also able to feed more successfully at a kill than the smaller ones from subordinate females.

When the cubs in a litter are all the same sex, siblicide may occur, especially in twins, when one cub will kill the other. While this is common in large raptors, siblicide is rare in mammals and its function there is unknown. Infanticide, when some or all the cubs are killed by individuals of their own kind, also occurs in spotted hyaenas. It usually involves male hyaena immigrants, but the resident females will attempt to defend their cubs against such a threat, often whooping vigorously in the process. At anywhere from 244 to 481 (mean: 357) days old, although usually when older than 1 year, young male spotted hyaenas in Serengeti will start to disperse, but the female young remain with their natal clan for life.

Range use

Each spotted hyaena clan uses a range which usually contains one communal den. Yet, because range and group size in social carnivores tend to be interrelated and flexible, both being influenced by the distribution and abundance of critical resources such as food and water, it is to be expected that the spotted hyaena ranges will also vary greatly in size from region to region. Even in the more mesic southern African savannas, prey animals usually occur at lower densities than in those of East Africa. Although the spotted hyaena's range size is similar in both areas, clan sizes are smaller in southern Africa. However, in the more arid and prey-poor savannas, the range size of a spotted hyaena clan must be considerably larger than in the more mesic ones to satisfy its energy requirements.

In Serengeti and the Ngorongoro Crater at least a portion of the large prey base is sedentary. Consequently their spotted hyaena clan ranges are relatively small, varying from 10 to 50 km² in size. In Timbavati the range size is some 25 km². Spotted hyaena range sizes in the Kruger National Park are surprisingly large at around 130 km², possibly because of increased competition for food from a large complement of other large carnivores. In Etosha the mean range size for a spotted hyaena clan is 360 km² in response to a temporarily variable and patchy food supply, and the widely scattered permanent waterholes. In Savuti a migrating prey resource and a sparse distribution of water in the dry season also lead to large range sizes for these hyaenas. In the southern Kalahari savanna with its poor prey and water resources, small clans of spotted hyaenas live in huge and variable ranges with a mean size of 1095 km². However, not all parts of these ranges are used with equal intensity, because these spotted hyaenas use the central and relatively more prey-rich parts of their ranges more regularly. The influence of the abundance and distribution of its vital resources on a spotted hyaena's clan range size, is clear when one considers that the smallest range of a clan in the southern Kalahari savanna is still some 55 times larger than the largest range of spotted hyaenas in the more mesic and prey-rich Hluhluwe-Umfolozi.

Some authors regard spotted hyaena ranges as territories in the true sense of the word, because they are actively defended by the clan members against intruders, as happens in the Ngorongoro Crater. Scent-marking is a common method of passive range defence, and it is done by pasting, scraping and often by the deposition of faeces in latrines. Other methods of defence include regular boundary patrols, vocal displays, and the aggressive eviction of intruders. In some areas such as the Masai-Mara, however, prey resources are patchy and scarce, and the spotted hyaena ranges are separated by wide buffer zones empty of hyaenas, as happens in the Namib Desert. Consequently the range boundaries are diffuse and rarely marked or defended, and aggressive encounters between clans are rare. In Savuti their range boundaries are also clearly marked, but because of an uneven distribution of prey in both time and space, disputes between clans do occur in areas of local prey abundance, often even involving fierce physical fights. These fights are extremely noisy, but severe injuries seldom occur. In the southern Kalahari savanna, where mainly the central or core areas of large ranges are used, range boundary disputes are rare.

11 cm

In the Kruger National Park range boundaries are actively maintained and aggressively defended. There the adult spotted hyaena females are most active in territorial defence. A clan will devote up to 20% of its activities to patrolling and scent-marking its range, particularly along its boundaries. These activities increase proportionally with the intrusion pressure from neighbours. Patrolling is done mainly along game trails, river-beds or roads. When marking the range, scent-marks are deposited 16 times more frequently than when foraging. Resident males on their own fail to evict intruding females, but in fact they sometimes end up by following such females back to their clans as prospective mates. The size of the clan, and consequently its number of adult females, is important in range defence. When the size of one clan studied in the Kruger National Park was reduced by 25%, its ability to defend its range declined, and two larger neighbouring clans appropriated 8 and 26 km² of its former range respectively.

Despite having discrete and defended ranges in most regions, the spotted hyaena is unique among carnivores in having developed an alternative survival strategy when food and water resources become scarce. This is called commuting, and it involves short-term trips lasting several days over distances of up to 80 km from a clan's own range

175

to find food or water. The term commuting was first used for the spotted hyaenas of Savuti where the availability of water in the dry season is unreliable and limited. However, the occurrence of long-term movements by spotted hyaenas in search of food had already been mentioned by H. Kruuk in 1972. In times of drought the spotted hyaenas from neighbouring ranges in Savuti cross into or over other ranges in search of water, returning to their own ranges to hunt. The system of commuting to a basic resource is most common in Serengeti where migrating prey regularly leave spotted hyaena clans with a need to find sufficient food to maintain the clan once the prey move out of their range. In Serengeti spotted hyaenas live in large, stable clans of up to 47 adults and subadults. Each clan's range contains a sedentary prey base with a mean density of some 3,3 animals per km² throughout the year. This density cannot, however, sustain a large clan indefinitely, being considerably lower than the prey base of 219 animals per km² which is available when the migratory herds of wildebeest, zebra and Thomson's gazelles pass through the area each year. In the absence of migratory herds, spotted hyaena clan members regularly leave their ranges to forage from the nearest available migratory herds, although the females usually have to return to their dens to feed their young. Consequently they only stay away from their dens for 3 to 4 days, compared with male absence of 6 to 10 days. Commuting does not occur in the Ngorongoro Crater where the resident herbivore population is about 95 animals per km².

Spotted hyaenas use a complex array of behavioural, morphological and physiological specialisations when they commute, to allow them to cross into or over neighbouring territories without evoking aggressive attacks from the residents. Nevertheless, commuters do try to avoid any resident clans at all costs. The resident clan members also adjust their behaviour to the context of the encounter by usually ignoring a commuter in transit, although they respond aggressively when finding a commuter on a kill. Members from different clans often meet in peace when commuting, and commuters do not show any aggression towards each other. The need to commute also declines as prey resources in a given clan's range increase. The spotted hyaenas of Serengeti spend 46 to 62% of their total foraging time in a given year on commuting between the clan's territory and the nearest herd of migrating herbivores. When commuting, the use of a communal den reduces the risk of cub predation in the mother's absence. Spotted hyaena cubs can survive for several days without nutrition, making up their deficiencies by drinking large quantities of milk when their mother returns. This allows a female to commute to food in order to survive and feed her cubs. Spotted hyaenas are highly mobile, making long-distance movements possible. To resident hyaenas, the presence of commuters is also beneficial, because residents can locate and take over the commuter's kills without fear of aggression.

Activity and movement

The spotted hyaena is highly mobile and mainly nocturnal, although its fastest pace is not a racing run but a bouncing gallop. Its activity is governed by that of its prey, and varies greatly between habitats and seasons. The spotted hyaena forages or hunts mainly at night, resting by day in some suitable shade. Where shade is not available, it will rest in an underground burrow during the day. When using a warthog burrow, the spotted hyaena and the warthog may even share the same burrow because the one is active at night and the other by day. In Serengeti the spotted hyaena spends up to 80% of its time resting. Because the spotted hyaena obtains a variable quantity of its food through scavenging, its nocturnal habits may have developed both to conserve its own body water and to reduce the necessity of competition with vultures which are the other dominant scavengers of the African savannas. Despite being mainly nocturnal, the spotted hyaenas of Savuti are nevertheless known to hunt successfully on cool days too. On extremely hot days, spotted hyaenas will also commonly enter waterholes and lie there for long periods to cool off.

Spotted hyaenas commonly lie-up in waterholes during the heat of the day. Photo: J. du P. Bothma.

An interesting variation in the general pattern of activity occurs in the Masai-Mara where the topi is a common prey animal. The topi grazes actively in the early morning, and by 10:00 a herd will begin to lie down, each animal with its head lowered and its chin resting on the ground. Spotted hyaenas then move in slowly, and settle down 50 to 100 m away from the resting topi. By about 11:00 the hyaenas start to wander towards the topi herd in a seemingly aimlessly manner, looking for any individuals which are deeply asleep. When the hyaenas start to move about, most of the topi will get up and move away. However, if one remains asleep, it will be stalked slowly until it can be attacked from 10 m away. Most of the topi escape the attack, but some do not and are killed in this unusual way.

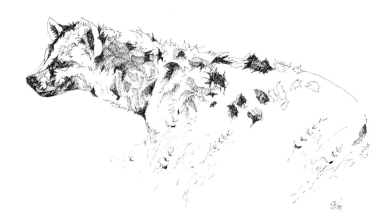

Much of a spotted hyaena's social activity is centred on the communal den which may be regularly moved to another location. A well-known den site near Kajiado in Kenya sometimes contained more than 80 hyaenas, and at this site they have made use of natural cavities in rocky cliffs, compacting the soil by their frequent passage. This den has been occupied by spotted hyaenas for as long as the local Masai can remember, and huge numbers of fleas cover any visitor to the den within the first few seconds of arrival. This is unusual, because most other dens are probably abandoned when they become too infested with fleas, as happens in the southern Kalahari savanna. New dens are usually free of fleas. At the den, the smaller cubs emerge only when the adults are present. In some areas, such as the Kruger National Park, the spotted hyaenas use the same den for 6 months or more, and may even do so for years. In other areas, such as the southern Kalahari savanna, den occupancy is short, and a particular den is used only once.

Whereas a brown hyaena normally moves about continuously while foraging because it eats various small food items, a spotted hyaena usually feeds on one larger food item, and then rests. When foraging or hunting, spotted hyaenas can travel considerable distances in a night. In the southern Kalahari savanna they travel a mean daily distance of 27,1 km at a mean speed of some 6,7 km/h. In one period of 10 hours and 20 minutes, one clan which was observed there moved 69,1 km. An earlier report based on circumstantial data also speculates that one of these clans could have travelled as much as 80 km in a single night on one occasion. In the Kruger National Park spotted hyaenas forage in small groups, and travel distances of up to 90 km between successive meals. In the southern Kalahari savanna the mean distance travelled between successive meals is 33 km. The actual distance moved by spotted hyaenas in a given night varies with the distribution of their food source in relation to their breeding dens, because although these hyaenas will follow their prey when foraging, they will attempt to return to their breeding dens as quickly as possible. Irrespective of the success of its foraging or hunting, however, a spotted hyaena in the southern Kalahari savanna will return to its den every day. Their movements are usually concentrated in the central areas of this range along the dry river-beds which have the highest prey density. Consequently the movement patterns of these spotted hyaenas are more linear than circular.

When spotted hyaena cubs are moved from den to den, those less than 4 weeks old are carried to the new den in their mother's mouth. The older cubs may walk there with their mother. In Serengeti a 6-week-old cub once walked 14,6 km in 4 hours and 18 minutes to get to a new den, remaining within 3 m of its mother who helped the cub by carrying it for brief periods. However, it was killed by a lion before it could reach the new den.

Spotted hyaenas live in large clans. Consequently they have to find food sources which are large enough to feed many hyaenas at the same time. Photo: C.H. Walker.

Feeding ecology

The development of large social groups such as wild dog packs and spotted hyaena clans, depends to a great extent on the type of food which an animal uses. The spotted hyaena is the most social of the living hyaenids. In consequence it must find food sources that are large enough to feed many hyaenas at the same time. Moreover, larger clans will exclude smaller ones from access to the best food resources and therefore spotted hyaenas specialise on large carcasses, which they can either kill or find when foraging as a clan. Amongst the hyaenids the spotted hyaena's teeth are the most specialised for meat-eating. However, it is not only what they eat, but how they obtain their food that determines the success with which spotted hyaenas can exist in large clans. Many people still regard them as scavengers rather than hunters. It is true that the spotted hyaena does scavenge and will eat anything that is even remotely digestible, but it is also an efficient hunter of fresh food. It is therefore best referred to as a hunter-scavenger. Although its prowess as a hunter has been known since 1884 when H.H. Johnston described it in his book, *The river Congo from its mouth to Bolobo,* its true hunting nature was first reported in 1964 by F.C. Eloff from the southern Kalahari savanna. Despite being a hunter, the spotted hyaena is also the most efficient scavenger of the African savannas, and is able to crush large bones and digest large amounts of bone.

As with most carnivores, the type of food eaten by a spotted hyaena varies from region to region according to the distribution and abundance of the major food items and the way in which it is obtained. For example, spotted hyaenas in Serengeti hunt and kill only 58% of their food whereas those in the Ngorongoro Crater hunt and kill 96% of theirs. Nevertheless, some clans may have distinct short-term and long-term prey preferences, and throughout their range spotted hyaenas feed mainly on large ungulates, killing 82% of all prey which is killed by the large predators of Serengeti and the Ngorongoro Crater. In the Masai-

The spotted hyaena is a hunter-scavenger which will consume anything that is remotely edible. Photo: C.H. Walker.

Mara spotted hyaena clans are found close to their main food resources. Nevertheless, they also scavenge, and this behaviour is reflected in their ability to travel long distances with low energy expenditure to obtain food when it is not readily available. This ability to travel long distances is also one of the reasons why the spotted hyaena population in Serengeti is not limited in size by the availability of the resident prey only. In that region the hyaenas can commute to migratory prey to obtain food through hunting or scavenging, as has been explained earlier under Range use.

In the bushveld savanna of South Africa the remains of lion kills are an important source of scavenged food for spotted hyaenas, and these hyaenas often scavenge more food than they hunt. However, they will utilise any temporally abundant food resource opportunistically. In the Kruger National Park, for example, they feed extensively (87,5% of all carcasses) on impalas during the lambing season, most of which they kill themselves. Of these impalas 92% are lambs. This is similar to their consumption of wildebeest calves during the calving season in Serengeti and the Ngorongoro Crater.

The spotted hyaenas in the Kruger National Park also feed on dead lions and other spotted hyaenas, and while they occasionally also eat other carnivores, they are not known to eat rodents. Although those in the Kruger National Park generally scavenge extensively, more than 50% of their food is still obtained by hunting, especially during times of drought when prey such as kudu, impala and warthog become highly

Impala lambs form the bulk of the spotted hyaena's diet during the lambing season in the Kruger National Park.
Photo: J. du P. Bothma.

vulnerable to predation. Spotted hyaenas only rarely eat plants, and when plant material appears in a scat, it usually comes from the rumen contents of a prey animal. However, they do eat wild fruit for its moisture and limited nutrition.

Occasional anthrax epidemics among the larger ungulates, but mainly in the blue wildebeest and Burchell's zebra of Etosha, provide the spotted hyaenas with an opportunistic food source. During an anthrax

In many African savannas adult impalas are highly vulnerable to predation by spotted hyaenas, especially during times of drought.
Photo: J. du P. Bothma.

epidemic, both the lions and the spotted hyaenas in Etosha do not have to hunt because of the abundance of carcasses for scavenging. Although the lions still continue to do some hunting, the spotted hyaenas then scavenge almost exclusively. At other times they hunt mainly blue wildebeest and springbok, because they are primarily hunters and only secondarily scavengers. In Etosha the spotted hyaenas normally kill 75% of their food and scavenge the rest. When hunting they rarely kill adult zebras, and foals younger than 3 months are killed only occasionally.

It normally requires a large hunting group of spotted hyaenas to hunt and kill an adult zebra successfully. Because those in Etosha usually hunt in small groups, they are mostly unable to kill adult zebras. Etosha's dry climate also influences their scavenging frequency, because it desiccates carcasses quickly, soon making them unacceptable to these scavengers.

In Savuti spotted hyaenas also hunt and kill 75% of their food, and the main prey animals killed there are various types of antelope and the warthog. In contrast to the spotted hyaenas of Etosha, zebra foals are hunted and killed regularly by these hyaenas. They form large groups when hunting adult zebras and also hunt prey selectively by age and type. Most of the larger prey killed, suffer from a previous injury and are therefore easier to hunt. Large groups of hyaenas also displace

In the Etosha National Park adult zebras are hunted only infrequently by spotted hyaenas. However, when the zebras die of anthrax, their carcasses are extensively scavenged by these hyaenas.
Photo: J. du P. Bothma.

183

female lions from some of their kills. However, the hyaenas in turn lose 25% of their kills to larger lion prides. In Savuti the spotted hyaenas also kill small prey such as the springhare and the occasional small carnivore when the opportunity arises, but they normally reject the flesh of other carnivores there. During the wet season they display their dietary opportunism even further by licking up fat-rich termites as they emerge from the ground. When scavenging these spotted hyaenas usually do not consume most of the bones of the carcass, possibly because they find enough to eat in their own kills.

The gemsbok is an abundant food resource for large carnivores in the southern Kalahari savanna. Consequently it is the major prey (43,3% of all kills) for spotted hyaenas there. However, of the gemsbok killed, 80,8% are calves. Nevertheless, the overall prey base is small, and the spotted hyaenas in that region eat a variety of food. This includes almost any kind of mammal, and different kinds of birds, reptiles, amphibians, invertebrates and even wild fruit. Ostrich eggs are also a prized food item, and the hyaenas will raid any nest they find, attacking the brooding birds to get at the eggs. A spotted hyaena is not able to bite open an ostrich egg as easily as a brown hyaena can, and therefore it often kicks one egg in a nest backwards against another, to get it to crack, after which it can be bitten open easily. Nevertheless, large and medium-sized mammals larger than 12 kg remain their main food. In one study of all the carcasses fed on, 53% were killed by spotted hyaenas, but this is probably an underestimation. Because they usually hunt larger prey, 73% of the actual weight of all food eaten is killed by the spotted hyaenas, and 27% scavenged. In the savannas of East Africa and the Kruger National Park with their large variety and number of other large carnivores, spotted hyaenas hunt less frequently and scavenge more often than in the areas with a poor prey base such as Etosha, Savuti and the southern Kalahari savanna. It is therefore clear that the spotted hyaena both hunts and scavenges for its food, but it is also obvious that the degree of each activity varies from region to region, as does its chief type of prey. Nevertheless, the spotted hyaena's main diet consists of vertebrate remains, whether hunted or scavenged. In summary, the spotted hyaena's food selection is so opportunistic and variable that it cannot be generalised over its range in Africa.

Despite scavenging when this is convenient for them, spotted hyaenas are true and most efficient pack hunters. As hunters they do not have the stealth and agility of the other larger carnivores of the African savannas to rely on. Nor are they capable of great speed, although they do have tremendous powers of endurance. When chasing its prey, a spotted hyaena's fastest pace is a bouncy gallop. Because a lone spotted hyaena cannot attack and kill a fleet-footed and vigorous prey, it has developed a hunting and foraging system which is unique to itself. Spotted hyaenas hunt or forage singly or in groups of varying size depending on local conditions, but the subadults rarely forage on their own. Although they do hunt often and effectively, spotted hyaenas also scavenge more frequently than most of the other large carnivores except the brown hyaena. In Serengeti spotted hyaenas will even dive under water to get at the carcasses of wildebeest which drown when crossing rivers during their annual migration. These hyaenas only come up to the surface to swallow and breathe, and then disappear below the surface again. Their hunting in the Serengeti-Mara ecosystem is done in groups of varying size, but scavenging usually involves a single hyaena only, which wanders around extensively for part of the day, making the discovery of a carcass for scavenging more likely. When hunting and scavenging, spotted hyaenas use their acute sense of hearing to detect potential live prey of their own, or to locate the scene of other predator's kills. In the Kruger National Park, they react strongly to lion roars when they hunt or kill, and they locate such potential carcasses for scavenging with pin-point accuracy. In Savuti spotted hyaenas find 78,5% of all lion kills, usually within 30 minutes of the kill being made, and in the southern Kalahari savanna they detect blue wildebeest herds by hearing them from a mean distance of 2,4 km (maximum: 6,0 km) away. These hyaenas also use their keen night vision for hunting, making 60,3% of their prey contacts in the dry bed of the Nossob River, by sight.

When detecting carrion, spotted hyaenas use their keen sense of smell, a sense which is common to all hyaenids. In the southern Kalahari savanna they detect carcasses downwind from a mean distance of 3,2 km (maximum: 4,2 km), yet they cannot detect even a strongly smelling carcass when they are upwind of it. Their keen sense of smell also allows them to discern live prey downwind from a mean distance of 1,1 km (maximum: 2,8 km) away. Pasting is used extensively by all the hyaenids to orientate themselves while foraging and hunting, especially to avoid moving through the same area repeatedly in the same night, in search of food. This also advertises the recent presence of an individual or group of hyaenas to the other members of the clan.

In several regions there is a clear relationship between the size of the hunting group and the nature and size of their prey. Unlike wild dogs, spotted hyaena clans often split into smaller groups to forage or hunt. In Serengeti individual hyaenas usually direct their hunting towards smaller prey only, and the larger prey is always hunted as a clan. In Savuti spotted hyaenas live in clans of up to 50 members, but they hunt in groups of two to four, increasing the chances of the clan to locate food in a region where the prey herds may be widely scattered at times. When a kill has been made, the other clan members are called, and they then all converge on the kill to feed. In Etosha they forage or hunt alone or in small groups of up to five, and in Timbavati spotted hyaenas also hunt or forage mainly alone or in pairs, but they do form larger groups to hunt larger prey. The spotted hyaena clans in the Kruger National Park also usually split into smaller groups to hunt or forage, rejoining at a carcass or a kill. Group hunting clearly increases hunting success. A spotted hyaena clan or group usually approaches the prey downwind in a fan formation when they hunt. An initial charge scatters the herd, and any vulnerable target is then selected visually, but the victim is only chased if it is really suitable. A vulnerable prey is usually a slower individual such as a calf, a young adult or a sick, injured or old adult. In Serengeti and the Ngorongoro Crater spotted hyaenas hunt wildebeest calves in particular when available, while in the Kruger National Park impala lambs are most at risk.

In the southern Kalahari savanna calves form 80,8% of all the gemsbok killed by spotted hyaenas. Up to subadult age the mean chase distance for these gemsbok calves increases with the age of the calf hunted, decreasing again for adults. Of the adult gemsbok hunted, there is some evidence that individuals in poor condition are selected in preference to others. When blue wildebeest are hunted, however, there is no relationship between the age of the prey and the distance chased. The mean chase distance for all successful blue wildebeest hunts is 1 km, and for unsuccessful ones 2,1 km. Wildebeest are hunted by spotted hyaenas as often in the southern Kalahari savanna as in those of East Africa, but in the southern Kalahari there is less pressure on the calves. The springbok is the most common prey animal in the dry riverbeds of the southern Kalahari, yet they are usually ignored by hunting spotted hyaenas because of their fleet-footedness and vigilance, except in the peak lambing season in January and February when the hyaenas can hunt the young lambs with ease. The mean chase distance for successful springbok lamb hunting is 644 m as opposed to 1,7 km for unsuccessful hunts. As with the small steenbok *Raphicerus campestris,* springbok lambs are also usually only hunted by solitary hyaenas because they do not provide enough food for the clan, or even for a small hunting group of hyaenas. The large and surprisingly mobile eland is rarely hunted by spotted hyaenas in the southern Kalahari savanna because they seldom meet each other. In one such instance reported by M.G.L. Mills, however, three spotted hyaenas chased an eland herd for 23,8 km, eventually killing a subadult bull after a severe struggle over a distance of 1 km.

The hunting strategies of different clans also vary considerably, but this seems to be related more to the type of prey selected than to the clan's hunting ability. An unusual hunting method occurs in Moremi, where single spotted hyaenas from different clans and parts of the range frequently pursue herds of lechwe into the water of the flood plains. In deep water a lechwe cannot swim as well as a spotted hyaena which is known to be an accomplished swimmer. The hyaena then catches and drowns its prey, dragging it to the water's edge where it is eaten. In the savanna areas of Comoé, spotted hyaenas are rare. Those that do occur, hunt alone or in pairs at most, to reduce competition with leopards. In Savuti the spotted hyaena takes advantage of the general lack of large males in lion prides, robbing these prides of many of their kills, especially when the hyaenas outnumber the lions by 4 : 1.

Some forms of prey are more difficult to hunt than others, some are dangerous to hunt, and others may even develop local defence strategies to counter-attacks by large predators such as spotted hyaenas. Outrunning the hyaenas is the most successful prey defence in most areas. In the southern Kalahari savanna the adult gemsbok is a potentially lethal adversary for any large predator. When attacked by a group of spotted hyaenas an adult gemsbok will back into a bush or tree, often defending itself successfully with its long, rapier-like horns, especially against smaller groups of hyaenas. The smallest group of hyaenas known to have killed an adult gemsbok in that area consisted of four members. In Savuti the blue wildebeest bulls have also developed a local defence strategy against spotted hyaena attacks which seems to be quite successful.

When killing prey, one or all of the hunting group of hyaenas bite at the legs and flanks of the prey on the run, much as wild dogs do. When the prey animal slows its pace, it is pulled down and killed. The innards may be pulled out and the hyaenas may even start to feed while the victim is still alive. To keep a prey animal such as a gemsbok at bay, various members of the hyaena attacking group will circle it, darting in to harass and bite at it, retreating when attacked. In retreating they try to entice the gemsbok into fleeing, because it can be killed more easily while on the run. A threatened gemsbok will charge and thrust at the attacking hyaenas, using its horns effectively in counter-attack to defend itself. When the hyaenas cannot get the gemsbok to flee from its protected position, they may either move off after a few minutes, or they may lie down nearby, waiting for as much as 5 hours for the gemsbok to move off again before finally giving up the hunt. The hunting technique of single spotted hyaenas who chase lechwe into the deep water of the flood plains of Moremi has already been described above.

Spotted hyaenas kill their prey with varying degrees of success, depending upon the type of prey, the conditions of the hunt, and sometimes the size of the hunting group. In Serengeti a single spotted hyaena which hunts wildebeest calves has a success rate of 15%, a group of two hyaenas has one of 23%, and a group of three or more a rate of 31%. In the southern Kalahari savanna the hunting success of different clans varies. However, the variations do not seem to be related to differences in hunting ability, but rather to differences in prey selection and abundance, the less successful clans selecting prey which is more difficult to find and kill. For example, blue wildebeest of all ages are killed with 39% success, which is similar to the 34% success rate for all ages of wildebeest in East Africa. When killing gemsbok calves, however, there is no relationship between hunting success and the gemsbok herd size, or the size of the hyaena hunting group. Nor is there an increased success rate as the size of the hunting group increases, because the spotted hyaenas in that region tend to hunt gemsbok calves as individuals rather than as a group. While gemsbok calves are killed effectively at a success rate of 82%, adults and subadults are more difficult to kill, such hunts being successful in only 14% of all cases. Other game are hunted with varying degrees of success too.

Spotted hyaenas are also known to kill more than they can eat, occasionally running into a milling herd and killing as many individuals as possible. This again occurs when local environmental conditions such as violent thunderstorms confuse the herd, or make detection of and escape from the hyaenas difficult. Surplus killing is more of a killing reflex than to satisfy hunger, because much of the prey killed in this way is not eaten. In one such incidence on the Serengeti Plains on 16 November 1966, which was reported by H. Kruuk, a dark night with heavy rain allowed a group of 19 spotted hyaenas to walk in among a sheltering herd of Thomson's gazelles. Because of the heavy rain, the gazelles did not react by fleeing as they normally would have done. As a result 82 gazelles were killed and another 27 seriously injured by the hyaenas. Although some were eaten, many were left untouched. Nevertheless, surplus killing is a rare event in nature.

Spotted hyaenas commonly feed for longer periods and on larger carcasses than brown hyaenas, often resting at the carcass, sometimes to continue feeding later. However, spotted hyaenas normally consume a carcass rapidly and completely. A clan of 38 spotted hyaenas in Serengeti, for example, is known to have consumed an adult zebra completely in only 15 minutes. A group of these hyaenas can also rapidly reduce any carcass smaller than a buffalo to a spinal skeleton in as little as 30 minutes. Competition among spotted hyaenas at a carcass takes place more in the speed of eating than in actual fighting, and there is little squabbling in a group feeding together. However, in the southern Kalahari savanna, they eat scavenged food more slowly than food which they have killed. Adult females with cubs at the den also often eat only for a while before abandoning the carcass to return to their cubs, even when there is still a lot of meat left. In the Kruger National Park competition at the feeding site is further reduced by individual spotted hyaenas carrying substantial pieces of the carcass as far as 1 km or more away from the feeding site before continuing to feed alone.

Unlike the striped and brown hyaena, the spotted hyaena does not carry meat from a scavenged carcass or a kill to its cubs at the den. Linear social dominance is most strongly expressed at feeding times and, because of their social dominance, adult females and their young have priority at any carcass. Consequently they obtain a high proportion of the meat, and have a better net energy economy than the adult males. Their preferential access to more food of better quality may also be one reason why the adult female spotted hyaenas are heavier, but not larger in the limb, than the males. The greater intake of good quality meat (protein) by the females benefits them and the survival of their cubs through their increased milk production. Male spotted hyaenas compensate for their poorer food-acquisition status by moving over greater distances when foraging, by consuming more quantities of low-quality food, and by feeding more readily under adverse conditions than the females.

Any large food source can attract large numbers of hyaenas. In Serengeti about 50 hyaenas have been seen to feed on a single carcass. A spotted hyaena will consume up to 30% of its own body weight in a single meal, eating easily 15 to 20 kg of food in the process. These hyaenas can deal with any foreign material such as grass which is accidentally consumed while feeding, by regurgitation and by means of their effective digestive system. It is difficult to measure a spotted hyaena's actual meat consumption accurately, but sodium and water turnover rates are useful for deriving reasonable estimates based on assessments of sodium influx. In one such study, a spotted hyaena's mean food intake was estimated at 3,8 kg per day. This is about twice as much as that arrived at from actual food consumption studies in Serengeti. In Etosha individual meals from hunted kills are usually larger than those from scavenged carcasses. When feeding, a spotted hyaena will often use one or both front paws to hold or manipulate its food, and the carnassial or shearing teeth are used more for processing skin, muscle and bone than for cutting muscle. Skin is consumed in greater quantities by the males than the females because of their lower feeding status. The speed of feeding and consequent lack of precision when feeding, lead to broken canines even in the spotted hyaenas with their strong teeth.

They are well known for their ability to crush and eat even the larger bones of most carcasses. As a result their characteristically white faecal droppings contain a high degree of calcium. In the Kruger National Park spotted hyaenas may carry bones and pieces of skin to their communal dens, but they still do so less often than those in East Africa where even young hyaenas carry bones to the den. In the process considerable bone assemblages may develop around such dens. The type of prey that these bones came from would then also reflect the relative abundance of their prey in a given area. However, spotted hyaena bone accumulations are usually much smaller than those of the striped and brown hyaena, both of which carry food to their cubs at the dens.

Food caching does occur with the spotted hyaena, but much less commonly than in the case of the striped and brown hyaena. In Serengeti, spotted hyaenas do store food occasionally, but only at waterholes. In the Kruger National Park larger pieces of food may be carried away from a carcass to avoid interference from other feeding hyaenas. These pieces of food may either be stored or are eaten as much as 1 km or more away. When stored, the food is hidden in grass clumps, under bushes, or in a waterhole. In the southern Kalahari savanna spotted hyaenas also use grass clumps, bushes or waterholes to store food. However, most stored food items there are probably never recovered and eaten.

Like the striped hyaena, the spotted hyaena is dependent upon the proximity of water for its survival. However, spotted hyaenas are less dependent on free water in areas where they kill their own prey regularly. This is because they can use the body fluids of their prey to recover their water loss as most of the other large carnivores do. For example, in Hluhluwe-Umfolozi, when the spotted hyaenas kill prey regularly they do not derive a significant proportion of their water intake from drinking, and when they do drink water, they are able to make do with small quantities. In the southern Kalahari savanna they also eat ostrich eggs which supply a source of nutrition and moisture. Unlike the brown hyaena, the spotted hyaenas in that area occasionally eat moisture-rich wild fruit such as the tsama melon and the gemsbok cucumber to obtain both water and nutrition. The spotted hyaenas in the southern Kalahari hunt their own prey quite often and therefore obtain much of their moisture needs from their own kills and from the widely scattered boreholes in the region. In Savuti each spotted hyaena clan has its own permanent water supply within its range. In times of drought they may sometimes abandon their range when their water supply runs out and there is no alternative source to commute to with safety.

The spotted hyaenas in the Chobe National Park are dependent upon a permanent supply of water for their survival, as they are elsewhere.
Photo: J. du P. Bothma.

Relationship with other wildlife

Because they live in large clans and are efficient hunters, the spotted hyaena's effectiveness as a predator of any particular type of prey will vary from region to region. The various factors involved in the nett effect of these hyaenas on their prey include the type of prey, their experience in being hunted, their availability at particular times, and the density of the hyaena population itself. While spotted hyaenas may influence the age structure and turnover rate of their major prey populations, they do not affect the population size to any great extent because the prey is usually present in large numbers in natural areas. In fact, all the large Serengeti predators combined could not regulate the number of potential prey there because these largely migratory herbivores are just too numerous. In Serengeti and the Ngorongoro Crater the wildebeest is the primary food source for the spotted hyaena, but in Serengeti many wildebeest also die from causes other than predation by

191

spotted hyaenas. The Serengeti hyaenas are resident, but they also move over vast distances depending on the prey movement. By contrast, the spotted hyaenas of Ngorongoro Crater are both resident and sedentary, and do not move about much. They therefore have a more local effect on their prey. The wildebeest of the Ngorongoro Crater are also fairly sedentary and stable, and therefore most of those that die there, are killed by spotted hyaenas. In Savuti spotted hyaenas are also believed to be able to control the numbers of some of the more sedentary prey. Spotted hyaena predation there is directed mainly at resident impalas and the foals of migratory zebras. Even in the southern Kalahari savanna with its low prey base, spotted hyaena predation has little impact on the prey.

The interaction between the various savanna predators and the spotted hyaena also varies from region to region according to the many ecological and sociological factors involved. In the northern Serengeti-Mara ecosystem, spotted hyaenas sometimes kill lions, leopards and caracals. In that region, however, they compete mainly with the African wild dog, driving small packs off their prey and even killing wild dog pups at times. Further south in Serengeti, spotted hyaenas drive wild dogs off a considerable proportion of their kills, and interference competition between these two large predators is severe.

Because of their mainly nocturnal habits, spotted hyaenas avoid direct competition with the vultures of the African savannas which scavenge mainly in the daytime.
Photo: J. du P. Bothma.

In the Kruger National Park and Hluhluwe-Umfolozi the spotted hyaenas interact most frequently with lions, leopards and black-backed jackals. They also compete seriously with African wild dogs, appropriating many of their kills and forcing the dogs to occupy less prey-rich areas with low spotted hyaena density. In Savuti these hyaenas succeed in driving smaller lion prides off their kills, when they outnumber the lions by at least 4:1. Although the lions are usually satiated to some degree before this happens, this interference by the hyaenas is a constant energy drain on the lions, forcing them to hunt more frequently than they would have done if they had not suffered such losses. In the South African bushveld savanna spotted hyaenas also compete with lions, leopards and cheetahs for food.

Spotted hyaena overlap in prey selection is avoided in the southern Kalahari savanna by means of the differential prey selection by age and species. Spotted hyaenas compete mainly with lions for ungulates weighing 12 kg or more, and in both predators, the blue wildebeest and gemsbok form 70% of their kills. However, the lions usually kill adult gemsbok and blue wildebeest, whereas the spotted hyaenas tend to focus on the calves of these animals. Because spotted hyaenas do kill adult gemsbok in other arid areas where lions are scarce, the southern Kalahari savanna lions may well be depriving spotted hyaenas of an important food source. In that region the spotted hyaenas scavenge food more often than the lions do, but by doing so they compete directly with the brown hyaenas. In Serengeti, the Ngorongoro Crater and elsewhere, spotted hyaenas and lions steal each other's kills aggressively, yet in the southern Kalahari savanna, the hyaenas usually wait some distance away until the lions leave a carcass, before moving in to scavenge the remains. The same thing happens with lions at hyaena kills. Clashes are rare, but when they do occur, the lions usually win. Moreover, spotted hyaenas actively avoid clashes when the lion pride contains a large adult male, but occasionally a pride of female lions will be chased off by a group of spotted hyaenas. A lion may even climb into a tree to escape from a pursuing group of hyaenas, because solitary lions are most at risk when competing with spotted hyaenas.

A leopard is usually dominated by two or more spotted hyaenas which will chase the leopard until it escapes down a burrow or up a tree. There is little competition for food between spotted hyaenas and cheetahs because they hunt different prey at different times. When a cheetah kills within 5 km of a spotted hyaena den, however, the spotted hyaenas may react to the kill by approaching and taking it over. Cheetahs may therefore sometimes be forced out of prey-rich hunting areas because of the presence of a spotted hyaena den. Black-backed jackals may occasionally compete with spotted hyaenas for springbok lambs, and they also scavenge from the hyaenas, often feeding with them at a carcass with little apparent fear. Because the brown hyaena mainly scavenges bits and pieces of old carcass, there is little competition between it and the spotted hyaena, but the spotted hyaenas may sometimes scavenge the food remains at a brown hyaena den, or rob brown hyaenas of their cached food.

Population dynamics

In Serengeti and the Ngorongoro Crater spotted hyaena mortality is closely linked to food competition, but in different ways. In Serengeti the major limiting factor is lack of sufficient food for the small cubs when the migratory herds are away from the area, and in the Ngorongoro Crater, by contrast, hyaena adults die at a younger age than in Serengeti because of competition among the adults for the available resident prey. Of all the yearlings in the Ngorongoro Crater, 30% die within 3 months of becoming independent, and of all the spotted hyaenas there, 16,7% die each year. The impact of food supply on spotted hyaena survival is clear from the fact that the Serengeti spotted hyaena population has more than doubled in response to the enormous increase in wildebeest numbers from 1969 to 1986. Following a recent increase in the wildebeest population to some 1,4 million, mainly because of constant control of rinderpest since the 1960s in addition to several years of abundant rainfall, there are now some 7200 to 7700 spotted hyaenas in Serengeti, of which about 5200 are out on the Serengeti Plains. Spotted hyaena cubs are occasionally killed by immigrant males (infanticide) and by same-sex litter mates (siblicide). Lions may ambush hyaenas at their communal den, and hyaena cubs are especially vulnerable to death when they are being moved from the birth den to the communal one. Lions are also the primary cause of death in older spotted hyaenas in the Masai-Mara. Of the 24 incidents of spotted hyaena deaths recorded by C. Moss in 1976 in that region, 13 were by lions, four by other hyaenas, five by disease or starvation, and two by man. Social ranking also plays a major role in spotted hyaena cub production and survival there, with the highest-ranking females producing surviving offspring two to three times more often than the lower ranking ones. Consequently a disruption of the social order in a spotted hyaena clan can have serious consequences from which the clan may take years to recover. In the Kruger National Park lions and spotted hyaenas were culled from 1974 to 1979 in an effort to stem a serious decline in zebra and blue wildebeest numbers. When it was realised that climate was the main causal factor in this decline, the culling was stopped. The lions recovered their former population size rapidly, but the spotted hyaena population took several years to do so.

In the southern Kalahari savanna, spotted hyaenas are occasionally killed when they attack a gemsbok which can defend itself vigorously with its long rapier-like horns. There the spotted hyaena has not developed a special hunting technique to cope with this threat as the lions have done. In the same region cub mortality amongst spotted hyaenas is low, but more adults die in their prime, mostly from rabies, which accounts for 43% of all the deaths in the adults. Consequently the spotted hyaena population in that region is young. Disease epidemics also do not spread easily between the various clans because of the low density of spotted hyaenas. In the Kruger National Park spotted hyaenas are highly resistant to anthrax. In fact, epidemics of this disease in the Kruger National Park and Etosha benefit the spotted hyaenas by making a large quantity of carcasses available for them. Blood samples taken from Serengeti spotted hyaenas contained antibodies for rinderpest, brucellosis and anaplasmosis. Trypanosomes, nematodes and tapeworms also occur in spotted hyaenas.

Spotted hyaena cubs in Serengeti leave their natal clan at an average age of 357 days, and most females remain with their natal clan for life. Therefore a spotted hyaena clan usually consists of matrilines of related females and immigrant males. In captivity, a spotted hyaena can live for 18 to 25 years, but in the Masai-Mara its life in the wild is closer to 16 years. In Serengeti the hyaenas have an estimated annual recruitment rate of about 5%. However, in the Ngorongoro Crater it is believed to be about 13,5%.

BIBLIOGRAPHY

Anyonge, W. 1996. Microwear on canines and killing behavior in large carnivores: saber function in *Smilodon fatalis. Journal of Mammalogy,* 77(4): 1059–1067.

Bailey, T.N. 1993. *The African leopard.* New York: Columbia University Press.

Bearder, S.K. 1977. Feeding habits of spotted hyaenas in a woodland habitat. *East African Wildlife Journal,* 15: 263–280.

Bearder, S.K. & Randall, R.M. 1978. The use of fecal marking sites by hyaenas and civets. *Carnivore,* 1(2): 32–48.

Berry, H.H. 1981. Abnormal levels of disease and predation as limiting factors for wildebeest in the Etosha National Park. *Madoqua,* 12(4): 242–253.

Bertram, B.C.R. 1979. Serengeti predators and their social systems. In: Sinclair,

A.R.E. & Norton-Griffiths, M. (Eds), *Serengeti, dynamics of an ecosystem.* Chicago: University of Chicago Press, 221–248.

Bothma, J du P. 1998. *Carnivore ecology in arid lands.* Berlin: Springer.

Brain, C.K. (Ed.). 1993. Swartkrans, a cave's chronicle of early man. *Transvaal Museum Monograph,* 8: 1–270.

Brocklesby, D.W. & Vidler, B.O. 1965. Observations on the behaviour of young spotted hyaena *(Crocuta crocuta)* in the burrow. *East African Wildlife Journal,* 3: 122–123.

Burrows, R. 1995. Demographic changes and social consequences in wild dogs, 1964–1992. In: Sinclair, A.R.E. & Arcese, P. (Eds), *Serengeti II: dynamics, management and conservation of an ecosystem.* Chicago: University of Chicago Press.

Child, G. & Robbel, H. 1975. Drowning of lechwe by spotted hyaena. *Mammalia,* 39(4): 705.

Cooper, S.M. 1990a. Clan sizes of spotted hyaenas in the Savuti region of the Chobe National Park, Botswana. *Botswana Notes and Records,* 21: 121–133.

Cooper, S.M. 1990b. The hunting behaviour of spotted hyaenas *(Crocuta crocuta)* in a region containing both sedentary and migratory populations of herbivores. *African Journal of Ecology,* 28: 131–141.

Cooper, S.M. 1991. Optimal hunting group size: the need for lions to defend their kills against loss to spotted hyaenas. *African Journal of Ecology,* 29:130–136.

Cooper, S.M. 1993. Denning behaviour of spotted hyaenas *(Crocuta crocuta)* in Botswana. *African Journal of Ecology,* 31: 178–180.

Deane, N.N. 1962. The spotted hyaena *Crocuta crocuta crocuta. The Lammergeyer,* 2: 26–44.

De Vos, V. & Bryden, H. 1997. The role of carnivores in the epidemiology of anthrax in the Kruger National Park. In: Van Heerden, J. (Ed.), *Lions and leopards as game ranch animals.* The Wildlife Group. Onderstepoort: South African Veterinary Association, 198–203.

Dinnick, J.A. & Sachs, R. 1969. Zystizerkose der Kreuzbeinwirbel bei Antilopen und *Taenia olngojinei* sp. Nov. der Tüpfelhyäne. *Zeitschrift fur Parasitenkunde,* 31: 326–339.

East, M.L. & Hofer, H. 1991. Loud calling in a female-dominated mammalian society. II. Behavioural contexts and functions of whooping in spotted hyaenas, *Crocuta crocuta. Animal Behaviour,* 42: 651–659.

East, M.L., Hofer, H. & Turk, A. 1989. Functions of birth dens in spotted hyaenas. *Journal of Zoology, London,* 219: 690–697.

Eloff, F.C. 1964. On the predatory habits of lions and hyaenas. *Koedoe,* 7: 105–112.

Estes, R.D. & Goddard, J. 1967. Prey selection and hunting behavior of the African wild dog. *Journal of Wildlife Management,* 31(1): 52–70.

Frank, L.G. 1986a. Social organization of the spotted hyaena *Crocuta crocuta.* I. Demography. *Animal Behaviour,* 34: 1500–1509.

Frank, L.G. 1986b. Social organization of the spotted hyaena *Crocuta crocuta.* II. Dominance and reproduction. *Animal Behaviour,* 34: 1510–1527.

Frank, L.G., Holekamp, K.E. & Smale, L. 1995. Dominance, demography, and reproductive success of female spotted hyaenas. In: Sinclair, A.R.E. & Arcese, P. (Eds), *Serengeti II: dynamics, management and conservation of an ecosystem.* Chicago: University of Chicago Press, 364–384.

Fuller, T.K. & Kat, P.W. 1990. Movements, activity and prey relationships of African wild dogs *(Lycaon pictus)* near Aitong, south-western Kenya. *African Journal of Ecology,* 28: 330–350.

Fuller T.K., Nicholls, T.H. & Kat, P.W. 1995. Prey and estimated food consumption of African wild dogs in Kenya. *South African Journal of Wildlife Research,* 25(3): 106–110.

Gasaway, W.C., Mossestad, K.T. & Stander, P.E. 1989. Demography of spotted hyaenas in an arid savanna, Etosha National Park, South West Africa/Namibia. *Madoqua,* 16(2): 121–127.

Gasaway, W.C., Mossestad, K.T. & Stander, P.E. 1991. Food acquisition by spotted hyaenas in Etosha National Park, Namibia: predation versus scavenging. *African Journal of Ecology,* 29: 64–75.

Green, B., Anderson, J. & Whateley, T. 1984. Water and sodium turnover and estimated food consumption in free-living lions *(Panthera leo)* and spotted hyaenas *(Crocuta crocuta). Journal of Mammalogy,* 65(4): 593–599.

Gorman, M.L., Mills, M.G.L., Raath, J.P. & Speakman, J.R. 1998. High hunting costs make African wild dogs vulnerable to kleptoparasitism by hyaenas. *Nature,* 391: 479–481.

Gould, S.J. 1981. Hyaena myths and realities. *Natural History,* 90(2): 16–20.

Grzimek, B.B. 1975. The African wild dog. In: Grzimek, B. (Ed.), *Grzimek's animal life encyclopedia.* New York: Van Nostrand Reinhold.

Gross, M. 1997. Leopards in Ivory Coast. *Cat News,* 27: 12–13.

Grimpe, G. 1916. Hyänölogische Studien. *Zoologischer Anzeiger,* 48: 49–61.

Henschel, J.R. 1986. *The socio-ecology of a spotted hyaena* Crocuta crocuta *clan in the Kruger National Park.* D.Sc. dissertation. Pretoria: University of Pretoria.

Henschel, J.R. & Skinner, J.D. 1987. Social relationships and dispersal patterns in a clan of spotted hyaenas *Crocuta crocuta* in the Kruger National Park. *South African Journal of Zoology,* 22(1): 18–24.

Henschel, J.R. & Skinner, J.D. 1990. The diet of the spotted hyaena *Crocuta crocuta* in the Kruger National Park. *African Journal of Ecology,* 28(1): 69–82.

Henschel, J.R. & Skinner, J.D. 1991. Territorial behaviour by a clan of spotted hyaenas *Crocuta crocuta. Ethology,* 88: 223–235.

Hill, A. 1980. Hyaena provisioning of juvenile offspring at the den. *Mammalia,* 44:(4): 594–595.

Hofer, H. & East, M.L. 1993a. The commuting system of Serengeti spotted hyaenas. I. Social organization. *Animal Behaviour,* 46: 547–557.

Hofer, H. & East, M.L. 1993b. The commuting system of Serengeti spotted hyaenas. II. Intrusion pressure and commuter's space use. *Animal Behaviour,* 46: 559–574.

Hofer, H. & East, M.L. 1993c. The commuting system of Serengeti spotted hyaenas: how a predator copes with migratory prey. III. Attendance and maternal care. *Animal Behaviour,* 46: 575–589.

Hofer, H. & East, M.L. 1995. Population dynamics, population size, and the community system of Serengeti spotted hyaenas. In: Sinclair, A.R.E. & Arcese, P. (Eds), *Serengeti II: dynamics, management and conservation of an ecosystem.* Chicago: Chicago University Press, 332–363.

Houston, D.C. 1979. The adaptations of scavengers. In: Sinclair, A.R.E. & Norton-Griffiths, M. (Eds), *Serengeti, dynamics of an ecosystem.* Chicago: University of Chicago Press, 263–286.

Johnston, H.H. 1884. *The river Congo from its mouth to Bolobo.* London: Low.

Kingdon, J. 1977. *East African mammals.* Vol. III, Part A: Carnivores. London: Academic.

Kruger, S. 1996. *The feeding ecology of the African wild dog* Lycaon pictus *in Hluhluwe-Umfolozi Park.* M.Sc. thesis. Pietermaritzburg: University of Natal.

Kruuk, H. 1966. Clan system and feeding habits of spotted hyaenas (*Crocuta crocuta* Erxleben). *Nature,* 209: 1257–1258.

Kruuk, H. 1970. Interaction between populations of spotted hyaenas (*Crocuta crocuta* Erxleben) and their prey species: animal populations in relation to their food resources. *British Ecological Society Symposium,* 10: 359–374.

Kruuk, H. 1972a. *The spotted hyaena.* Chicago: University of Chicago Press.

Kruuk, H. 1972b. Surplus killing by carnivores. *Journal of Zoology, London,* 166: 233–244.

Kurten, B. 1958. The bears and the hyaenas of the interglacials. *Quaternaria,* 4: 69–81.

Laurenson, M.K. 1995. Implications of high offspring mortality for cheetah population dynamics. In: Sinclair, A.R.E. & Arcese, P. (Eds), *Serengeti II: dynamics, management and conservation of an ecosystem.* Chicago: University of Chicago Press, 385–399.

Lindeque, M. & Skinner, J.D. 1982. Aseasonal breeding in the spotted hyaena (*Crocuta crocuta* Erxleben) in southern Africa. *African Journal of Ecology,* 20: 271–278.

Macdonald, D.W. 1983. The ecology of carnivore social behaviour. *Nature,* 301: 379–384.

Matthews, L.H. 1939. Reproduction in the spotted hyaena, *Crocuta crocuta* (Erxleben). *Philosophical Transactions of the Royal Society of London,* Series B. 230(565): 1–78.

Mills, M.G.L. 1978. The comparative socio-ecology of the Hyaenidae. *Carnivore,* 1(1): 1–7.

Mills, M.G.L. 1989. The comparative behavioral ecology of hyaenas: the importance of diet and food dispersion. In: Gittleman, J.L. (Ed.), *Carnivore behavior, ecology and evolution.* London: Chapman & Hall, 125–142.

Mills, M.G.L. 1990. *Kalahari hyaenas.* London: Unwin Hyman.

Mills, M.G.L. & Gorman, M.L. 1987. The scent-marking behaviour of the spotted hyaena *Crocuta crocuta* in the southern Kalahari. *Journal of Zoology, London,* 212: 483–497.

Mills, M.G.L. & Gorman, M.L. 1997. Factors affecting the density and distribution of wild dogs in the Kruger National Park. *Conservation Biology,* 11(6): 1397–1406.

Mills, M.G.L. & Mills, M.E.J. 1977. An analysis of bones collected at hyaena breeding dens in the Kalahari Gemsbok National Park. *Annals of the Transvaal Museum,* 30(14): 145–149.

Moss, C. 1976. *Portraits in the wild.* London: Collins.

Pienaar, U. de V. 1969. Predator-prey relationships amongst the larger mammals of the Kruger National Park. *Koedoe,* 12: 108–187.

Pournelle, G.H. 1965. Observations on birth and early development of the spotted hyaena. *Journal of Mammalogy,* 46: 503.

Racey, P.A. & Skinner, J.D. 1979. Endocrine aspects of sexual mimicry in spotted hyaenas. *Crocuta crocuta. Journal of Zoology, London,* 187: 315–326.

Rainy, M. & Rainy, J. 1989. High noon on the Masai Mara. *New Scientist,* 9 December: 48–52.

Rieger, I. 1978. Social behavior of striped hyenas at the Zürich Zoo. *Carnivore,* 1(2): 49–60.

Rieger, I. 1981. Hyaena hyaena. *Mammalian Species,* 150: 1–5.

Sachs, R., Staak, C. & Groocock, C. 1968. Serological investigation of brucellosis in game animals in Tanzania. *Bulletin of Epizootological Diseases of Africa,* 16: 93–100.

Skinner, J.D., Funston, P.J., Van Aarde, R.J., Van Dyk, G. & Haupt, M.A. 1992. Diet of spotted hyaenas in some mesic and arid southern African game reserves adjoining farmland. *South African Journal of Wildlife Research,* 22(4): 119–121.

Skinner, J.D., Henschel, J.R. & Van Jaarsveld, A.S. 1986. Bone-collecting habits of spotted hyaenas *Crocuta crocuta* in the Kruger National Park. *South African Journal of Zoology,* 21: 303–308.

Skinner, J.D. & Smithers, R.H.N. 1990. *The mammals of the southern African subregion.* Pretoria: University of Pretoria.

Skinner, J.D. & Van Aarde, R.J. 1981. The distribution and ecology of the brown hyaena *Hyaena brunnea* and the spotted hyaena *Crocuta crocuta* in the central Namib Desert. *Madoqua,* 12(4): 231–239.

Smuts, G.L. 1978. Interrelations between predators, prey and their environment. *BioScience,* 28(5): 315–320.

Smuts, G.L. 1979. Diet of lions and spotted hyaenas assessed from stomach contents. *South African Journal of Wildlife Research,* 9: 19–25.

Sutcliffe, A.J. 1970. Spotted hyaena: crusher, gnawer, digester and collector of bones. *Nature,* 227: 1110–1113.

Tilson, R.L., Von Blottnitz, F. & Henschel, J.R. 1980. Prey selection by spotted hyaenas *(Crocuta crocuta)* in the Namib Desert. *Madoqua,* 12(1): 41–49.

Turner, A. 1993. New fossil carnivore remains from Swartkrans. *Transvaal Museum Monograph,* 8: 151–165.

Van Heerden, J., Mills, M.G.L., Van Vuuren, M.J., Kelly, P.J. & Dreyer, M.J. 1995. An investigation into the health status and diseases of wild dogs *(Lycaon pictus)* in the Kruger National Park. *Journal of the South African Veterinary Association,* 66(1): 18–27.

Van Jaarsveld, A.S., Henschel, J.R. & Skinner, J.D. 1987. Improved age estimation on spotted hyaenas *(Crocuta crocuta). Journal of Zoology, London,* 231: 758–762.

Van Jaarsveld, A.S. & Skinner, J.D. 1987. Spotted hyaena monomorphism: an adaptive "phallusy"? *South African Journal of Science,* 83: 612–615.

Van Jaarsveld, A.S., Skinner, J.D. & Lindeque, M. 1988. Growth, development and parental investment in the spotted hyaena, *Crocuta crocuta. Journal of Zoology, London,* 216: 45–53.

Van Valkenburgh, B. 1996. Feeding behavior in free-ranging African carnivores. *Journal of Mammalogy,* 77(1): 240–254.

Von Richter, W. 1972. Remarks on present distribution and abundance of some South African carnivores. *Journal of the Southern African Wildlife Management Association,* 2: 9–16.

Watson, R.M. 1965. Observation on the behavior of young spotted hyaena *(Crocuta crocuta)* in the burrow. *East African Wildlife Journal,* 3: 122–123.

Wells, M.E. 1968. A comparison of the reproductive tracts of *Crocuta crocuta, Hyaena hyaena* and *Proteles cristatus. East African Wildlife Journal,* 6: 63–70.

Werdelin, L. & Solounias, N. 1991. The Hyaenidae: taxonomy, systematics and evolution. *Fossils and Strata,* 30: 3–104.

Wozencraft, W.C. 1993. Order Carnivora. In: Wilson, D.E. & Reeder, D.M. (Eds), *Mammal species of the world,* 2nd ed. Washington, DC: Smithsonian Institution, 279–348.

8

The striped hyaena

The striped hyaena *Hyaena hyaena* is the second largest of the living hyaenas in the world. The male is larger than the female. An adult striped hyaena weighs from 25 to 55 kg, those in Africa being smaller than the striped hyaenas in Eurasia. It is the only living hyaena to retain the generic name *Hyaena,* and this name has an interesting origin. It is based on the Middle English word *hyena* which is Old French and derived from the word *hyene,* which in turn is a Latin derivation of the Greek word *huaina,* which is the feminine form of *hus,* meaning pig. Like the spotted hyaena, the striped hyaena was originally thought to be a dog when it was first described as *Canis hyaena* by C. Linnaeus in 1758 from a specimen originally thought to have been collected in India, but later attributed to the Benna Mountains in Iran. The generic name *Hyaena* was first used by M.J. Brisson in 1762. However, the credit for this classification has since been given to Brünnich, who is now recognised as the originator of the name. The striped hyaena was renamed *Hyaena striata* by E.A.W. von Zimmerman in 1777. It has now been given the name *Hyaena hyaena* in accordance with the International Rules on Zoological Nomenclature.

The striped hyaena is built much like the spotted and brown hyaena, with powerful shoulders and neck, and the typical hyaena carnassial teeth. Like the brown hyaena and the aardwolf, an excited striped hyaena can erect its long dorsal crest which runs along the back to end in the bushy tail. Its body and legs are boldly striped in black against a light buff to grey background. It has a black face mask and throat patch, and dark ears. It is the only living hyaena to occur outside Africa, being found from as far south as the Tarangire National Park (3°50' S) in Tanzania to the Arabian Peninsula in the north, and from there to Eurasia as far east as India and Nepal. In Eurasia it also occurs as far north as southern Siberia and the Caucasus. There are not as many superstitions nor is there as much mysticism in man's beliefs concerning the striped hyaena as there are about the spotted one. Nevertheless, almost every body part of the striped hyaena is used in many regions for medicine or as an aphrodisiac. Moreover, in ancient Egypt the striped hyaena was tamed and fattened for food. It was also used to hunt game. In Afghanistan fights between striped hyaenas and dogs were held for entertainment.

Although it no longer occurs in southern Africa, there is some fossil evidence of striped hyaenas having lived in South Africa, Tanzania, Kenya and Ethiopia in the past. These fossils indicate that the striped hyaena originated in southern Africa together with the brown hyaena in the late Miocene, and only recently invaded Eurasia, possibly crossing the savanna-like land bridge which formed between Africa and Eurasia during the most recent Ice Age some 18 000 years ago, when sea levels dropped worldwide. However, there is also some fossil evidence of a possible Pleistocene *Hyaena* species in Florida in the United States of America, and earlier fossils from elsewhere. These fossils show that various *Hyaena* species had a much wider range in previous times than they have today. There is no evidence to suggest that the striped hyaena is the most primitive of the three scavenging species of hyaena alive in the world at present. The similarity in the striped pattern of the aardwolf and the striped hyaena also does not indicate close relatedness. Instead, it is probably a phylogenetic remnant of a cryptic colour pattern which has been retained by both from some ancient, common ancestor.

In their distribution there is no current contact between the brown and striped hyaena, but there is considerable overlap in range between the striped and spotted hyaena, and to a lesser extent between the striped hyaena and the aardwolf. The largest degree of ecological overlap occurs between the striped and brown hyaena, both of which forage for food scraps widely but alone. However, the striped hyaena rarely lives in small clans, unlike the brown hyaena which has a well-developed clan system. Yet, many of the behavioural adaptations which occur in spotted hyaenas are also found in the striped hyaena, although they are not all as prominently developed in the latter.

Like the brown hyaena, the striped hyaena prefers arid savannas. It

also often inhabits rocky, mountainous regions, living mainly in deserts, arid open *Acacia* savannas, and sparse open grasslands. However, an unusually reddish specimen has been collected from a rocky region of the Lake Victoria coast west of the Nile. This specimen suggests that the striped hyaena may be able to live in a more mesic climate, and that a rocky terrain and not aridity may be the essential habitat component.

Social behaviour

The striped hyaena is a crepuscular scavenger which usually forages alone and rarely lives in small groups in the African savannas. When a small group is found, it usually consists of a female and her subadult young, or a female in oestrus with one or more males in attendance. However, in the deserts of Israel the striped hyaenas live in pairs more often than not. Nevertheless, striped hyaenas have several behavioural adaptations to living a largely solitary life. In East Africa as many as 12

203

striped hyaenas may congregate at a large carcass as brown hyaenas do elsewhere. Such groupings are of short duration and do not imply the existence of any formal group ties. Although individual striped hyaenas meet each other frequently while moving about, such meetings are usually incidental and, unlike the spotted and brown hyaena, the striped hyaena does not have any bonding mechanisms which would favour the formation of more permanent groups. There is little information on striped hyaena density in the northern and eastern African savannas, but their normally prey-poor and arid environment would suggest low densities in most parts of their range. In the Negev Desert in Israel, for example, there is only 1 striped hyaena per 300 km^2 (0,3 per 100 km^2) compared with 1,7 striped hyaenas per 100 km^2 in the Serengeti-Mara ecosystem.

The presence of a wide range of communication systems, some of which are agonistic in nature, indicates that some form of social dominance does occur between various striped hyaenas. They also scent-mark their ranges extensively to orientate themselves and to convey signals of their presence to other striped hyaenas. Although they are relatively silent animals, the striped hyaena does have vocalisations which resemble those of the spotted hyaenas, although the spotted hyaenas' are louder, more varied and more frequent in comparable situations. Its relative silence and solitary life may be one reason why the striped hyaena often escapes the attention of people and of other large carnivores, especially in remote and inaccessible rocky habitats. In Israel, where it is not exposed to the same degree of competition from the spotted hyaena as in East Africa, the striped hyaena is decidedly noisier than its African counterpart.

The calls of juvenile and subadult striped hyaenas are similar in nature and context to those of the spotted hyaena. When it becomes excited, a striped hyaena will cackle and whine, while adults may also communicate with a soft 'hoo'. Threat calls start with a low rumble and culminate in a roaring growl. When a threat leads to snapping at each other, the snap is usually directed at the legs of the opponent. The legs seem to be most vulnerable in a striped hyaena, and at the first snap, both antagonists usually fold back their front paws, and drop onto their carpal joints to prevent damage to their legs. A subordinate striped hyaena sometimes also backs away from a dominant one rather than turning around and risking attack. When two striped hyaenas meet, they do not have the elaborate greeting ceremony of the brown and spotted hyaena, and visual displays are also infrequent. Nevertheless, two striped hyaenas will sniff each other's anal pouch and mane when they meet, possibly to establish their identities. Subordinate striped hyaenas also extrude their anal pouch by way of appeasement.

Like all other hyaenas, a striped hyaena has active anal glands and scent-marking occurs frequently in both sexes. Unlike the brown hyaena and the aardwolf, however, but in common with the spotted hyaena, the striped hyaena has only one type of paste. Pasting is done by the striped hyaena in the same way as the spotted hyaena. However, the striped hyaena has the least elaborate pasting system of all the hyaenas. It also often pastes over a spotted hyaena mark on a grass stalk, and this seems to be part of a clear mutual attraction which exists between these two types of hyaena. As in other hyaenas, a striped hyaena's scent-marks elicit different responses from individuals of the same or opposite sex, and they must convey specific messages about the individual who did the pasting. Pasting seems to be done at random over the range, but usually not close to the den. Faecal deposits are generally more peripheral in the range. The faeces are not deposited in latrines, and appear to have no scent-marking function. The urine of a striped hyaena also does not seem to have a scent-marking function, as in other hyaenas.

Reproduction and young

There is little published information on reproduction in the striped hyaena, but there seems to be some evidence that the female may be reproductively dominant as in the spotted hyaena. However, morphologically the reproductive tract of a female striped hyaena differs vastly from that of a female spotted hyaena, while that of a male striped hyaena resembles the male aardwolf. All male hyaenas have internal testes and lack the baculum, a bone found in the penis of some other carnivores such as dogs, bears and weasels. As in the brown hyaena, a female striped hyaena is polyoestrous and breeds throughout the year, although there may be a slight breeding peak in summer. Both sexes become sexually mature when about 2 to 3 years old. When a female comes into oestrus, she is followed around by up to three males for several days before allowing one of them to mate with her. Oestrus lasts for one day only. Once mated, the pair stay together until the cubs have been raised. Striped hyaenas copulate four to five times per day, in bouts of 15 to 45 minutes. The intercopulation interval is around 20 minutes. Gestation lasts for 90 to 92 days, and the litter size varies from one to six young (mean: 2,4), with litters of four occurring most frequently in East Africa. Unlike the spotted hyaena, where the cubs are born in an advanced stage of development and with their eyes open, striped hyaena cubs are born helpless and with their eyes closed like the brown hyaena cubs. The eyes open when they are 5 to 8 days old, and they are mobile from 8 days. The sex ratio of cubs is equal at birth, and postpartum oestrus occurs 20 to 21 days after the birth of the cubs.

A small striped hyaena cub looks exactly like an adult because it does not have a natal coat. The cubs are born in a natal den which, by prefer-ence is in a small cove or a cavity on a rocky slope or in the burrow of some other animal, which the female enlarges. The cubs first emerge from their den when 10 to 14 days old. Males show no antipathy towards the cubs and will help to raise their young, visiting the cubs alone or in the company of the female. The cubs suckle until they are 10 to 12 months old, but because the adults also bring food to the den, they are much less dependent on a milk-supplemented diet than the cubs of a spotted hyaena. The cubs start to eat meat when they are 30 days old. Both sexes bring food to the cubs at the den, although the female appears to do so more often than the male. This is in striking contrast to what happens in a spotted hyaena. However, food is not regurgitated to the cubs, and they usually suckle at nightfall. Occasionally a subadult striped hyaena will also carry food to the den. The cubs may start to accompany the adults on foraging trips when they are 6 months old. As in many other carnivores, the more experi-enced the mother, the more successful she is in rearing her cubs. Nevertheless, only one litter is raised at the same time in a given den.

Range use

In one study in Serengeti, two radio-tagged striped hyaenas used a range which varied from about 44 km² in a subadult female, to 72 km² in an adult male. However, this is a food-rich habitat, and striped hyae-nas may well have much larger ranges in the more arid and prey-poor savannas. The striped hyaena range does not appear to be defended, and consequently it is not regarded as a territory. As in the other hyaenas, a striped hyaena's range use centres on the breeding den, yet a small ter-ritory may well be defended around the den. A permanent supply of water within 10 km of the den is essential. When a stranger ventures too close to the den, it is chased away, but there is considerable range use overlap in the striped hyaena.

Activity and movement

The striped hyaena is mainly crepuscular by nature, being most active immediately before nightfall and again before dawn. It also spends much of the early part of the night in foraging around. By day it rests in a rocky lair or under a shady, rocky overhang. In areas near people, striped hyaenas may become more nocturnal. When they move about, those in Serengeti rarely use footpaths as they do on the Dead Sea coastal plains in Israel where their food resources are much more localised. In Serengeti most of their food will be distributed at random, and any footpaths which may be present will not lead these hyaenas to such resources.

Feeding ecology

Like the brown hyaena, the striped hyaena is an effective scavenger, but also occasionally hunts ineffectively. It has an unspecialised and broad diet. Over their entire range striped hyaenas mainly scavenge the bony remains of carcasses left over by other large predators. There is also a large amount of plant material in the striped hyaena's diet throughout its range. In Serengeti and on the Arabian Peninsula they are more omnivorous than elsewhere, eating insects, wild fruit and small verte-brate prey in addition to carrion. Among the hyaenas, the striped hyae-na is more omnivorous than the spotted hyaena, and its diet overlaps more closely with that of the brown hyaena in terms of the broad food categories used. Serengeti striped hyaenas are especially fond of the fruit of the wild plum tree *Balanites aegyptiaca*. However, they do not eat the fruit of the marula tree *Sclerocarya birrea* although it is nutri-tious and also abundant there. In Serengeti in general the striped hyaena's diet overlaps the spotted hyaena's in terms of gazelles and impalas, whether scavenged or hunted. The remains of large mammals occur in 26% of the faeces of Serengeti striped hyaenas, the remains of medium-sized mammals in 68%, and those of small mammals in 28%. In addition, 78% of the scats contain insect remains, 44% contain birds, 40% reptiles, and 36% wild fruit. Sometimes a striped hyaena's entire stomach contents consist of splintered dry bones that have obviously been exposed to the sun for some time before being eaten. In agricultural areas striped hyaenas may also attack and kill domestic stock.

Striped hyaenas usually forage alone, but they may sometimes do so in small groups of two or more. They also hunt occasionally, but are not effective at it. Insects are caught on the wing or on the ground, and a striped hyaena is adept at running after an insect on the wing, leaping up into the air to catch it with a snap of the jaws. When it does hunt, the striped hyaena probably uses much the same primitive chase-and-grab sequence as the brown hyaena, although the striped hyaena's hunting has not yet been described in any detail. When a striped hyaena forages, it probably covers more ground and finds food more quickly than a spotted hyaena, trotting rapidly for long distances and moving to and fro between foraging sites. In Serengeti a striped hyaena forages for 26% of every day as opposed to 16% in the spotted hyaena. Some of the pastoral Karamojong people in East Africa also believe that the striped hyaena acts as a foraging pilot for the spotted hyaena, directing it to large prey which it cannot hunt for itself, but from which it may scavenge after the spotted hyaena has killed the prey. The same people also believe that the striped hyaena will direct spotted hyaenas to large carcasses which it cannot feed upon easily before they are dismembered by the more powerful spotted hyaenas. Whatever the case, the striped and spotted hyaenas of Serengeti do have a clear and mutual attraction to each other, and one often follows the other about, but the striped hyaena does not really benefit from this much in terms of the volume of food gained. Despite the fact that they are often found in each other's proximity, striped hyaenas usually forage on their own, or occasionally in pairs.

All three of the scavenging hyaenas alive today have large and powerful teeth to crush large bones, enabling them to obtain nutritious marrow. They can also digest all the organic matter contained in such bones, and they therefore obtain the maximum energy from any carcass. The spotted, striped and brown hyaenas are the only large carnivores in existence which are known to be able to do this. Amongst the hyaenids, however, the spotted hyaena's teeth are the most specialised for eating meat, followed by those of the brown hyaena and then by the striped hyaena. The aardwolf, of course, has a much reduced dentition, and it is the most specialised feeder because it feeds mainly on termites. The striped hyaena easily cracks bone with its third premolar teeth, although its dentition is less specialised for this task than that of a spotted hyaena. Digestion is thorough and the striped hyaena's droppings are often chalky-white after a meal containing a large quantity of bone. Excess fur and feathers are regurgitated in pellets, and defecation occurs at random, and not in middens or latrines as in the aardwolf, spotted hyaena, and brown hyaena. Excess food is cached for later use, but spotted hyaenas may find and rob striped hyaenas of some of these

caches. Occasionally up to 12 striped hyaenas may gather at a large carcass, but such a grouping is rare and of short duration.

A striped hyaena's den is usually within 10 km of a permanent water
supply, although it can go without drinking water for long periods. A
striped hyaena's fast, trotting gait allows it to find and utilise relatively
distant sources of food and water.

Relationship with other wildlife

Because it is mainly a scavenger that forages alone, the striped hyaena
has no influence on the prey populations that exist in its range. It also
usually stays away from the other large carnivores of the African savannas. In Serengeti smaller carnivores are either ignored or regarded as
possible prey. Amongst the larger carnivores of Serengeti the striped
hyaena seems to be at the same dominance level as the leopard.
Nevertheless, a pair of striped hyaenas have been known to take over
some leopard kills in Serengeti, and elsewhere they may even do so
with the occasional tiger kill.

In Serengeti there seems to be something more in the relationship
between the striped hyaena and spotted hyaena than between either of
these two and other large carnivores. The spotted hyaena often seems
to follow the striped hyaena about. Because the latter is more mobile
and wanders widely in any given night, it often finds food which the
spotted hyaena may later appropriate. Spotted hyaenas also rob striped
hyaenas of cached food supplies. Conversely, the striped hyaena may
feed on carcasses found and dismembered by spotted hyaenas. When a
spotted and a striped hyaena meet, the spotted one will invariably
approach the striped hyaena, but they seldom react aggressively towards
each other. Striped hyaenas often approach spotted hyaenas, but then
show fear and lie down flat in the grass to escape attention. It is possible
that the spotted hyaenas of Serengeti exclude striped hyaenas from the
best habitats, and that the unobtrusiveness of the striped hyaena in the
area may well be a product of this competition.

Population dynamics

Little is known about the dynamics of striped hyaena populations. This
is surprising, given the wealth of information on the other large carnivores of Serengeti, and the wide geographical distribution of the striped
hyaena. Research into this matter is therefore a high priority. From the
limited information available, man is the striped hyaena's main adver-

sary. Under natural circumstances the low density at which the striped hyaena occurs probably protects it to some extent from the worst effects of mortality agents such as disease, competition and predation. Their large ranges also probably help them to obtain sufficient food, even in the event of severe changes in their habitat.

BIBLIOGRAPHY

Bothma, J. du P. 1998. *Carnivore ecology in arid lands.* Berlin: Springer.

Bouskila, Y. 1984. The foraging groups of the striped hyaena *(Hyaena hyaena syriaca). Carnivore,* 7: 2–12.

Dorst, J. & Dandelot, P. 1970. *A field guide to the larger mammals of Africa.* London: Collins.

Fox, M.W. 1974. *The wild canids.* New York: Van Nostrand Reinhold.

Hamilton, P.H. 1976. *The movements of leopards in Tsavo National Park, Kenya, as determined by radio-tracking.* M.Sc. thesis. Nairobi: University of Nairobi.

Howel, F.C. & Petter, G. 1980. The *Pachycrocuta* and *Hyaena* lineages (Plio-Pleistocene and extant species of the Hyaenidae). Their relationship with Miocene ictitheres: *Palhyaena* and *Hyaenictitherium. Geobis,* 13: 579–623.

Kingdon, J. 1977. *East African mammals.* Vol. III, Part A: Carnivores. London: Academic.

Kruuk, H. 1972. *The spotted hyaena.* Chicago: University of Chicago Press.

Kruuk, H. 1975. *Hyaena.* Oxford: Oxford University Press.

Kruuk, H. 1976. Feeding and social behaviour of the striped hyaena *(Hyaena vulgaris* Desmarest). *East African Wildlife Journal,* 14: 91–111.

Macdonald, D.W. 1978. Observations on the behaviour and ecology of the striped hyaena, *Hyaena hyaena* in Israel. *Israel Journal of Zoology,* 27: 189–198.

Mills, M.G.L. 1978. The comparative socio-ecology of the Hyaenidae. *Carnivore,* 1(1): 1–7.

Mills, M.G.L. 1990. *Kalahari hyaenas.* London: Unwin Hyman.

Nader, I.A. 1996. Distribution and status of five species of predators in Saudi Arabia. *Saudi Arabia Journal of Wildlife Research,* 1(2): 210–214.

Ognev, S.I. 1931. *Mammals of eastern Europe and northern Asia.* Vol. II, Carnivora. Jerusalem: Israel Programme for Scientific Translations (1962).

Owens, D.D. & Owens, M.J. 1979. Notes on social organization and behavior in brown hyaenas *(Hyaena brunnea* Thunberg) of the central Kalahari Desert. *Journal of Mammalogy,* 60: 405–408.

Owens, M.J. & Owens, D.D. 1978. Feeding ecology and its influence on social organization in brown hyaenas *(Hyaena brunnea* Thunberg) of the central Kalahari Desert. *African Journal of Ecology,* 17: 35–44.

Palgrave, K.C. 1993. *Trees of southern Africa,* 2nd ed. Cape Town: Struik.

Rieger, I. 1978. Social behavior of striped hyaenas at the Zürich Zoo. *Carnivore,* 1(2): 49–60.

Rieger, I. 1979a. A review of the biology of striped hyaenas, *Hyaena hyaena* (Linné, 1758). *Säugetierkundliche Mitteilungen,* 27: 81–85.

Rieger, I. 1979b. Breeding the striped hyaena *Hyaena hyaena* in captivity. *International Zoo Yearbook,* 19: 193–198.

Rieger, I. 1981. *Hyaena hyaena. Mammalian Species,* 150: 1–5.

Skinner, J.D. & Ilani, G. 1979. The striped hyaena *Hyaena hyaena* of the Judean and Negev Deserts, and a comparison with the brown hyaena *Hyaena brunnea. Israel Journal of Zoology,* 28: 229–232.

Skinner, J.D. & Smithers, R.H.N. 1990. *Mammals of the southern African subregion.* Pretoria: University of Pretoria.

Watson, M. 1950. The wild animals of Teso and Karamoja. Part V. *Uganda Journal,* 14.

Wells, M.E. 1968. A comparison of the reproductive tracts of *Crocuta crocuta, Hyaena hyaena* and *Proteles cristatus. East African Wildlife Journal,* 6: 63–70.

Werdelin, L. & Solounias, N. 1991. The Hyaenidae: taxonomy, systematics and evolution. *Fossils and Strata,* 30: 3–104.

Wozencraft, W.C. 1993. Order Carnivora. In: Wilson, D.E. & Reeder, D.M. (Eds), *Mammal species of the world,* 2nd ed. Washington, DC: Smithsonian Institution, 279–348.

9

The brown hyaena

The distribution of the brown hyaena *Parahyaena brunnea* is limited to the drier parts of the savannas of southern Africa in Zimbabwe, Mozambique, Namibia, Botswana and South Africa. It was first recorded by A. Sparrmann in 1783 when it still ranged around Table Bay and Cape Town. However, it was described scientifically as *Hyaena brunnea* by C.P. Thunberg only in 1820 from a stuffed specimen, with its type locality given as the Cape of Good Hope of South Africa. Thunberg apparently never saw a live brown hyaena during his travels, which is not entirely surprising in view of this animal's secretive and nocturnal nature. When it was first described, the brown hyaena was considered to be a true *Hyaena,* but on closer study enough differences were found for Q.B. Hendey to rename it *Parahyaena brunnea* in 1974. Moreover, if the brown hyaena were to be named *Hyaena brunnea* as it was in the past, this would contravene the International Rules on Zoological Nomenclature, because it would create a paraphyletic group among extant and/or fossil taxa. The scientific name *Hyaena* is based on the Middle English word *hyena* which is derived from the Old French word *hyene*. This in turn is a Latin derivation of the Greek word *huaina* which is the feminine form of *hus,* meaning pig. The name *Parahyaena* simply means 'similar to *Hyaena'*.

The brown hyaena is only a little smaller than a large striped hyaena. It has long hair over most of its body, and not just a long mane like the striped hyaena. Its long hair has pilo-erection capabilities, which gives a brown hyaena excellent thermal insulation. This allows it to inhabit

The brown hyaena is limited in distribution to the more arid savannas of southern Africa. In the southern Kalahari savanna, the interior dune habitats are an important part of their range. Photo: J. du P. Bothma.

quite cold regions such as the Namib Desert coast successfully. The brown hyaena is quite a bit smaller than the spotted hyaena, an adult male weighing about 47 kg and an adult female 42 kg. Moreover, in contrast with the spotted hyaena, the female brown hyaena follows the usual mammal pattern in being smaller than the male. The brown hyaena is the third largest of the four species of hyaena living in the world today, and it is also the rarest large carnivore in Africa. It is well adapted physiologically, morphologically and behaviourally to exist on the meagre food it eats, and to live in arid savannas and other such regions where large herbivores are often thinly and erratically distributed.

The brown and the striped hyaena both seem to have developed in South Africa in the late Miocene, making them some of the oldest living carnivores in Africa. It also makes them different from many of the other large carnivores in the world today, many of which have also

Eurasian origins. Although some possible brown hyaena fossils have also been found in Ethiopia, these fossils are ill-defined and may well represent another taxon, especially because there are no other brown hyaena fossils known outside southern Africa. This may be because the evolving brown hyaena was not successful enough to spread northward into areas already occupied by the strongly competitive spotted hyaena.

Social behaviour

Brown hyaenas are much more social than they have previously been thought to be, and they also live in clans. Among the carnivores, only the brown hyaena has a social system similar to that of the spotted hyaena. The original impression that they were not social probably stems from the solitary nature of their foraging. It is now known that the brown hyaena has an advanced social system with intricate relationships existing between the various members of a clan. It also has a well-developed communication system which includes vocalisations, visual displays, elaborate rituals, and extensive scent-marking. Individual brown hyaenas meet regularly, greeting each other in a ritualised way. Carcass sites are important socialising places for meeting and greeting each other. The brown hyaena, however, has a flexible social system because, although it forages alone, it also has all the social mechanisms necessary for exploiting a concentrated food resource communally, and for socialising at other times. Brown hyaenas also have extensive ranges which are defended territories, and the den is the centre of their society.

In the southern Kalahari savanna brown hyaena clans can be much larger than those of spotted hyaenas, because the brown hyaena is more effective in capitalising on ephemeral changes in food availability than the spotted hyaena. However, spotted and brown hyaena clans in the southern Kalahari savanna are usually quite similar in size, numbering five to 15 members. Their degree of social organisation is affected by the quality of the food available in the range. Yet, it is not so much how many carcasses are available from the kills of other predators, but the size of the available carcasses that is significant. Although food is important, the most influential determinant of brown hyaena clan size in the southern Kalahari savanna is subadult emigration. The brown hyaena is the most common large carnivore in the southern and central Kalahari savannas. In the southern Kalahari there are 1,8 brown hyaenas per 100 km^2, which is twice the density of the spotted hyaenas in that region. Where brown hyaenas do occur in natural areas in the more mesic savannas, they live at low densities, partly because the water availability allows for food competition to develop between the more timid brown hyaena and the other large carnivores of the African savannas such as the spotted hyaena.

Although to date little evidence of a dominance hierarchy has been found in the brown hyaenas of the southern Kalahari savanna, it is known that immigrant males dominate natal males in the central Kalahari savanna clans. There is little aggression between the clan members, and clan cohesion is maintained mainly through various forms of communication. In the central Kalahari savanna one clan of 13 members studied, consisted of five adult females, an adult and dominant male, two subordinate males, two subordinate females, and three young hyaenas. Nomadic males play an important role in the brown hyaena society. Approximately 8% of all the brown hyaena males in the southern Kalahari savanna become nomadic when they reach adulthood at about 30 months of age. Some of these nomads join other clans later. A nomadic male is received less aggressively than neighbouring clan members when it enters a clan's range. Once a nomadic immigrant male has become assimilated into a clan, he plays an important role in foraging, and frequently leads a foraging group. Nomadic males also do most of the mating with the clan females. Females and males born in the same clan show no mating interest in each other.

When communicating, brown hyaenas do not have as wide a range of vocalisations and visual displays as the spotted hyaenas. This is because the brown hyaena usually forages alone which substantially reduces the need for communication with other clan members, especially concerning sources of food. However, the brown hyaena does have a well-developed communication system which it uses to convey information to itself when foraging, and to other brown hyaenas when they meet. When meeting, pilo-erection of the long hair of its coat conveys a clear submissive or aggressive message to other brown hyaenas, depending on the circumstances. Cohesion within the clan is maintained by means of a highly ritualised greeting ceremony through some forms of muzzle-wrestling and a variety of grooming actions. Muzzle-wrestling or neck-biting seems to be used mostly to recruit new subadults into the clan, and for the expulsion of natal subadults from the clan. The brown hyaena's greeting ceremony is not as elaborate as that of the spotted hyaena. Yet it does involve elaborate and prolonged sniffing, smelling and appeasement, especially among the cubs, or when adults or subadults approach the den after a period of absence. In the central Kalahari savanna aggressive encounters between brown hyaenas are stereotyped and directed specifically towards the necks of the combatants. They therefore appear to be as ritualised as those of the canids. In the process of neck-biting, wounds as large as 1 cm or more in diameter may be inflicted on subordinates whose necks may become heavily scarred over time. In response to repeated neck-biting the subordinate may extrude its anal pouch in an appeasement gesture. Neck-biting most frequently occurs at waterholes where strange brown hyaenas may meet. It also occurs primarily in animals of the same sex, and less often between the sexes.

Individual brown hyaenas can definitely recognise each other, and in the central Kalahari savanna there is a well-defined social order which is not sexually delineated. Scent-marking is used extensively by the brown hyaena, and it has an extrudable anal pouch like all hyaenids. However, unlike the spotted and striped hyaena, but in common with the aardwolf, the brown hyaena pastes using two distinct types of paste. One of them is a long-lived, lipid-rich white secretion which is used mainly at latrines, and functions as a communication system between the clans. The other component is a short-lived, black and watery secretion which seems to be unique to a specific individual, and which is used to help a foraging brown hyaena to identify areas over which it or another brown hyaena has recently foraged, so that unproductive foraging can be avoided. Although the aardwolf also has two types of paste which are used for different purposes, it does not scent-mark at latrines or middens.

The two types of paste and the higher frequency of pasting found in the brown hyaena as opposed to only one type of paste deposited at a lower frequency by the spotted hyaena, suggest that pasting has a broader function in the brown hyaena than in the spotted one. A brown hyaena scent-marks its whole range by pasting and depositing droppings in latrines, but it does so more often over a given time in the interior areas of its range where it spends most of its time. Nevertheless, when near its range boundary an individual brown hyaena scent-marks more frequently per unit distance moved than elsewhere. Because of the relative abundance of such regular scent marks placed along the range boundaries, an intruder is likely to encounter a fresh scent mark soon after entering another clan's range. Pasting is the most important means of communication between brown hyaenas. Therefore, adults paste soon after arriving at and just before leaving the communal den. Pastes are usually placed on grass stalks at the brown hyaena's nose height in areas of interest to the hyaenas, maximising their chance of discovery. Scent-marking by pasting requires a significant energy investment because the long-lived white paste or secretion is 97% lipid (fat), and an individual brown hyaena may deposit 2900 such secretions in a year. The number of active scent marks in a brown hyaena's territory at any given time, depends upon the rate of decay of the old scent marks and the rate of deposition of new ones. Male and female brown hyaenas paste at the same overall rate of 264 pastes per 100 km moved. Along the boundary of the range the frequency increases to 446 pastes per 100 km moved. Any brown hyaena in the southern Kalahari savanna is usually within 250 m of a scent mark in most of its territory, and 500 m away from one over its entire range. When foraging in the central Kalahari savanna, brown hyaenas use an extensive network of pathways which connect carcasses up to 3 months old. These pathways are also maintained by pasting.

Brown hyaenas use faecal latrines as scent marks as well. These latrines are placed next to a prominent landmark, usually near to but not next to, the territory boundary. In the southern Kalahari savanna most brown hyaena range boundaries are located in the dunes away from the river-beds which are most frequented by the spotted hyaenas. In these dunes the shepherd's tree is common. It is also the most frequent landmark selected by the brown hyaena near to which it places a latrine (66% of all latrines). Up to 50 droppings may accumulate at a brown hyaena latrine. The lifespan of such a latrine possibly varies, but most of them are used for short periods only. The frequency of an individual hyaena's visits to a latrine is significantly higher when the hyaena is near its range boundary than elsewhere. Not all defecation occurs in latrines, however, and brown hyaenas occasionally do defecate less frequently elsewhere in their range. A brown hyaena's urine does not appear to have a scent-marking function.

Reproduction and young

Most brown hyaena clans consist of a related group of individuals of both sexes, but the clan's resident males show little sexual interest in any females, whether from their own or another clan. Immigrant males always dominate the clan's resident males. Mating occurs only between the nomadic males who have left their own clans and the resident clan females, with each male's mating tenure lasting only some 26 months. He therefore seldom sires more than two successive litters before he is replaced by another immigrant male. Unlike the spotted hyaena, the female and male brown hyaenas differ vastly in outward appearance, but a male brown hyaena resembles a male aardwolf and also a striped hyaena. As the spotted and striped hyaena, the brown hyaena has no baculum in the penis.

A brown hyaena becomes sexually mature when about 30 months old, and as is the case with a spotted hyaena male, a brown hyaena male has three reproductive options: to remain with his natal clan and be reproductively inactive, to become nomadic, or to emigrate to a new clan and become reproductively active. A female brown hyaena has two reproductive options: to remain with her natal clan or to leave and establish her own clan and territory. Female brown hyaenas are poly-oestrus, with anoestrus periods during lactation. A female usually produces her first litter when she is about 2 years old. The female's oestrus period lasts for several days, and mating may stretch over a period of up to 15 days, when the male follows the female about. When copulating the male gently bites the female's neck. In the southern Kalahari savanna the male mounts the female at a mean rate of once every 7,7 minutes, resting for a mean interval of 6,6 minutes between successive mounts. Not all the mounts lead to copulation because the female may move off, or the male may be poorly positioned. The mean period during which mounting is attempted is 42 minutes.

Reproduction appears not to be restricted to a specific season because the cubs are born at different times in different regions. The mean interval between successive litters for a given female is 16,5 months. However, when her litter dies, a female will come into oestrus sooner and have cubs again within 9 to 10 months. Gestation in the brown hyaena lasts for some 90 days. In the central Kalahari savanna it is usual for only one female in a clan to give birth to cubs each year, and there seems to be some degree of competition for breeding opportunities. Both the dominant and the subordinate females may produce litters, but they usually do so at different times. On the rare occasions when they do produce cubs together, the dominant female may harass a subordinate one to such an extent that the latter may abandon her own cubs and start to suckle those of the dominant female. However, because the full sexual cycle of a brown hyaena female and the development of her cubs lasts for more than a year, even the most subordinate female occasionally succeeds in rearing her cubs successfully.

Litter size in the brown hyaena usually varies from one to four young, with an occasional maximum of six. The young are born in a natal den, with their eyes closed and with short hair, but with a coat colour similar to that of an adult. Therefore cubs of both the brown hyaena and the striped hyaena do not have a natal coat. The eyes open when the cubs are 8 days old. The den is usually an underground burrow, but it can also be in a rocky lair, in dense bush or in tall grass. When establishing a natal den, the brown hyaena excavates an aardvark burrow to meet the needs of her cubs, although a brown hyaena is also able to dig its own den. When in a burrow, the brown hyaena's natal den is similar to that of the spotted hyaena, allowing only the cubs to enter the deeper, resting chamber through a narrow tunnel which excludes the female and any other large predator. The cubs are carried by their mother to the clan's communal den when they are 2 to 3 months old where helpers assist in looking after and raising the cubs.

All female brown hyaenas irrespective of social rank and degree of relatedness suckle and provide for cubs other than their own. A brown hyaena cub suckles for up to 10 months, but it eats meat and other scraps of solid food from about 12 weeks of age. This is much earlier than in a spotted hyaena where the adults do not carry solid food to the cubs. However, a brown hyaena does not regurgitate food to its cubs like the canids. A brown hyaena's cubs are weaned when they are 12 to 16 months old as are those of the spotted hyaena. When a brown hyaena female or another adult arrives at the den, it puts its head into the cavity while uttering a soft growl to call the cubs out. A female brown hyaena rarely stands when suckling and will usually lie down on her side, with the uppermost hindleg raised. She rolls on her stomach to terminate the suckling. Although a female will suckle other cubs, she clearly favours her own.

Other forms of assistance by males and females include providing the older cubs with solid food at the den, maintaining and cleaning the den, defending the cubs against attacks from predators, playing with the cubs, and even adopting orphans. This strategy ensures better cub survival in the arid savannas which these hyaenas usually inhabit, where a mother may have to travel long distances for food. Although the natal males also provide for the young, they do so less often than the natal females. The females provide for all young as distant as a second cousin. Males, however, only provide for first cousins. Such discrimination in non-parental aid among mammals has previously only been known in primates.

Brown hyaenas usually raise one litter per den, and the cubs stay at the den until they are about 8 months old. Small cubs only emerge from the den when an adult, usually their mother, is present. Brown hyaena dens normally have fewer entrances than those of the spotted hyaena because the brown hyaena den usually contains fewer cubs. In addition, brown hyaenas may have one or two minor dens up to 500 m away from the main communal den, which the spotted hyaena does not have. In the southern Kalahari savanna brown hyaenas usually occupy the dens for short periods, possibly because severe flea infestations develop during long-term occupancy. However, when they do move to a new den, it is usually in the same vicinity as the old one. By contrast, brown hyaenas in the central Kalahari savanna often use the same den for long periods. During their time at the den the cubs develop vital social ties with the clan.

A brown hyaena cub spends about 15 months at its den, but it may start to spend some time away from the den when 10 months old. One of the most important functions of the communal den is the protection of the cubs. Although the cubs can escape from predators such as wild dogs and lions by darting underground into the den, they are occasionally killed at the den by these predators, especially on windy days when they fail to hear the attackers approaching. The cubs therefore usually spend windy days underground, venturing out only when the wind subsides. In the southern Kalahari savanna brown hyaena cub mortality is usually low, and most adults live to an old age. In the central Kalahari savanna, however, one of six litters studied by D.D. and M.J. Owens did not survive. Subadults of both sexes will disperse from their natal clans. Sometimes the dominant ones force the subadult females to leave the clan by repeatedly biting their necks.

Range use

The resources available to brown hyaenas also determine their range size as they do with all carnivores. Even for a given clan, the size of its range and the location of its boundaries are adjusted in response to changes in abundance and distribution of food. It was originally thought that a brown hyaena does not defend any portion of its range, and therefore that its range cannot be a territory. This was probably because the brown hyaena was regarded as a solitary animal whose range widely overlaps those of other individuals. However, it has now been realised that although the brown hyaena forages alone, it is also a member of a closely knit clan of varying size with a communally defended range. This range overlaps those of its neighbours a little, and it is scent-marked. Consequently a brown hyaena clan is truly territorial.

On the more mesic savannas of the Rustenburg Nature Reserve, the individual brown hyaenas studied used ranges with a mean size of 21,1 km², but they had been recently translocated to that area and did not yet form part of a clan. In the central Kalahari savanna the mean range size of individual hyaenas during the dry season was 40 km², but that of a clan was approximately 170 km². In the more arid southern Kalahari savanna, the range size of various clans varies from 235 to 480 km². These ranges never overlap by more than 20%. The mean range size of six brown hyaena clans studied in the southern Kalahari savanna was 308 km², which is 3,5 times smaller than the mean range size of six spotted hyaena clans studied in the same area. The degree of range overlap between various brown hyaena clans is greatest in areas where their food is more abundant.

Activity and movement

The brown hyaena is a nocturnal, solitary forager which lives mainly on scavenged vertebrate food. As is the case with spotted and striped hyaenas, there are two activity peaks, one early in the evening soon after sundown, and a later one just before dawn. The nocturnal habits of all the hyaenas probably reduce competition from vultures which are exclusively diurnal, and also help to conserve water by making them inactive during the hotter parts of the day. Brown hyaenas are active for longer periods at night than spotted hyaenas, because a foraging brown hyaena has to move about continually from one small food item to the next. By contrast, a spotted hyaena usually feeds for long periods at a scavenged carcass or a kill, and it then rests. When not active by day, a brown hyaena rests in a burrow or under a densely foliated tree with considerable shade, such as the shepherd's tree in the southern Kalahari savanna. An adult brown hyaena is active for 43% of the 24-hour cycle. In winter it may occasionally also move about by day.

When a brown hyaena does move about, it may cover vast distances alone in a single night while searching for food. In the southern Kalahari savanna a brown hyaena travels a mean distance of 31,1 km per

During the day a brown hyaena will rest in an underground burrow or in some convenient shade. Photo: J. du P. Bothma.

night. In one study the maximum known distance travelled there was 54,4 km in a little less than 14 hours at a mean speed of 3,9 km/h. The movement pattern of a brown hyaena varies with the distribution and abundance of its food. Therefore its movements are usually random because the main food resource for these brown hyaenas also occurs at random. In the normally dry Nossob river-bed of the southern Kalahari savanna, however, a brown hyaena may also often follow the river-bed itself because that is where most of the lions and spotted hyaenas occur. The remains of kills from these two large predators form an important food source for a brown hyaena. The river-bed also contains a considerable number of herbivores some of which die naturally and are then scavenged by the brown hyaena.

Most if not all of the males leave their natal clans when they are subadult, moving some distance away. All four brown hyaenas relocated to the Rustenburg Nature Reserve some 100 to 190 km south of their capture site moved out of the reserve within 14 days of release, establishing themselves 8 to 17 km away on farmland. Another marked female moved 530 km from her release site in 4 months. However, she did so in a direction away from her original capture site. Therefore it could not be rated as a homing activity.

Feeding ecology

The type of food which a carnivore eats, is one of the most important driving forces in its social evolution. Both the brown and striped hyaena eat smaller and more isolated food items than the spotted hyaena, often scavenging scraps of food. This means that they usually forage alone because there is no advantage in acquiring food by foraging in large groups, especially when a clan has a large range containing scarce food resources. The brown and striped hyaena's diet is the most varied in all the hyaenids. The brown hyaena is an opportunistic scavenger with a generalised diet. It concentrates mainly on the kill remains of the other large predators which coexist with it in the savannas. Consequently its scavenged food overlaps with the type of food selected by these other large carnivores. For example, in the Kruger National Park it overlaps with that of the cheetah by 72%, followed by the spotted hyaena (32%), the lion (29%), the leopard (24%) and the African wild dog (21%). Wild fruit is eaten occasionally by the brown hyaena, but mainly for moisture, although this type of fruit does have a nutritional value as well.

In the southern Kalahari savanna, the brown hyaena scavenges 96% of its food, but sometimes hunts its own small prey such as small birds and mammals. Insects form an important part of the brown hyaena's diet in the southern Kalahari savanna, and a bat-eared fox *Otocyon megalotis* was once killed and eaten there by a brown hyaena. Occasionally a single type of prey may be killed habitually by brown hyaenas. For example, in one study three different brown hyaenas are known to have learned to hunt the black korhaan *Eupodotis afra* successfully in the southern Kalahari savanna. Such habitual kills may be more widespread amongst brown hyaenas than was originally thought. However, most of its prey is probably killed opportunistically. The only time that a brown hyaena makes a purposeful search for live prey in the southern Kalahari savanna, is when it hunts small springbok lambs. Even then its hunting success is only 6% compared with 31% in the spotted hyaena for the same prey. Ostrich eggs are a valuable and prized food resource for the brown hyaena although it will not attack the brooding birds as a spotted hyaena does. In contrast to the spotted hyaena, a brown hyaena can easily bite open the top of an ostrich egg, lapping up the contents, even when it spills onto the sand. In the southern Kalahari savanna it is not the biomass of other large predators' potential prey which is most important to a foraging brown hyaena. The size of the carcasses that become available is the vital factor. The mammal remains most commonly eaten by these brown hyaenas are those of the blue wildebeest, gemsbok, springbok, steenbok and the small canids. Of all the large mammal remains consumed by a brown hyaena, 83% are eaten in the wet season, a period when the large herbivores also have most of their young.

Although wild fruit is a primary moisture resource, the tsama melon and gemsbok cucumber are also especially important secondary food resources for the brown hyaena, comprising 29% of all the food items eaten. Nevertheless, they have a low energy value. The tsama melon and the gemsbok cucumber both become available late in the wet season, from March onwards, but the tsama melon remains available for a much longer time into the winter than the gemsbok cucumber. A tsama melon has an edible mass of some 300 to 700 g which is considerably more than the 100 to 200 g of a gemsbok cucumber. Tsama melons can remain edible for over a year, but the gemsbok cucumber usually disappears after the first frost which can occur as early as the latter part of May, and they are usually all gone by mid-winter in July. Both the tsama melon and the gemsbok cucumber have a low caloric value of 30 to 100 kJ/100 g, and 22 tsama melons have the energy equivalent of 1 kg of fresh meat. Both these wild fruits are also rich in mineral trace elements and vitamin C, and they consist of 90% water by weight. Other types of wild fruit eaten by the brown hyaenas of the southern Kalahari are the raisin bush *Grewia flava* and the wild cucumber. Brown hyaenas may therefore be important agents for the dispersal of tsama melon and gemsbok cucumber seeds through their faeces. The 'nabba or Kalahari truffle *Terfezia pfeilii,* a wild fungus, is available for a short period in late summer when it may also be dug up and eaten by brown hyaenas. The cubs also eat this truffle, but less frequently than the adults.

The brown and striped hyaena are similar in their foraging behaviour, but remarkably different from the spotted hyaena. These differences are also reflected by the variations in their diet. Although the brown hyaena lives in different sized clans, it is a solitary forager because its main diet of small and isolated scraps of food cannot support a group foraging together. When searching for food it wanders widely through the clan's range, investigating a variety of potential food items. When scavenging the food is located either upwind or downwind. Carrion is usually found by smell, and fresh carcasses either by smell or by listening for the noise of the kills and feeding activities of other predators. Subadult brown hyaenas rarely forage on their own, usually doing so in the company of an adult. Because a brown hyaena feeds on such small and widely scattered food items, it is important for other members of the clan to know whether another brown hyaena has recently searched a given area for food. Such messages are relayed by

In the southern Kalahari savanna the tsama melon is an important source of water for many of the large carnivores, including the brown hyaena.
Photo: J. du P. Bothma.

the short-lived pastes which a brown hyaena secretes every 1 to 3 minutes while foraging, much as an aardwolf also does. These secretions are unique to each individual and are recognisable as such by other brown hyaenas.

When foraging, a brown hyaena in the central Kalahari savanna uses a network of extensive pathways throughout the clan's range, often meeting other brown hyaenas along the way. These pathways are used by all the members of the clan. The trails are maintained by pasting, and they connect waterholes and carcasses up to 3 months old from which scraps of food can still be scavenged from time to time. During the dry season a brown hyaena's foraging distances are great, varying from 20 to 30 km per night. During the rainy season, however, brown hyaenas forage mainly in areas where the game and their attendant large predators congregate, travelling only 10 to 20 km per night. Although it is mainly an opportunistic, general scavenger, it does hunt its own food occasionally. However, its hunting technique is unsophisticated and poorly developed, although it does stalk its prey on rare occasions. Although it is primitive, such hunting is important because it provides individuals with an occasional highly nutritious food item. Hunting normally occurs when carrion is scarce. When it does take place, it is usually carried out in areas of sufficient grass and/or bush cover to conceal the hunter.

When catching a flying insect a brown hyaena does not run or jump up into the air to snap up the insect as the striped hyaena does, and when it hunts other prey it is usually nothing more than a primitive chase-and-grab affair. The only time a brown hyaena in the southern Kalahari savanna purposefully looks for and hunts live prey, is when it seeks out small springbok lambs, but even this is rare. Usually when a springbok herd and a brown hyaena meet, they simply ignore each other. The brown hyaena never hunts large herbivores in the southern Kalahari savanna, but elsewhere it may learn to hunt and kill smaller livestock or the calves of larger ones. Even in natural areas brown hyaenas may learn to kill a specific type of prey by preference. In the southern Kalahari savanna, for example, three different brown hyaenas learned to hunt both the black and the red-crested korhaan *Eupodotis ruficrista* successfully. In the central Kalahari savanna, only 16% of their vertebrate prey eaten, was killed by the brown hyaenas themselves. The inefficiency of a brown hyaena hunt is clear from one study which gave a low kill rate of 4,7% of 128 small mammals hunted by them in the southern Kalahari savanna. Only 6% of all the hunts are successful when they specifically hunt small springbok lambs.

When it feeds on a fresh carcass, a brown hyaena eats the entrails first, and its carnassial or shearing teeth are then used to cut the skin away before the meat is eaten. The carnassial shear is also used effectively to wedge the ball of the femur from its socket. The forelegs are separated from the rest of the carcass in a similar way. When a fresh carcass is available, a brown hyaena will eat in a more leisurely way, consuming smaller quantities of meat than a spotted hyaena. It usually consumes 4,5 to 5 kg of fresh meat and 1,5 to 3 kg of bone and skin per sitting. As many as six brown hyaenas may meet to socialise at a carcass or waterhole. When they congregate at a larger carcass, some or all of them will feed peacefully together. In one study at the central Kalahari savanna, two or more brown hyaenas fed together at 58,6% of all the large carcasses, yet other brown hyaenas visited such a carcass only to socialise with the rest of the hyaenas and not to feed. Also in the central Kalahari savanna, a subordinate brown hyaena is believed to visit a carcass simply to socialise and not to feed when the more dominant clan members are present. These dominant hyaenas spend the greatest proportion of their time at a carcass in actual feeding. However, in the southern Kalahari savanna all the brown hyaenas will feed equally on a carcass, regardless of their social rank.

Most of the brown hyaena's food items are so small when it scavenges, that they can only provide food for one brown hyaena at a time. As predators which scavenge most of their food, the spotted, brown and striped hyaena all have large and powerful jaws and teeth which allow them to crush large bones. In the process they obtain nutritious marrow from the long bones. The brown hyaena's teeth are less specialised for eating meat than the spotted hyaena's, but a brown hyaena is able to digest bone more completely. Consequently it obtains maximum energy from a carcass which no other large carnivore including the other hyaenas can do. Much of the brown hyaena's food consists of small pieces of bone and old legs and skulls which are eaten alone. They also feed extensively on other smaller food items, because an analysis of brown hyaena faeces shows that 60,1% of them contain some insect remains, and 19,6% reptile remains. Many brown hyaena droppings also contain wild fruit rinds and seeds. In the southern Kalahari savanna up to 50% by volume of all brown hyaenas' faeces found in the late winter may contain such rinds and seeds.

Brown hyaenas commonly carry pieces of food away from a carcass to cache them for later use. This is done to avoid competition while feeding at a carcass, or to take the food to the den in order to feed the cubs later on. One study in the central Kalahari savanna showed that of all the carcasses eaten, 70% had a portion carried away by brown hyaenas for caching purposes. Some of these food items were carried 2 km or more closer to the den. In the southern Kalahari savanna, adult and subadult brown hyaenas carry food to the cubs younger than 9 months at the den from a mean distance of 6,4 km away. Cubs older than 9 months forage for themselves, and in the process they also carry food to the den. Consequently large accumulations of bone are assembled near the den which reflect the type and abundance of the food available to the hyaenas. Food carried to the den is eaten inside or outside, but there is one pile or midden where most of the bones and other old food remains are discarded. However, a brown hyaena adult or subadult never regurgitates food for the cubs.

When a brown hyaena finds a large quantity of food, it will quickly eat some of it and then set about carrying away and caching some of the rest before returning to feed on what remains. Such food caching is common among brown hyaenas, and they always seem to have a reserve of cached food to fall back on when food becomes scarce. However, most fresh stored food is eaten within 24 hours of being cached because the African climate and numerous vertebrate and invertebrate scavengers do not allow fresh meat to be cached or preserved for long, as other carnivores in the colder climates in other parts of the world are able to do. Nevertheless, bones and ostrich eggs can be, and indeed are, stored for long periods by brown hyaenas in the southern Kalahari savanna. Food caching is a form of direct competition among brown hyaenas of the same clan, but not all the cached food is necessarily eaten by the hyaena who did the caching. Other brown hyaenas in particular, but also other scavengers, may find and eat such a cache, as is known to occur in the central Kalahari savanna.

For caching purposes ostrich eggs are prized items for brown hyaenas because they last long. In the southern Kalahari savanna a brown hyaena has been observed to carry an ostrich egg in its mouth with ease for distances of up to 6,8 km. In one such incident recorded by M.G.L. Mills, a female brown hyaena discovered a nest containing 26 ostrich eggs. She immediately picked one up, carried it 50 m, put it down on the sand, and returned to the nest where she bit open and ate two eggs. She then carried 13 more eggs for distances of 150 to 600 m, hiding them in various spots in tall grass clumps or under bushes. Returning to the nest to eat another egg, she then carried off one more egg, before moving away.

Brown hyaenas are equipped to live in the arid savannas of Africa and are consequently independent of free water, although they do drink water when it is available. When water is available in the central Kalahari savanna, a brown hyaena will not only drink at least once a night when foraging, but often two to three times each night. They often meet and socialise at waterholes, neck-biting each other in the process. In the southern Kalahari savanna a brown hyaena will also eat moisture-rich wild fruit when it is available to maintain its own water balance. Of all the wild fruit the tsama melon and gemsbok cucumber are most often consumed. They both have a moisture content of 90%. In the central Kalahari savanna the above fruit and also the wild cucumber become vital water sources for brown hyaenas, especially in the dry season when the rinds and seeds of these fruits form as much as 50% of their faeces. Its almost exclusively nocturnal habits also help the brown hyaena to prevent excessive water loss in its arid savanna habitat.

Relationship with other wildlife

Because it is largely a scavenger, the brown hyaena has no impact on the prey populations which share its habitat. This is also probably true of the striped hyaena with which the brown hyaena share the largest degree of ecological overlap. This overlap, however, can be one of the reasons why the brown hyaena is limited to the southern African savannas and the striped hyaena to the northern and eastern ones.

In the more mesic savannas of southern Africa, the spotted hyaena is dominant and more common whenever it occurs in the same area as the brown hyaena, although as a scavenger of smaller food items, the brown hyaena does not really compete with the spotted hyaena for much of its food. The degree of competition also depends on water availability. Because a spotted hyaena needs a permanent water supply in order to take up residence in an area and a brown hyaena is largely independent of free water, brown hyaenas can inhabit largely waterless areas while spotted hyaenas cannot. This difference has serious conservation implications. For example, when boreholes were sunk in large areas of the Kruger National Park to supply herbivores with a more permanent water source during prolonged droughts, this also made it possible for the spotted hyaena clans to settle there. In consequence, the brown hyaena is probably now extinct as a breeding population in the Kruger National Park because of increased competition from the spotted hyaenas.

In the southern and central Kalahari savannas, brown hyaenas do not approach spotted hyaenas which are feeding at a carcass. Even in range use, the southern Kalahari savanna brown hyaenas generally avoid the dry river-beds which have a high spotted hyaena density. For example, 93% of all the brown hyaena dens in the area are found in the dunes away from these river-beds, while 63% of all the spotted hyaena dens can be found in the river-beds. Even when denning in a river-bed, a brown hyaena clan's range still includes a large proportion of dune habitat which the spotted hyaenas venture into less frequently. When they do meet, spotted hyaenas are socially dominant over brown hyaenas, and therefore a dune component in the southern Kalahari savanna is probably essential for the successful habitation of that arid savanna by brown hyaenas. Furthermore, in the southern Kalahari savanna with its extensive dune habitat, the brown hyaena is ecologically more successful than the spotted hyaena. In the central Kalahari savanna there is little range overlap between the spotted and the brown hyaena clans.

Of all the larger carnivores of the southern African savannas, the brown hyaena ranks low in the dominance hierarchy. It usually dominates only the cheetah, but then provided that the cheetah is alone. In the central Kalahari savanna a brown hyaena may possibly dominate a single leopard too. It may follow the leopard's tracks, presumably to scavenge from its kills. When lions are at a kill, a brown hyaena will not come closer than 200 m, approaching the carcass cautiously only after the lions have left. On rare occasions lions will chase brown hyaenas away from prey carcasses which have died of causes other than predation. Brown hyaenas may be killed by lions, but the lions do not eat them. In general, however, the brown hyaena probably receives more benefit from the lion than it loses, especially when the lion population is small.

Where African wild dogs are present with brown hyaenas in a natural area such as the central Kalahari savanna, they also dominate the brown hyaenas, but they do not usually attack and kill any. There is usually little contact between brown hyaenas and wild dogs because they live in different habitats. However, when they do meet, the wild dog does not tolerate brown hyaenas at a kill, and a wild dog pack in the central Kalahari savanna once took over a kill which a brown hyaena had in its turn appropriated from a cheetah. Leopards usually have little influence on brown hyaenas in the arid Kalahari savannas, but in the central Kalahari savanna a brown hyaena will occasionally take over a leopard's kill. Normally, however, a leopard will take its prey up a tree to evade scavenging brown hyaenas, making all but the scraps which drop down, unavailable to them. When a leopard and a brown hyaena do meet while both are moving about, they simply ignore each other.

The only large savanna carnivores which a brown hyaena can dominate are the caracal and a cheetah on its own. In the central Kalahari savanna, a brown hyaena easily appropriates a single cheetah's kill, and it does not fear the cheetah at all. In the dry bed of the Auob River in the southern Kalahari savanna, cheetahs are abundant, and their kills provide brown hyaenas with a substantial amount of food. Any springbok carcass killed by cheetahs during the day which is not consumed fully by nightfall, is usually scavenged at night by the brown hyaenas. Elsewhere cheetahs are scarcer and consequently the carcass supply for brown hyaenas from cheetah kills is more sporadic. When a cheetah makes the occasional kill close to nightfall, it may even be displaced from its fresh kill by a brown hyaena. Caracals are comparatively rare in the southern Kalahari savanna. However, when they do make a kill they may also be forced away from the carcass by a brown hyaena. In doing so the brown hyaena merely moves towards the caracal which then withdraws without any show of resistance.

The brown hyaena is a timid carnivore that is easily chased off by other large carnivores.
Photo: J. du P. Bothma.

Concerning the smaller carnivores in the Kalahari savannas, there is considerable competition for food between the brown hyaena and the black-backed jackal. Both their diet and their life habits overlap considerably, and they frequently interact. In a dispute over food, the brown hyaena usually dominates the jackal, but at larger carcasses in the central Kalahari savanna up to eight jackals may join a brown hyaena in feeding at the carcass. This competition for food is somewhat tempered by the jackal's inability to eat large bones, and jackals also pick up scraps of food after the brown hyaenas have fed. Therefore both gain and lose food from each other, but because of their greater numbers the jackals eventually gain more than the brown hyaenas. Brown hyaenas are also alert to the movements of foraging black-backed jackals, moving over towards a jackal when they sense that it has discovered something to eat. In the southern Kalahari savanna brown hyaenas also readily eat dead black-backed jackals.

Population dynamics

In a brown hyaena society the clan size may fluctuate markedly from time to time, and different brown hyaena clans in the same area may at the same time vary greatly in size and composition. Fluctuations in litter size do not explain these variations, but there may be some link with the degree of emigration by both sexes. Most, if not all the males eventually leave their natal clan, and also some of the females, but the rate and degree of emigration varies within and between clans. Immigration is not a major factor because only a few males manage to emigrate and join new clans. On average, the brown hyaena population in a given area will consist of 8% nomadic, immigrant males and 30% of non-breeding dispersing subadults.

The mortality rate among young and adult brown hyaenas is low, and most adults live to an old age. When mortality does occur, violent attacks by other large predators such as the lion and spotted hyaena are the most common cause of death for the brown hyaena. Some old brown hyaenas will also die of starvation because tooth wear will eventually prevent proper scavenging and feeding. In the central Kalahari savanna, 16,7% of litters do not survive to adulthood, and in the southern Kalahari savanna the same applies to 11% of the litters. Rabies, a major mortality factor among spotted hyaenas, is apparently not an issue among brown hyaenas in the southern Kalahari savanna.

BIBLIOGRAPHY

Bothma, J. du P. 1998. *Carnivore ecology in arid lands.* Berlin: Springer.

Bothma, J. du P. & Nel, J.A.J. 1980. Winter food and foraging behaviour of the aardwolf *Proteles cristatus* in the Namib-Naukluft Park: *Madoqua,* 12(3): 141–149.

Cooper, S.M. 1993. Denning behaviour of spotted hyaenas *(Crocuta crocuta)* in Botswana. *African Journal of Ecology,* 31: 178–180.

Eaton, R.L. 1976. The brown hyaena: a review of biology, status and conservation. *Mammalia,* 40(3): 377–399.

Eloff, F.C. 1984. Food ecology of the Kalahari lion *Panthera leo vernayi.* Supplement to *Koedoe,* 27: 249–258.

Frank, L.G. 1986. Social organization of the spotted hyaena *(Crocuta crocuta).* I. Demography. *Animal Behaviour,* 34: 1500–1509.

Gorman, M.L. & Mills, M.G.L. 1984. Scent-marking strategies in hyaenas (Mammalia). *Journal of Zoology, London,* 202: 535–547.

Mills, M.G.L. 1977. Foraging behaviour of the brown hyaena (*Hyaena brunnea* Thunberg, 1820) in the southern Kalahari. *Zeitschrift für Tierpsychologie,* 48: 113–141.

Mills, M.G.L. 1978a. The comparative socio-ecology of the Hyaenidae. *Carnivore,* 1(1): 1–7.

Mills, M.G.L. 1978b. The diet of the brown hyaena *Hyaena brunnea* in the southern Kalahari. *Koedoe,* 21: 125–149.

Mills, M.G.L. 1982a. *Hyaena hyaena. Mammalian Species,* 194: 1–5.

Mills, M.G.L. 1982b. Factors affecting group size and territory size of the brown hyaena, *Hyaena brunnea* in the southern Kalahari. *Journal of Zoology, London,* 198: 39–51.

Mills, M.G.L. 1982c. Notes on age determination, growth and measurements of brown hyaenas *Hyaena brunnea* from the Kalahari. *Koedoe,* 25: 55–61.

Mills, M.G.L. 1982d. The mating system of the brown hyaena, *Hyaena brunnea* in the southern Kalahari. *Behavioural Ecology and Sociobiology,* 10: 131–136.

Mills, M.G.L. 1983. Behavioural mechanisms in territory and group maintenance of the brown hyaena, *Hyaena brunnea,* in the southern Kalahari. *Animal Behaviour,* 31: 503–510.

Mills, M.G.L. 1989. The comparative behavioural ecology of hyaenas: the importance of diet and food dispersion. In: Gittleman, J.L. (Ed.), *Carnivore behavior, ecology and evolution.* London: Chapman & Hall, 125–142.

Mills, M.G.L. 1990. *Kalahari hyaenas.* London: Unwin Hyman.

Mills, M.G.L. & Gorman, M.L. 1987. The scent-marking behaviour of the spotted hyaena *Crocuta crocuta* in the southern Kalahari. *Journal of Zoology, London,* 212: 483–497.

Mills, M.G.L. & Gorman, M.L. 1997. Factors affecting the density and distribution of wild dogs in the Kruger National Park. *Conservation Biology,* 11(6): 1397–1406.

Mills, M.G.L. & Mills, M.E.J. 1977. An analysis of bones collected at hyaena breeding dens in the Kalahari Gemsbok National Park. *Annals of the Transvaal Museum,* 30(14): 145–159.

Mills, M.G.L. & Mills, M.E.J. 1982. Factors affecting the movement patterns of brown hyaenas, *Hyaena brunnea*, in the southern Kalahari. *South African Journal of Wildlife Research*, 12(4): 111–117.

Owens, D.D. & Owens, M.J. 1979a. Notes on social organization and behavior in brown hyaenas *(Hyaena brunnea)*. *Journal of Mammalogy*, 60: 405–408.

Owens, D.D. & Owens, M.J. 1979b. Communal denning and clan associations in brown hyaenas (*Hyaena brunnea*, Thunberg) of the central Kalahari Desert. *African Journal of Ecology*, 17: 35–44.

Owens, D.D. & Owens, M.J. 1984. Helping behaviour in brown hyaenas. *Nature*, 308: 843–845.

Owens, M.J. & Owens, D.D. 1978. Feeding ecology and its influence on social organization in brown hyaenas (*Hyaena brunnea*, Thunberg). *East African Wildlife Journal*, 16: 113–115.

Rieger, I. 1978. Social behavior of striped hyaenas at the Zürich Zoo. *Carnivore*, 1(2): 49–60.

Rieger, I. 1981. *Hyaena hyaena*. *Mammalian Species*, 150: 1–5.

Skinner, J.D. 1976. Ecology of the brown hyaena *Hyaena brunnea* in the Transvaal, with a distribution map for southern Africa. *South African Journal of Science*, 72: 262–269.

Skinner, J.D., Henschel, J.R. & Van Jaarsveld, A.S. 1986. Bone-collecting habits of spotted hyaenas *Crocuta crocuta* in the Kruger National Park. *South African Journal of Zoology*, 21: 203–308.

Skinner, J.D. & Smithers, R.H.N. 1990. *Mammals of the southern African subregion.* Pretoria: University of Pretoria.

Skinner, J.D. & Van Aarde, R.J. 1987. Range use by brown hyaenas *Hyaena brunnea* relocated in an agricultural area of the Transvaal. *Journal of Zoology, London*, 212: 350–352.

Skinner, J.D., Van Aarde, R.J. & Van Jaarsveld, A.S. 1984. Adaptations in three species of large mammals *(Antidorcas marsupialis, Hystrix africaeaustralis* and *Hyaena brunnea)* to arid environments. *South African Journal of Zoology*, 19: 82–86.

Von Richter, W. 1972. Remarks on present distribution and abundance of some South African carnivores. *Journal of the Southern African Wildlife Management Association*, 2: 9–16.

Wells, M.E. 1968. A comparison of the reproductive tracts of *Crocuta crocuta*, *Hyaena hyaena* and *Proteles cristatus*. *East African Wildlife Journal*, 6: 63–70.

Werdelin, L. & Solounias, N. 1991. The Hyaenidae: taxonomy, systematics and evolution. *Fossils and Strata*, 30: 3–104.

Wilson, E.O. 1975. *Sociobiology: the new synthesis.* Cambridge: Belknap.

Wozencraft, W.C. 1993. Order Carnivora. In: Wilson, D.E. & Reeder, D.M. (Eds), *Mammal species of the world,* 2nd ed. Washington, DC: Smithsonian Institution, 279–348.

Yost, R.A. 1980. The nocturnal behaviour of captive brown hyaenas *(Hyaena brunnea)*. *Mammalia*, 44: 27–34.

10

The aardwolf

The aardwolf *Proteles cristatus* is one of Africa's most specialised carnivores. It also is the smallest living hyaena in the world today, with an adult male and female weight of about 9 kg each. Until recently there has been considerable controversy over whether the aardwolf, with its highly specialised termite diet, was indeed a form of hyaena. Because it has the same size and number chromosomes as the other living hyaenas and also some morphological similarities, the aardwolf is now recognised as a hyaena, but as an exceedingly primitive one which may have split off from the rest of the hyaena branch very early in their evolution.

The aardwolf was first described scientifically as a type of civet in 1783, when it was called *Viverra cristata* by A. Sparrmann based on a specimen collected near the Little Fish River at Somerset East in the Eastern Cape Province, South Africa. Its original name means maned civet. It was renamed *Proteles lalandii* by É. Geoffrey Saint-Hillaire in 1824, and as *Proteles cristatus* in 1987 in accordance with the International Rules on Zoological Nomenclature. In coloration the aardwolf looks much like a small striped hyaena. It has three vertical black stripes on the trunk of the body against a pale buff to yellowish-white background, with one or more diagonal black stripes across each of the fore- and hindquarters, running from the mid-back and tail to the underparts of the body. Black spots or stripes may occasionally appear on the neck. There is a thick, black-tipped mane of long hair which runs from the back of the head to the base of the tail. An aardwolf's most striking features are its large eyes and ears, its peculiar naked and leathery muzzle which is an adaptation to its feeding habits, and its long crest of erectile hair which forms a mane from its ears to its tail.

In terms of the fossil evidence, which has to date been found only in South Africa, the aardwolf has existed for some 1,5 million years, making it one of the more recent carnivores of the African savannas. However, the *Proteles* fossil remains from the Swartkrans and Kromdraai Pleistocene deposits in South Africa are larger than the living aardwolf. In these fossils the teeth were also not as reduced as those of a living aardwolf, and they may possibly represent a different species. The true origins of the aardwolf are still unknown. Whether the aardwolf developed from a primitive hyaenid or directly from a civet-like ancestor, is still a matter of debate. This is not really important, however. What is important is that, like all the other hyaenids, the aardwolf developed from an ancient civet-like ancestor. Civets are known to be able to eat food that is toxic or distasteful to most mammals. If the aardwolf developed from such an ancestor and retained this ability, as it seems to have done, it explains the mechanism which led it to specialise in a termite food source which contains high levels of distasteful terpenes. The exact manner in which an aardwolf tolerates these terpenes will be dealt with in more detail in the feeding ecology section.

The aardwolf occurs in two discrete areas today, with one subpopulation in southern Africa and another in east and north-east Africa. These two subpopulations are at present separated by a more mesic band of habitat which is about 1500 km wide and in which no aardwolves occur. There is no doubt that during the drier climate of the Pleistocene there was once a single, continuous aardwolf population from southern to north-eastern Africa. The aardwolf was probably always absent from West Africa because of the rarity of its main food source consisting of various species of surface-foraging, nocturnal termites of the genus *Trinervitermes*. It usually inhabits dry, open savannas with a rainfall of between 100 and 600 mm per year, where the *Trinervitermes* species of termites is abundant. Traditionally an aardwolf pelt is used as a head-dress by the Karamojong people of East Africa, and as medicine and meat for some of the people of South Africa. The pelts are often used to construct fur mantles or karosses.

It is interesting that in South Africa the aardwolf seems to mimic the brown hyaena morphologically to some degree. In East Africa, where the aardwolf and the striped hyaena occur together, the aardwolf looks much more like a striped hyaena. However, their range in eastern and north-east Africa does not overlap totally. Whether this is possible mimicry, or has any advantages for the aardwolf at all, remains unclear.

However, by looking like the larger, more robust and aggressive striped or brown hyaena, an aardwolf may certainly gain a survival value in times of a physical confrontation with the other larger predators of the African savannas. It is also possible that this apparent mimicry is nothing more than the retention of some ancestral feature by these hyaenids.

Social behaviour

The aardwolf is a highly solitary animal, except when mating or being accompanied by young cubs. Adults are normally intolerant of each other's company. Nevertheless there are some scattered reports of several females and their young being found together on rare occasions. Little is known about their prevalence, although one study at the Rustenburg Nature Reserve reported a density of some 250 aardwolves per 100 km^2 for all sexes and ages. Another study reports 100 aardwolves per 100 km^2 for adults only.

Despite being solitary for most of its life, the aardwolf has a whole range of communication systems which includes body postures, vocalisations and scent-marking. Defensive displays are particularly exaggerated, and in times of physical conflict, the aardwolf also drops onto its knees and folds it paws back for protection as the striped hyaena does. The aardwolf's facial expressions are limited mainly to the eyes and ears because the leathery muzzle is not conducive to snarling or grinning. The long and conspicuous mane around the neck can be fanned out independently of the dorsal crest, which emphasises the head. Simultaneous erection of the mane and dorsal crest makes the aardwolf appear to be almost twice its size. This allows the rather timid carnivore to bluff its way out of possible threatening situations with great apparent ferocity. It has a variety of calls, including a kind of roar, and a howl similar to that of the striped hyaena. It also makes whistling calls to other aardwolves, grunts and growls defensively, and occasionally barks thinly like a dog.

Like the other hyaenids, the aardwolf scent-marks extensively using the typical hyaenid pasting method. However, like the brown hyaena, it has two types of paste, a short-acting one used to orientate it while foraging, and a longer-lived one used to delineate its range. An aardwolf is individually recognisable from its paste, which is extruded from the anal glands, and contains volatile short to medium-chain fatty acids which occur in markedly different relative concentrations in different individual aardwolves. An aardwolf usually scent-marks on a grass stalk at nose height within its range. Apart from serving to mark its range, an

aardwolf's scent-marking also plays a role in its reproductive strategies, as will be explained later. The latter leads to fewer than 5% of all the scent marks being placed outside an aardwolf's territory. When scent-marking its territory, the message relayed depends greatly on the size of the territory, the frequency of the territorial encounters, and the defensive behaviour of the resident. The greater the territory size, and consequently the more difficult it is to defend, the greater the threat of a scent mark needs to be. This implies that fresh scent marks should always be present in sufficient quantities in such areas to ensure that any likely intruder will encounter and heed them. In the aardwolf scent marks are therefore concentrated around the range boundaries and, the smaller the territory, the more scent marks occur at increasingly higher densities.

4,5 cm

An aardwolf does not use a latrine in the sense that a spotted and brown hyaena would do. However, it does defecate in up to four middens which are scattered throughout its range. A midden is a round or oval depression of about 1 m in diameter. Each midden is thickly carpeted with droppings and a strong and distinctive smell emanates from them. Although the biological role of a midden is still uncertain, aardwolves do visit them often, and they also frequently paste close to it. In addition, the aardwolf often urinates on its buried faeces in a midden, but it will also urinate elsewhere in its range. Urination therefore does not seem to be a form of scent-marking, but it may be involved in reproduction when the males test a female's urine for olfactory clues to her state of reproductive receptivity.

5 cm

Reproduction and young

Aardwolves form monogamous pairs for mating and raising the cubs. Each mated pair occupies a well-defended territory throughout the year, but extra-pair copulation also occurs in as many as 40% of all the mated pairs, resulting in the distinct possibility that a given male may be cuckolded into raising at least some cubs which are not his own. This aspect will be dealt with in more detail later. In the aardwolf both sexes are similar in size. A male aardwolf closely resembles a male striped hyaena. Mating occurs over a 2-month period in the winter, and as the mating season approaches, the adult males begin to make frequent scouting excursions into their neighbouring territories. Initially they do not paste there, but they do so as the actual mating time gets closer. The males make these excursions to test the aggressiveness of the other territorial males, not to displace them territorially but to gain access to additional females in oestrus. Male pasting in neighbouring territories increases in frequency the closer the female gets to oestrus. It is a form of advertisement of the intruding male's qualities as an additional mate, and it is directed at both the neighbouring male and the resident female. If the resident male responds aggressively, the intruding male soon ceases to paste in the former's territory and retreats to his own territory and female. However, if the intruder is more aggressive than the resident male, he continues pasting outside his own range, and may eventually mate with his own female as well as with the neighbouring resident male's female.

About a week before a female allows copulation, numerous males will visit her, pasting frequently in the process. Those females paired with less aggressive males will then also begin pasting extensively outside their own range, to advertise their receptivity to more aggressive extra-pair males. However, at the time of actual oestrus, only the resident male and perhaps an aggressive intruder remain, both of whom may copulate with the female. When an intruder also copulates with a resident female, she may produce young from the intruder and from her own male in the same litter. Because a resident male will care for all his mate's cubs regardless of their origin, he may be cuckolded into raising young other than his own.

The occurrence of cuckoldry in the aardwolf is an established feature of its biology. It is not known in any other mammal but man, although it does occur in some birds. The reason that it does not occur more often in other monogamous mammals may be found in the social structure of the aardwolf. In other monogamous carnivores such as the foxes and jackals the most recent offspring remain with the adult pair into the next breeding season to help raise the next generation of young, especially when food supplies are abundant. These helpers may also assist in preventing intruders from gaining access to the female. In the aardwolf, all the subadults leave their natal range, leaving an intruding male with only the resident male to subdue by intimidation. This intimidation is done by frequent scent-marking to advertise himself to the female. When the female comes into oestrus, the intruder may even physically fight with the resident male, especially when he is larger than the resident.

Cuckoldry is a form of genetic competition which operates through the male's sperm. It leaves the cuckolded male to unknowingly raise at least some young which he did not inseminate. It only occurs in animals which are monogamous and show extensive male parental care. Clearly, there is no way for the male to distinguish his own young from that of an intruder when they are born from the same female at the same time. But why does it occur at all? In the aardwolf it seems that the more aggressive a male is, the better he guards his young. This increases the cub's chances of survival, and creates the possibility that a less aggressive male may desert his own mate when she is mating promiscuously with both her own mate and her neighbour's. In doing so, at least some of her cubs will also receive the genetic material of a more aggressive male which may in turn make these cubs more aggressive when they become sexually active. In the process she is increasing the chances of establishing her own genetic material in the population at large, as dominant spotted hyaena females will also do, but she uses a different reproductive strategy. In the process of being fertilised by different males, a promiscuous female increases the genetic variability of future aardwolf populations.

Copulation lasts from 1 to 4,5 hours, and although the penis remains inserted for all this time, there is no copulatory lock or tie as is found in the canids. The first ejaculation occurs after an hour, and then at about hourly intervals. An aggressive intruder may displace a resident male during copulation. Copulation ends when the female enters the den, forcing the male to dismount. Gestation lasts for 90 to 110 days. Most litters contain two to four young, and the male guards the cubs at the den while the female forages for most of the night. The guarding male usually only forages for 2 to 3 hours per night just before dawn.

An aardwolf cub is born helpless and with its eyes closed. It suckles until it is at most 5 months old, but it does start to forage and feed on termites from an age of 3,5 months. Its termite diet precludes an aardwolf from carrying food to its cubs at the den and it also does not regurgitate food to its cubs. Therefore, the only way in which a male aardwolf can help raise the cubs is by defending the den. The cubs remain in the vicinity of the den until they are 3 months old, but the den site may be changed several times during this period. All the subadults of both sexes leave their natal range, and most of the cub deaths occur in winter from food stress when the main *Trinervitermes* food source for aardwolves is less active. The cubs become physically mature when they are about 9 months old.

Although a male aardwolf may unwittingly be raising some cubs which are not his own, mate desertion is rare in the socially monogamous aardwolf. However, it does happen on those occasions when the male in an adjacent pair dies a natural death during the short time that the female who has lost her mate is still reproductively receptive. Because the aardwolf male is opportunistic in mating, the potential always exists for him to respond to such local conditions by deserting his own mate and attempting to breed with another female. However, given the high energetic costs of parental care, this will remain a rare occurrence.

Range use

In Serengeti where the correct termite food supply is abundant and evenly distributed, each aardwolf pair spaces itself out in a small territory of some 1,5 km^2 (range 1 to 4 km^2) which is shared by the pair in a classically territorial way. The actual size of the range depends to some degree on the available food supply, but breeding requirements are the main determinants of an aardwolf's range size. Its range has to allow each member of the mated pair easy access to the food. These territories are defended fiercely by both members and no known overlaps occur, although the territorial integrity of the pair may be breached during the mating season, as was explained above. Elsewhere, aardwolf territories seem to be of a similar size and nature as is found in Serengeti. When a midden is located on a territory boundary, both pair members use the midden, and they paste over each other's marks in the vicinity. Elsewhere they also scent-mark over the marks of intruders. It is believed that such marking is a direct threat of aggression, and that proper perception of this threat is of vital survival value to any intruder. Male aardwolves seem to spend more time along their territory boundaries, while the females spend most of their time near the centre of the range.

Each aardwolf territory has at least one active den where the pair has protection from excessive cold in the winter and heat in the summer. Old aardvark, porcupine or any other suitable burrows are used as dens, but an aardwolf can dig its own den in soft soil. Most aardwolf dens are oval with an entrance some 420 mm wide and 320 mm high. This entrance cavity rapidly narrows to a tunnel about 300 mm wide and 200 mm high. At the end of this tunnel, which may be as long as 5 m, there is a resting chamber 1 m long, 400 mm wide, and 250 mm high. A specific den is used for 6 to 8 weeks, before the aardwolves move to a new one. An aardwolf under threat knows exactly where its den is, and will dash straight to it from distances of 1 km or more to escape from any possible danger.

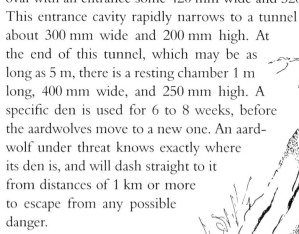

Activity and movement

During the summer when its main food source in the form of various *Trinervitermes* species of harvester termites is active at night, the aardwolf is mainly nocturnal, and only emerges from its den at or after sunset, returning to it before dawn. However, at sunset on cold winter nights of below 18°C, the temperature may become too cold for *Trinervitermes* to forage at night. Then the aardwolf becomes more diurnal because it has to supplement its diet with another harvester termite *Hodotermes mossambicus* which is mainly active in daytime during winter. The midden is a focal point of activity when the aardwolf forages at night. In summer, an aardwolf may defecate three to six times per night in one or more of the middens spread throughout its range. It buries its faeces after defecating, and sometimes urinates on top of them as well. The middens with their abundant droppings smell strongly of terpenes because of the type of food eaten, and they may well be frequently used landmarks to orientate the aardwolf within its own territory.

In the Lichtenburg Nature Reserve an aardwolf forages over a distance of some 1,5 to 9,1 km (mean: 4,2 km) per night. In an *Acacia* savanna in north-western South Africa, the mean speed of an aardwolf's movement is 2,3 km/h when it is not foraging, and 1,0 km/h when it is foraging. The actual foraging speed is determined by the quantity of termites available as food and their distribution. In another open *Acacia* savanna area of South Africa a tagged male aardwolf moved 35,4 km in a straight line from its release site in 24 days. An aardwolf

An aardwolf defecates in clearly defined middens with numerous old droppings on the surface.
Photo: J. du P. Bothma.

245

relocated there moved 9,7 km back towards its original territory in 3 days, despite having lost a front leg from below the knee.

Feeding ecology

The aardwolf is probably best known for its highly specialised diet and its use of a food source which differs markedly from that of any of the other living hyaenas. In fact, the very distribution of the aardwolf in Africa seems to be determined mainly by the presence of its main food source. This food source consists of various species of ecologically equivalent *Trinervitermes* or long-nosed harvester termites which forage for dry grass in columns on the ground surface mainly at night, and are active for most of the year. By contrast, most other species of termite in Africa forage underground or under the protection of mud galleries on woody vegetation. The only other termite which also always forages on the ground surface is the common harvester termite *Hodotermes mossambicus,* but it is mostly active in the day. It is used by the aardwolf as an emergency food supply during cold winters when *Trinervitermes* may become inactive or less active. Because of its remarkably reduced molars an aardwolf does not have much capacity to kill and eat anything other than termites, although it is known to eat the occasional insect, reptile, bird, rodent and even honey. When its usual food source becomes inactive in the winter, an aardwolf may experience a weight loss of up to 20% because it has to eat less nutritious or abundant foods. In Serengeti the variability of an aardwolf's diet also increases during the rainy season when the army ants of the *Dorylus* species and the termite *Odontotermes badius* may be eaten. The aardwolf's preference for the *Trinervitermes* species is remarkable, even more so because these termites are known to have a powerful chemical defence mechanism against being preyed upon. During foraging it is the workers who are mainly exposed to aardwolf predation at first. However, as soon as the foraging column is disturbed, the soldiers emerge in greater numbers. These soldiers squirt fine threads of noxious and distasteful terpenes at any predator, yet an aardwolf seems to be able to tolerate these secretions up to a point before it ceases feeding on a particular column and moves off to find a new one. The aardwolf's leathery and naked muzzle also protects it against these chemicals. The terpene secretions persist in the aardwolf's droppings, giving them a strong characteristic smell which is especially noticeable at an aardwolf midden.

The presence of its main food source has a strong impact on the aardwolf's geographic distribution in Africa. Within its range, temperature clearly has the most important influence on the availability of its main food resource. Where various species of the nasute or long-nosed harvester termites of the genus *Trinervitermes* occur abundantly, the aard-wolf is also abundant. However, in the more mesic West Africa these termites are rare because they do not have access to the dry grass matter which is vital to their survival. The large quantity of green grass which grows throughout the wet season in West Africa therefore greatly reduces the presence, abundance and activity levels of the *Trinervitermes* termites. This would place a severe stress on the aardwolf if it were to live there, which is why it does not occur in that area. The aardwolf's nocturnal habits are also linked to its main food resource. Because the *Trinervitermes* termites are poorly pigmented, they cannot tolerate direct sunlight, and are therefore nocturnal foragers. Consequently the aard-wolf is also a nocturnal forager. Nevertheless, in regions where they do occur abundantly, these termites are such a reliable food resource for most of the year, except during the coldest winter nights, that their presence has allowed the aardwolf to specialise almost exclusively on them as a single food resource.

This aardwolf food specialisation was made even more possible by the fact that all the *Trinervitermes* species of nasute harvester termites are a food resource which is all but unexploited by any other mammal preda-tors in the African savannas. Consequently the aardwolf faces no com-petition concerning its choice of food, provided that it can overcome the chemical defence system used by these termites, which has enabled them to keep other termite-eaters at bay. It is believed that the ability to tolerate the terpene secretions of the *Trinervitermes* soldiers was present in the aardwolf from the earliest times, and that it only became more refined over time. The aardwolf is considered to have evolved from an ancestral civet-like viverrid ancestor. The civet is well known for its abil-ity to eat noxious and even toxic foods. These characteristics may there-fore have preadapted the evolving aardwolf to enable it to specialise on this single food resource which can evidently defend itself against all the other mammal termite-eaters, but not against the aardwolf.

An aardwolf in Serengeti moves about alone when foraging, slowly searching for food at a speed of 2 to 3 km/h with the ears cocked for-ward and the head bent down. It covers an irregular route unrelated to wind direction. In an open *Acacia* savanna in South Africa aardwolves forage at a mean speed of 1 km/h, but this depends on the number of termites available. There the aardwolf's nutritional requirements and its food abundance influence its range size. About 3000 termite mounds per territory are required for a mated pair of aardwolves to survive.

Termite feeding columns are always located upwind and primarily by their terpene scent which is secreted at low concentrations, but the food is also located by hearing. Food location distances vary from 0,5 to 1 m, but may be as much as 2 m. As soon as it starts to rain the foraging termite sounds are blanketed, and when the rain is heavy and prolonged, the termites also move back underground which is why aardwolves seldom forage in the rain. The aardwolf's use of middens to concentrate its buried droppings in few specific locations in its range may well be part of its foraging strategy. Its faeces smell strongly of the terpenes excreted by its food source in an attempt at chemical defence, and this same smell is used by the aardwolf to locate that food source. By burying its faeces in selected, known spots, an aardwolf may well be avoiding the olfactory confusion which would arise when foraging for fresh sources of food over a range where its faeces are scattered in the open. The aardwolf's use of faecal middens may therefore be a strategy employed to reduce the wasting of time and energy when foraging.

Having discovered a column of foraging termites, the aardwolf licks them up rapidly for a minute or two with its broad, spatulate tongue before moving on to find a new column. However, wear on the front of the lower incisors of most adults seems to indicate that aardwolves may also bite at columns of termites, taking them up into their spade-like lower jaws. In the process of licking up or biting its food from the ground surface, the aardwolf ingests a large volume of sand. The result is that its large droppings often contain as much as 50% sand, and the

The aardwolf forages mainly at night for surface-feeding *Trinervitermes* termites which it licks up from the ground with its broad, spatulate tongue.
Photo: J. du P. Bothma.

rest the indigestible carapaces of the termites eaten. However, the more abundant the termites are, the less sand is ingested. In Serengeti there are therefore conspicuous regional and seasonal differences in the amount of soil found in aardwolf droppings. Apart from probably being preadapted to handle the terpene defence secretions in its food, an aard-wolf has also developed a range of other features linked to its specialised diet over time. Internally, these include its broad, spatulate tongue which is covered with large, hardened papillae; a broad palate and large mandibular salivary glands which neutralise the terpenes. A muscular pyloric region in the stomach also aids in the mastication of food which may contain large quantities of sand. There is also a short intestine for rapid food passage. Its degenerated cheek teeth developed because an aardwolf no longer has to chew its food. A keen sense of hearing and smell has also developed. Externally the most obvious adaptation is the development of a leathery and hairless muzzle which makes it difficult for the terpene secretions to stick to the skin when the aardwolf feeds. The aardwolf's most significant adaptation to its termite diet remains its ability to overcome the chemical defence of these termites. This ability also sets the aardwolf apart from all the other insectivorous carnivores.

In protecting a foraging column of termites, the termite soldiers secrete most of the chemical defences which eventually force even an aardwolf to move on, once its threshold of tolerance has been reached. Nevertheless, an aardwolf ingests a vast number of termites in a given night. In East Africa, one stomach which was examined, contained 1 kg of termite remains and very little sand or debris. It has also been esti-mated that an aardwolf in East Africa can gather 40 000 termites within 3 hours. In South Africa, one stomach examined contained the heads of some 124 000 termites, and it has been estimated that one aardwolf will eat as many as 300 000 termites in a single night. Because a typical for-aging column of *Trinervitermes* contains some 4000 termites of which 30% are soldiers routinely protecting the foraging party by lining the route and facing outwards, the need to forage widely from different ter-mite columns becomes clear. However, on cold winter nights when *Trinervitermes* become inactive and the aardwolf shifts to *Hodotermes mossambicus* as an alternative food resource, the reduced foraging time, the enforced daytime foraging, and the use of a specialised food resource, allow the aardwolf to consume only 20% of the number of termites which it would normally take in a given night in summer. Although *Hodotermes mossambicus* is larger than *Trivervitermes,* the fact remains that during the winter the aardwolf loses up to 20% of its body weight, and that some cubs may die of food stress.

Termites are rich in protein and fat, and the flesh of an aardwolf in peak condition may contain so much fat that it appears yellow. After feeding well an aardwolf may remain inactive for a day or so. In focusing on termites as its main food source, it has lost the general hyaenid characteristic of strong jaws and bone-crushing molar teeth, and it has also now incurred the penalty of being restricted to areas where its main food supply is found. This implies that if ever anything were to destroy its *Trinervitermes* food source, the aardwolf would become extinct. The aardwolf is independent of free water because it gets all the moisture it needs from its food. However, during long cold spells when its main food source becomes inactive, an aardwolf may walk long distances to drink water, but this is the only time that it does so.

Dynamics and relationship with other wildlife

The aardwolf does not compete with any other mammal for its main food, but it may follow the aardvark around for the occasional leftovers. The aardwolf is timid, and it is often preyed upon by other carnivores including the leopard and the python *Python sebae*. Nothing is yet known about the dynamics of aardwolf populations.

BIBLIOGRAPHY

Anderson, M.D., Richardson, P.R.K. & Woodall, P.F. 1992. Functional analysis of the feeding apparatus and digestive tract of the aardwolf *Proteles cristatus*. *Journal of Zoology, London,* 228: 423–424.

Apps, P.J., Viljoen, H.W., Richardson, P.R.K. & Pretorius, V. 1989. Volatile components of the anal gland secretion of the aardwolf *(Proteles cristatus). Journal of Chemical Ecology,* 15(5): 1681–1688.

Bothma, J. du P. 1965. Random observations on the food habits of certain Carnivora (Mammalia) in southern Africa. *Fauna and Flora,* 16: 16–22.

Bothma, J. du P. 1971a. Notes on movement by the black-backed jackal and the aardwolf in the western Transvaal. *Zoologica Africana,* 6(2): 205–207.

Bothma, J. du P. 1971b. Food habits of some Carnivora (Mammalia) from southern Africa. *Annals of the Transvaal Museum,* 27: 15–26.

Bothma, J. du P. 1998. *Carnivore ecology in arid lands.* Berlin: Springer.

Bothma, J. du P. & Nel, J.A.J. 1980. Winter food and foraging behaviour of the aardwolf *Proteles cristatus* in the Namib-Naukluft Park. *Madoqua,* 12(3): 141–149.

Eaton, R.L. 1976. Support of the hypothesis that aardwolves mimic hyaenas. *Mammalia,* 40(2): 342–343.

Kingdon, J. 1977. *East African Mammals.* Vol. III, Part A: Carnivores. London: Academic.

Kruuk, H. & Sands, W.A. 1972. The aardwolf (*Proteles cristatus* Sparrmann 1783) as predator of termites. *East African Wildlife Journal,* 10: 211–227.

Linley, T.A. 1965. Aardwolf at East London Zoo. *International Zoo Yearbook,* 5: 145.

Mills, M.G.L. 1978. The comparative socio-ecology of the Hyaenidae. *Carnivore,* 1(1): 1–7.

Mills, M.G.L. 1990. *Kalahari hyaenas.* London: Unwin Hyman.

Nel, J.A.J. & Bothma, J. du P. 1983. Scent marking and midden use by aardwolves *(Proteles cristatus)* in the Namib Desert. *African Journal of Ecology,* 21: 25–39.

Richardson, P.R.K. 1985. *The social behaviour and ecology of the aardwolf* Proteles cristatus *(Sparrmann 1783) in relation to its food resources.* Ph.D. dissertation. Pretoria: University of Pretoria.

Richardson, P.R.K. 1987a. Aardwolf: the most specialized myrmecophagous mammal? *South African Journal of Science,* 83: 643–646.

Richardson, P.R.K. 1987b. Aardwolf mating system: overt cuckoldry in an apparently monogamous mammal. *South African Journal of Science,* 83: 405–410.

Richardson, P.R.K. 1987c. Food consumption and seasonal variation in the diet of the aardwolf *Proteles cristatus* in southern Africa. *Zeitschrift für Säugetierkunde,* 52(5): 307–325.

Richardson, P.R.K. 1990. Scent marking and territoriality in the aardwolf. In: Macdonald, D.W., Müller-Schwarze, D. & Natynczuk, S.E. (Eds), *Chemical signals in vertebrates* 5. Oxford: Oxford University Press, 378–387.

Richardson, P.R.K. 1991. Territorial significance of scent-marking during the non-mating season in the aardwolf *Proteles cristatus* (Carnivora: Protelidae). *Ethology,* 87: 9–27.

Richardson, P.R.K. & Coetzee, M. 1988. Mate desertion in response to female promiscuity in the socially monogamous aardwolf *Proteles cristatus. South African Journal of Zoology,* 23(4): 306–308.

Richardson, P.R.K. & Levitan, C.D. 1994. Tolerance of aardwolves to defence secretions of *Trinervitermes trinervoides. Journal of Mammalogy,* 75(1): 84–91.

Shortridge, G.C. 1934. *The mammals of South West Africa.* London: Heinemann.

Skinner, J.D. & Smithers, R.H.N. 1990. *The mammals of the southern African subregion.* Pretoria: University of Pretoria.

Skinner, J.D. & Van Aarde, R.J. 1986. The use of space by the aardwolf *Proteles cristatus. Journal of Zoology, London,* 209: 299–301.

Smithers, R.H.N. 1966. *The mammals of Rhodesia, Zambia and Malawi.* London: Collins.

Smithers, R.H.N. 1983. *The mammals of the southern African subregion.* Pretoria: University of Pretoria.

Turner, A. 1993. New fossil carnivore remains from Swartkrans. *Transvaal Museum Monograph,* 8: 151–165.

Von Ketelhodt, H.F. 1966. *Proteles. Zeitschrift für Säugetierkunde,* 31: 300–306.

Von Richter, W. 1972. Remarks on present distribution and abundance of some South African carnivores. *Journal of the Southern African Wildlife Management Association,* 2: 9–16.

Wells, M.E. 1968. A comparison of the reproductive tracts of *Crocuta crocuta, Hyaena hyaena* and *Proteles cristatus. East African Wildlife Journal,* 6: 63–70.

Werdelin, L. & Solounias, N. 1991. The Hyaenidae: taxonomy, systematics and evolution. *Fossils and Strata,* 30: 3–104.

Wozencraft, W.C. 1993. Order Carnivora. In: Wilson, D.E. & Reeder, D.M. (Eds), *Mammal species of the world,* 2nd ed. Washington, DC: Smithsonian Institution Press, 279–348.

11

The larger carnivore guild

Konrad Gesner was the first author to group all the meat-eating animals into one scientific category in his book *Historiae animalium,* in 1551. He was followed by C. Linnaeus in 1758, who placed all the meat-eating animals in the Order Ferae when he published the tenth edition of his *Systema naturae,* a scientific classification system of all the living organisms known at that time. This classification system for the carnivores was later refined by various authors. All the original classification systems made particular use of morphological similarities in the carnivore's dentition to describe the relationships among species and between groups of species. Gradually it became apparent that the ability to eat meat and the resulting morphological implications could not be used exclusively to classify the carnivores because bats and various insectivores would then also be included, an error which first appeared in the sixth edition of C. Linnaeus' *Systema naturae* in 1748.

Various characteristics were used to refine the carnivore classification. These initially included separating the carnivorous mammals from the herbivorous ones on the grounds that the carnivores walk on their soles (plantigrade) as opposed to walking on the toes (digitigrade) as is the case with the herbivores. In the carnivore classification, skull morphology, post-cranial features and the soft anatomy were then all used to define similarities and differences. The comparison of living carnivores with fossilised ones, however, still relied heavily on the characteristics of the teeth which remain well preserved. From these studies one clear distinctive characteristic emerged for defining all the members of the Order Carnivora. This is the presence of the principal carnassial shear on the fourth upper premolar and first lower molar teeth, despite its secondary loss in some groups. More recently carnivore classification systems have also used the characteristics of the basicranium, and this places the extinct species into perspective. The basicranium is important because many functional aspects of a carnivore's biology can be inferred from this part of the skull where several organ systems such as cranial nervation, blood circulation, balance, mastication, head and neck muscle attachment and hearing are concentrated. Detailed biochemical and cytogenetic studies have now been added wherever possible to refine the carnivore relationships even further. It is now generally accepted that the Order Carnivora has two main lineages: the cat-like Suborder Feliformia which includes the mongooses, civets, hyaenas and cats amongst others, and the dog-like Suborder Caniformia which includes the dogs, bears, fur seals, true seals, racoons, otters, polecats, weasels, badgers and others. The most recent classification of the Order Carnivora was done by W.C. Wozencraft in 1993.

The origins of the Order Carnivora

The Order Carnivora has developed relatively recently in geological time. The earliest mammals are known to have lived some 200 million years ago, but they were small and only rarely reached the size of a domestic cat. Most of the early mammal fauna disappeared together with the dinosaurs about 65 million years ago. However, a few species survived, but none was a specialised terrestrial carnivore. Moreover, at that time the savanna grasses had only just started to develop, and the savannas did not yet exist. Therefore the main herbivore prey base of the living savanna carnivores had also not yet come into existence. The basic carnivore prototype was an archaic, ferret-sized genus *Cimolestes,* but the earliest known members of the Order Carnivora were small, arboreal viverrids. They were arboreal probably because the forests were well developed and extensive at that time – trees having been in existence for some 150 million years. As the tropics of the world retracted in the Tertiary, a latitudinal zonation of climates formed, creating new climatic zones for mammal evolution which included the savannas and their carnivores. The earlier land-bridge connections between the emerging continents were mainly between Eurasia and North America until the middle of the Eocene, a time when tropical conditions existed even in the higher latitudes of the earth. The southern continents, which included Africa, were substantially isolated during much of the Tertiary, and Africa contained no true Carnivora up to and during the early Oligocene. The first true Carnivora crossed to Africa from Eurasia in the early to middle Miocene some 30 to 25 million years ago when the ancestors of some civets, mongooses and cats arrived there. They were followed by the ancestors of other carnivores such as the bears, dogs and more cats in the late Miocene and early Pliocene about 7 to 2,5 million years ago. These two main waves of colonisation allowed the modern African carnivore community to evolve, eventually leading to a rich complement of mammal carnivores. For many of these carnivores the savannas with their rich herbivore prey formed an ideal habitat, and they thrived there.

Of the large carnivores, the jaguar genus *Pseudaelurus* is considered to be the origin of all the cats. Furthermore, the ability to extend the claws from sheaths may predate the emergence of the modern cats. Of the large cats, the members of the genus *Panthera* occurred at some time in Eurasia, Africa and South America. Leopards have a long history in Africa, first appearing there in Villafranchian deposits. The earliest cheetahs are known from Villafranchian deposits in Eurasia, but cheetah-like cats also occurred in North America. The hyaenas developed from small civet-like ancestors at some time in the Miocene, with the genus *Progenetta* from the lower European Miocene as the probable common ancestor. The most important phylogenetic changes in hyaenas were in their size and body proportions. There are at least 10 species of hyaena which are known from the African fossil deposits. They soon became more dog-like. The earliest canid fossils were found in North America, but the modern canids only began to radiate in the late Miocene. Of all the dogs, the black-backed jackal is the geologically oldest member of the genus *Canis,* having been identified from fossils dating back to the Pleistocene at least.

Comparative characteristics

The large carnivores of the African savannas display a variety of social groupings which vary from the highly gregarious spotted hyaena and African wild dog to the mainly solitary leopard, caracal and the striped hyaena. Those carnivores living in groups enjoy the benefits of increased hunting efficiency and access to larger prey because the mass of the prey which they hunt, increases with the combined mass of the hunters. Predation is therefore greatly affected by group size. Despite the fact that 85 to 90% of the carnivores of the world live solitary lives, only the leopard, the caracal and the striped hyaena in the African savannas are truly solitary. The spotted hyaenas form the largest groups, but the clans may split into smaller groups to hunt. In many savannas such as those of Serengeti the spotted hyaena is the most numerous of all the large carnivores. There is now an estimated population of 7700 spotted hyaenas in the Serengeti-Mara ecosystem. This hyaena also kills the vast majority of all the prey there. The whole African wild dog pack functions as a unit, although it too may split up on rare occasions, but then only to hunt. The lion is also gregarious, but it usually lives in smaller prides than the spotted hyaena and the wild dog. Lions may also live in pairs or alone. The brown hyaena lives in small clans, but it usually forages alone, because the nature of its food which is mainly scavenged, often precludes feeding in a large group. The cheetah occasionally forms small groups of dependent young and their mothers, or of male litter-mates which stay together for life. The aardwolf lives in monogamous, mated pairs, and although the striped hyaena lives alone in the African savannas, it may also live in pairs elsewhere. The leopard and the caracal live alone and only make contact with one another when mating or when rearing their young.

All the carnivores use a wide array of systems to communicate with each other and to gather information for themselves. The large felids and the African wild dog scent-mark their ranges mainly with urine mixed with glandular secretions. By contrast, the hyaenas use anal pastes when scent-marking. The spotted and brown hyaena also use their latrines for scent-marking, but the aardwolf's midden probably does not function in such marking. Striped hyaenas rarely use latrines. The spotted and striped hyaena only have one type of paste, whereas the brown hyaena and the aardwolf have both a short-lived and a long-lived paste. Scrapes, which leave secretions from the interdigital glands as markers, are also often used as a form of communication in many of the carnivores. In general, scent-marking has more than one function in a given species and it may have different functions in different species. In the canids the status of an individual is governed by social dominance and submission, and effective communication becomes of prime importance.

The reproductive systems of the large carnivores of the African savannas are clearly varied. They depend to some degree on the presence or absence of grouping, and on the social structure of any groups which may occur. Communal rearing of the young occurs in the more social large carnivores such as the lion, the spotted hyaena, the brown hyaena, and the wild dog. An aardwolf male may also be cuckolded into rearing young other than his own when his mate is promiscuous. In the wild dog and the spotted and brown hyaena, the communal den is the focus of attention where helpers of various ages and sexes assist in rearing the young. Such assistance may also take place to some degree in lions where all the females may help to rear the cubs of other females.

The lion, leopard, cheetah, and wild dog, and the spotted, brown and striped hyaenas all use large ranges which vary in size depending on the resources available. The caracal uses a smaller range, and the aardwolf a limited one. The cheetah is the only large cat in Africa which has smaller ranges for males than females. In the aardwolf, a mated pair share exactly the same range. A permanent supply of water within the range is essential only for the African wild dog, and the spotted and striped hyaena. Most of the large carnivores are active mainly at night, the aardwolf almost exclusively so. The cheetah and the wild dog hunt mainly by day, but most of the other large carnivores will also hunt by day if the opportunity arises and conditions permit. Gregarious carnivores are generally more diurnal than the solitary ones who are mainly nocturnal.

All the large carnivores of the African savannas either forage, hunt or scavenge for their food. Some are both hunters and scavengers, making them true opportunists who can exploit a wide variety of food resources. The type and size of the food items eaten depend to some extent on the size of the individual and the group involved, but most of the carnivores are opportunistic in their food selection. Because the size of the prey selected increases with the combined mass of the predators involved, the more gregarious hunters such as the lion, spotted hyaena and wild dog, are able to hunt and kill larger prey than the other large carnivores of the African savannas. Prey selection becomes less possible in the more arid savannas where all possible prey must be hunted in order for a large carnivore to survive. The large cats are the most carnivorous of the large mammals, and except for the cheetah and the caracal, which do not readily eat carrion, they all hunt and scavenge for food. The African wild dog also usually hunts and kills fresh food daily. The spotted hyaena hunts much more frequently than is generally believed, but the striped and brown hyaena are primarily scavengers. Scavenging requires the ability to travel long distances with a low energy expenditure. This ability and their digestive efficiency make the spotted, brown and striped hyaenas successful scavengers. It is believed that the African savannas now have their full ecological complement of large scavenging carnivores, and that there are no vacant niches for another large mammal scavenger. The development of bone-crushing teeth and the ability to extract nourishment from bone was a secondary development in hyaenas. Bone-crushing teeth also developed in some canids in North America where so-called hyaena dogs are known from the fossil history. The fact that these dogs have now become extinct there, implies that the bone-eating niche was much more important for the early hyaenids than it is now for the spotted, striped and brown hyaenas. The aardwolf is rare among carnivores in having a highly specialised diet consisting mainly of various species of the termite genus *Trinervitermes* which is occasionally supplemented by the termite *Hodotermes mossambicus* in midwinter in the colder southern latitudes.

On the African savannas, therefore, the large carnivores avoid exploiting the same hunted food resources through variations in food choice which are linked to their distribution and individual and group size. However, when scavenging for food there is much more interference for the same food resource. It is also clear that most of the large carnivores of the African savannas cannot be divided clearly into those that kill their own prey and those that only scavenge, as has been done in earlier studies. Moreover, migratory prey systems were once found in most of the African savannas, but today there are only a few such systems intact. Consequently most of the African savannas now have resident prey populations which may support a higher sustained predator-prey ratio than was commonly found there when a large proportion of the prey biomass still migrated annually, unless the predators present were able to switch to alternative abundant sources of food when the other prey migrated.

The advantages gained from group hunting have for some time been considered to be the most important factor which leads to the development of social groups under certain circumstances in carnivores. However, this is no longer believed to be the case because such sociability is often not only the consequence of group hunting, but of a complex of factors which includes group hunting, phylogeny, the size of the individual and the prey resource utilised. The methods used by those large carnivores which hunt on the African savannas differ widely. The African wild dog and the spotted hyaena can chase and exhaust their prey over long distances, while the others prefer to hunt over short distances, although occasional longer distance hunts do occur. These differences are also related to the social organisation of both the predator and its prey, and they all contribute to the coexistence of the large predators of the African savannas in relative ecological harmony.

In the large carnivores the predator's familiarity with its prey and the reaction of the prey to predation largely determine the killing response. Large cats kill most of their prey with a throat or neck bite, or by suffocation. The spotted hyaena and the wild dog run their prey down, biting at it on the run, and exhausting or weakening it before pulling it down for the kill. Striped and brown hyaenas rarely hunt, but when they do, it is done in a primitive way. The aardwolf licks up its food, ingesting the termites without necessarily killing them first. The carnivores possess a diverse array of teeth which may be adapted for specific feeding functions. The aardwolf does not chew its food, and therefore has only rudimentary molar teeth. However, the teeth of some fossilised aardwolves were better developed. Surplus killing is known among the lion, the leopard, the caracal and the spotted hyaena, but given the appropriate circumstances, it may well occur occasionally in the other hunters too. Under normal circumstances, where prey resources are abundant, surplus killing is a needless waste of energy. Some predators may also learn to use a specific or modified habitual killing technique for a given type of prey. When feeding, the large-group carnivores differ in their speed of food ingestion, their response to each other, and in the feeding hierarchy of the young. Generally, the larger the predator the less the need to chew the food. The African wild dog, and the spotted, striped, and brown hyaenas all eat more bone than the lion, leopard, cheetah and caracal. The leopard and the brown and striped hyaenas are especially adept at caching food for later use, but spotted hyaenas and wild dogs occasionally also do so. The caracal rarely returns to its food once it has been disturbed while feeding.

Over time, each of the large carnivores of the African savannas has adapted its ecology and behaviour to allow it to coexist successfully as a member of a large and varied guild of large carnivores. The lion and the spotted hyaena compete for dominance in this guild with the size of the group being a primary determinant of the result. However, the spotted hyaena is by far the most numerous large carnivore in the African savannas. Interference at a kill or scavenged food source is more severe than competition for the various food resources of the African savannas. In addition to food selection the activity cycles, social structure and the size of the prey consumed, all serve to reduce competition among the large carnivores. In many of the African savannas the sheer abundance of prey further reduces exploitation competition between its large carnivores.

Most of the large carnivores of the African savannas need large natural areas with abundant prey resources to survive. In such areas the large carnivores do not severely influence their prey populations, and they certainly do not regulate the quantity of prey. Rather, the prey is regulated by dry season food availability, parasites and disease. In areas with migratory prey, some of the larger predators can adapt their feed-

259

ing ecology to the regular dispersion of their food resources, but others are unable to do so because of social and behavioural limitations. In terms of their own dynamics, the abundance and vulnerability of their food sources and the survival of their young are the major contributing factors to population survival in the large carnivores of the African savannas.

Conclusion

The large carnivores of the African savannas have developed over a long time in harmony with the large herbivores and the vegetation of these habitats. Today, these three components form a varied but well-balanced ecological system which serves to maintain these vast natural habitats of Africa. However, the savannas of Africa and their attendant predators and prey are changing continually, as has happened over millennia. Although it may be difficult for modern man to envisage such an event, it may well happen one day that this wonderful spectacle may be altered permanently by some major imbalance imposed naturally or by man, and it may then ultimately disintegrate. For now, however, the larger carnivores of the African savannas remain one of the wonders of the world. We should cherish and protect this resource with determination and tenacity.

BIBLIOGRAPHY

Bearder, S.K. & Randall, R.M. 1978. The use of faecal marking sites by hyaenas and civets. *Carnivore,* 1(2): 32–48.

Belsky, A.J. 1987. A flexible body mass in social carnivores. *American Naturalist,* 129(5): 755–760.

Bertram, B.C.R. 1979. Serengeti predators and their social systems. In: Sinclair, A.R.E. & Norton-Griffiths, M. (Eds), *Serengeti, dynamics of an ecosystem.* Chicago: University of Chicago Press, 221–248.

Bosman, P. & Hall-Martin, A. 1997. *Cats of Africa.* Vlaeberg: Fernwood.

Bothma, J. du P. 1998. *Carnivore ecology in arid lands.* Berlin: Springer.

Caro, T.M. 1994. *Cheetahs of the Serengeti Plains.* Chicago: University of Chicago Press.

Cooper, S.M. 1990. The hunting behaviour of spotted hyaena *(Crocuta crocuta)* in a region containing both sedentary and migratory populations of herbivores. *African Journal of Ecology,* 28: 131–141.

Eaton, R.L. 1976. The brown hyaena: a review of its biology, status and conservation. *Mammalia,* 40(3): 377–399.

Hanby, J.P. & Bygott, J.D. 1979. Population changes in lions and other predators. In: Sinclair, A.R.E. & Norton-Griffiths, M. (Eds), *Serengeti, dynamics of an ecosystem*. Chicago: University of Chicago Press, 249–262.

Hofer, H. & East, M.L. 1995. Population dynamics, population size, and the community system of Serengeti spotted hyaenas. In: Sinclair, A.R.E. & Arcese, P. (Eds), *Serengeti II: dynamics, management and conservation of an ecosystem*. Chicago: University of Chicago Press, 332–363.

Houston, D.C. 1979. The adaptations of scavengers. In: Sinclair, A.R.E. & Norton-Griffiths, M. (Eds), *Serengeti, dynamics of an ecosystem*. Chicago: University of Chicago Press, 263–286.

Kingdon, J. 1977. *East African mammals.* Vol. III, Part A: Carnivores. London: Academic.

Kleiman, D.G. & Eisenberg, J.F. 1973. Comparisons of canid and felid social systems from an evolutionary perspective. *Animal Behaviour,* 21: 637–659.

Kruuk, H. 1972. Surplus killing by carnivores. *Journal of Zoology, London,* 166: 233–244.

Martin, L.D. 1989. Fossil history of the terrestrial Carnivora. In: Gittleman, J.L. (Ed.), *Carnivore behavior, ecology and evolution*. London: Chapman & Hall, 536–568.

Mitchell, B.L., Shenton, J.B. & Uys, J.C.M. 1965. Predation on large mammals in the Kafue National Park, Zambia. *Zoologica Africana,* 1(2): 297–318.

Rautenbach, I.L. & Nel, J.A.J. 1978. Coexistence in Transvaal Carnivora. *Bulletin of the Carnegie Museum of Natural History,* 6: 138–145.

Schaller, G.B. 1972. *The Serengeti lion.* Chicago: University of Chicago Press.

Sinclair, A.R.E. & Arcese, P. (Eds). 1995. *Serengeti II: dynamics, management and conservation of an ecosystem*. Chicago: Chicago University Press.

Turner, A. 1993. New fossil carnivore remains for Swartkrans. *Transvaal Museum Monograph,* 8: 151–165.

Van Valkenburgh, B. 1996. Feeding behavior in free-ranging African carnivores. *Journal of Mammalogy,* 77(1): 240–254.

Wozencraft, W.C. 1989. The phylogeny of the recent Carnivora. In: Gittleman, J.L. (Ed.), *Carnivore behavior, ecology and evolution*. London: Chapman & Hall, 495–535.

Wozencraft, W.C. 1993. Order Carnivora. In: Wilson, D.E. & Reeder, D.M. (Eds), *Mammal species of the world,* 2nd ed. Washington, DC: Smithsonian Institution, 279–348.

Wright, B.S. 1960. Predation on big game in East Africa. *Journal of Wildlife Management,* 24(1): 1–15.

INDEX

Larger Carnivores of the African Savannas

SPONSORS' EDITION

A

FNB – a Division of FirstRand Bank Limited

B

Bales, Steve

C

Nel, Jan & Elizabeth

D

Pieterse, Dion Wayne

E

Aan Christo van der Merwe
Ter herdenking van 25 jaar as die dryfveer van Trinamics Ing
1 Augustus 1999

COLLECTORS' EDITION

1

Clarke, Gary K.

2

Gee, Rob

3

Watt, Ronnie

4

The Hidden Family

5

Garonga Safari Camp

6

Krachler, Friedrich

SUBSCRIBERS: STANDARD EDITION

Alberts, M.
Barnes, Bert
Beck, Dr. Achim
Beneke, J.C.
Boll, Katja
Brand, Marius
Braun, K.W. – Switzerland
Breyer-Menke, Honor
Conservation International Okavango Programme
Currie, Keith & Barbie
Dabchick Wildlife Reserve
Daly, Debbie & Vernon
Dennill, Michael & Ingrid
Dumbrill, Graham
Evans, Fiona
Evans, Gareth & Robyn
Friedman, Russel, Bonnie & Gabriella
Frost, Willem P.
Gettliffe, Shirley
Gilbert, T.J.
Goott, Mel
Graham, Ken
Greyvensteyn, Chris & Sonja
Grobbelaar, Dr. N.J.
Grohovaz, A.J.
Hammond, Christopher A.
Harvey, R.A.
Heather, R.A.
Hough, Wendel James
Human, D.W.
Ingwe Productions
Jacana Education
Kemp, P.C.
Klagsbrun, Steven & Gaby
Knickelbein, Roy & Erica
Krone, Franci & Mariaan
Larsen, Per & Thelma
Laubscher, Nico & Maud, Stellenbosch
Lawrie, R.M.

Lindsay, Lionel
Livingstone, Brian & Dawn
Lohmann, Ingrid U.
Louw, H.A.
MacQuilkan, Peter & Yvonne
Mansfield, Jack B.H.
Marais, Deon & Penny
Marques, R.M.
Matos-Lopes, Carlos
McDonald, Ian Ramsay
Moritz, Saskia & Sabine
Morrison, Bruce, Sharon, Brett & Nicole
Roedean School (SA)
Ross, Dr. K.
Ryder, Marc & Lorna
Ryder, Samantha & Gray
Sandy, Glynn & Hannetjie
Sarkin Family
Sartorius von Bach, Helmke & Dagmar
Scott, C.E.L.
Sellmann, Roy, Agneta & Angie
Skawran, D. & H.
Smit, P.L.
Stathoulis, Ines & Basil
Stewart, Bruce (J.W.B.)
Steyn, Pieter
Tame, Barry
Teasdale, Grant J.
Terblanche, Stefan & Venessa
Toerien, G.P.
Topham, Steve
Van den Hoven, Pieter F.
Van de Wetering, A.
Van der Jagt, Dick & Liz
Van Rijswijck, M. & M.A.
Van Schaik, Theo
White Elephant Lodge – Pongola Game Reserve
Williams, Jumbo
Williams, Peter & Jeffe